Ireland's Professional Amateurs

Ireland's Professional Amateurs

◆

A Sports Season At Its Purest

Andy Mendlowitz

iUniverse, Inc.
New York Lincoln Shanghai

Ireland's Professional Amateurs
A Sports Season At Its Purest

Copyright © 2007 by Andrew Mendlowitz

All rights reserved. No part of this book may be used or reproduced by any means, graphic, electronic, or mechanical, including photocopying, recording, taping or by any information storage retrieval system without the written permission of the publisher except in the case of brief quotations embodied in critical articles and reviews.

iUniverse books may be ordered through booksellers or by contacting:

iUniverse
2021 Pine Lake Road, Suite 100
Lincoln, NE 68512
www.iuniverse.com
1-800-Authors (1-800-288-4677)

Because of the dynamic nature of the Internet, any Web addresses or links contained in this book may have changed since publication and may no longer be valid.

The views expressed in this work are solely those of the author and do not necessarily reflect the views of the publisher, and the publisher hereby disclaims any responsibility for them.

Cover photo: "Kilkenny's Henry Shefflin (left) battles with Cork's Seán Óg Ó hAilpín during the 2004 All-Ireland final."

ISBN: 978-0-595-45684-0 (pbk)
ISBN: 978-0-595-89986-9 (ebk)

Printed in the United States of America

To my parents and brother, who else for my first book?

Contents

Prologue 1

Hurling & Gaelic Football Primer 9

Chapter 1 Hoosier's, Irish-style 15
 February: Kilmurry-Ibrickane, County Clare

Chapter 2 End of a Hex? 39
 March: Ballina, County Mayo

Chapter 3 From Hell to Riches 59
 April to early May: County Leitrim

Chapter 4 Northern Ireland 79
 Mid-May to late June: More Than a Game

Chapter 5 The Hidden Language 113
 July: Gaeltacht, west County Kerry

Chapter 6 The Gamble 129
 Early August: Kilnadeema/Leitrim, County Galway

Chapter 7 Hurling Under Bright Lights 143
 Mid-August to mid-September: Cork city

Chapter 8 A Sporting Battlefield 165
 Late September to early October: Dublin city

Epilogue GAA in America & What I Learned 187

Acknowledgments 195

Note on Sources 197
Final Note..199

Prologue

Buzzed by jet lag, I arrived in Ireland with a friend for my summer 2002 vacation on a cool Sunday afternoon in July. We took a double-decker bus into downtown Dublin and looked for our hotel, rather unsuccessfully, near the Ha'penny Bridge. People were roaming the streets in anticipation of a big game. As a sportswriter, I took interest and assumed they were soccer-mad. Eventually on our stroll, my full, oversized backpack began ripping into my shoulder and we ducked to a semi-dark pub for directions, nourishment and our first pint. Customers lined up for food, and as I waited for the soda bread and stew, I noticed more fans wearing yellow jerseys with black stripes.

I asked them what football team was playing—carefully not saying soccer as I tried to appear savvy. No, it turned out, they were fans of hurling.

Hurling?!?

The only hurling I ever heard of was the American version. The one that took place around three o'clock in the morning on your knees after a night of drinking. But the locals explained that here in Ireland it was a popular sport played with a stick similar to ice hockey on grass. The action, though, mostly stayed in the air. They also told me about Gaelic football, another native Irish sport that was a mix between soccer and rugby. Surprised and curious, my friend and I decided to add a game to our itinerary during our two-week trek.

We soon found our hotel and immediately took a nap. It was enough to invigorate us for the week we spent in the Emerald Isle's capital enjoying the pubs, old churches and cool breezes. No, we didn't have to worry about the furnace fed heat that blistered us back home. All week we wore pants and light jackets, enjoying the mild temperatures as if it was early autumn.

On Friday, we rented a car and drove cross-country past the hundreds of sheep and cows munching on flat, cloud-injected lands to the rocky beaches of the West Coast. Sunday, we had an important stop to make—an All-Ireland hurling elimination game between County Wexford and County Clare at neutral Portlaoise, in the middle of the country approximately where Missouri would sit. We arrived hours early for the 6:25 p.m. start to get tickets. Good thing—the 20,000-seat stadium sold out, packed with fans wearing the blue and saffron of

Clare or the purple and yellow of Wexford. The stadium's concessions lacked beer and offered only basic snacks like potato chips. Fans of both teams sat side-by-side. They didn't bicker or croon "asshole" chants to one another. In other words, they were better behaved than I expected. Then it started.

To my untutored eye, hurling seemed shockingly dangerous as players' flung sticks high into the air at a little ball. They didn't wear any equipment—no chest protectors, kneepads or shin guards. Unbelievably, helmets were optional. Mysteriously, no one's skull was crushed, no one was carried off the field as a hushed crowd of fanatics momentarily joined in shock and fear looked on. But it was more than just brutes yielding billy clubs going around whacking each other. The action was lightening-quick without timeouts or offside penalties. The players, fifteen to a side, displayed awesome skills in balancing the peach-size ball on the flat end of their stick, then passing or shooting it with a pinpoint strike. Up close, you could hear the smashing of the sticks, or the "clash of the ash." Tackling was illegal, but defenders harshly jammed their shoulders into the opponent's to jar any sense of balance. While I didn't understand everything, this brute force made some of our coddled American athletes, I'm sad to say, seem downright pansy-like. Sports like basketball, while equally as fast, or football, equally as dangerous, didn't have this in-your-face violence where a player could seemingly lose his front teeth at any time.

The next day, I bought newspapers that flashed banner headlines and featured pullout sections wrapping up the weekend's action. The biggest game was the Leinster provincial Gaelic football final that drew 78,000 fans in Dublin's historic Croke Park—a place equivalent to a combination of Yankee Stadium, the Boston Garden and the Rose Bowl rolled into one. Pictures showed smiling Dublin players and coaches raising the winning cup with blue and white ribbons streaming out after their victory over Kildare. Action shots captured runners clutching the ball, trying to elude their opponent with a stiff arm to the chest. Television station RTÉ nationally aired the game and ran a highlight show in the evening as commentators broke down the six major Gaelic football and hurling contests. These sports, which I had never heard of until the week before, were clearly big deals.

I asked someone the next day how much the players were paid. I thought since Ireland was a smaller country than the United States, the salaries might not reach the 10 million euros a year mark, but could be around €500,000 for the stars. He just laughed.

"Nothing. They do it for the love of the game."

Huh? *They don't get paid?*

I couldn't believe it. These players were amateurs?!? They could play in front of 78,000 fans one day and then had to return the next day to their jobs as plumbers, salesmen, police officers or whatever they did. I came to understand that they train like professionals, but must juggle their sport with fulltime jobs, families, social lives and in some cases, college. The strategic X's and O's collide with trying to pay a mortgage. A study by an actuary found that the average top-level player loses between €100,000 to €150,000 in earnings over a career due to missing things like overtime and advancement opportunities. They're more average Joes than prima donnas. I could just imagine if Barry Bonds had to wake up after a World Series game to sell insurance.

I learned a few more things in the next week about the sports' governing body, the Gaelic Athletic Association (GAA). There are no trades or free agency. Players compete for their church parishes in county leagues. The all-stars form the inter-county squad and square off against thirty-one other counties in a fierce All-Ireland tournament each summer. Hence, the top players are on two teams: club and county. And both are equally as important to the athlete.

The GAA isn't just a sporting organization—it is a way of life. In earlier decades, the Association often provided the main social outlet for rural areas cut off from the cities and towns. Now, with paved roads and major highways, cell phones and Internet access, video games and cable TV across the country, the GAA still provides an identity in the modern world. Clubhouses host birthday parties, bingo nights and dances. If you throw a dart at a map, chances are it will land on one of the 2,600 clubs throughout Ireland, each one supporting several teams based on its size. Everything is done on a volunteer basis. The community essentially owns the club, whether it's in Sixmilebridge of County Clare, Mayobridge of County Down or Silverbridge of County Armagh.

I also learned that the games are intertwined with Ireland's struggle for independence. Nationalists formed the GAA in 1884 to preserve a part of Irish heritage in the face of English opposition. Imagine, if you can, the National Basketball Association popping up in 1770 to help advance the colonies' ideas of freedom against the British loyalists. Forget Washington crossing the Delaware. Instead the famous painting would feature John Adams and Thomas Jefferson twirling whistles while teaching the young patriots how to hit a perfect crossover dribble or play zone defense to fight unfair taxation. Sounds far-fetched, but in Ireland, holding onto the sporting culture played an important role. The GAA banned its members from also playing the "foreign" games of soccer or rugby—both internationally and domestically—until 1971. In Northern Ireland, playing the GAA sports immediately identifies you as a Catholic (even though the organization is nonsectarian and nonpolitical). Protestant paramilitary groups have murdered GAA members and vandalized fields.

After my brief visit to Ireland, I returned to my job as a sportswriter for a small paper in Virginia. People asked about the trip. Sure, I told them about the Rock of Cashel in Tipperary, with its gray Medieval buildings and round tower, and the Birr Castle in Offaly, the site of a mega telescope and trim gardens and the spectacular Cliffs of Moher hanging over the Atlantic Ocean. The thing that excited me the most, though, was the Irish sporting world. *Yeah, we went to castles and saw breathtaking cliffs, but let me tell you about this game called hurling.* I had discovered this little enclave that none of my friends knew anything about. It differed so much from the American sporting world of me-first athletes and greedy owners. It was as if the Irish players were stuck in a grainy black and white newsreel, romantically playing for the love of the game and the honor of their people. It seemed so fresh, but also a little naïve. Why shouldn't they get paid? Obviously, someone was making money off of them—our tickets for the hurling game cost €20 and prominently displayed the Guinness logo as the All-Ireland tournament's sponsor. Were the players getting taken advantage of? Were they suckers? Were they really content not earning a dime for their efforts? I had grown so used to bloodthirsty agents conniving against thrifty owners and seeing players' mug shots, the Irish setup seemed bizarre.

The thing that stuck with me the most was the pure pride the players carried with them. I admired that because I was in sort of a rut before my vacation, and quickly fell back into one after the excitement of my trip waned. What had been my *passion*—writing—was becoming just a *job* where I did the minimum and skated by. It was never like that before. Back in college, I wanted to be a great, to be mentioned in the same breath as nonfiction writers I enjoyed like Hunter S. Thompson, Tom Wolfe or Gay Talese. A few years later, I'd be lucky to be mentioned along with Snoopy.

My inertia, more than anything, was holding me back. I'd become excited once in a while and find a good story, and even won some awards from the state press association, but trying to be great just took too much effort.

What happened to my ambition? I couldn't claim that life beat me down, but somehow I had settled into a routine that was comfortable and easy. It extended from hearing daily "one game at a time" quotes to taking trips to the break room and praying that peanut M&M's would be available from the vending machine. I was stuck in mediocrity, and more troubling, didn't care. I had to question what I was doing with my life. I had friends who were doctors, lawyers and businessmen, and here I had a fear that one day I'd wake up and still be doing this at fifty-five. I needed a jolt of energy. A purpose. A feeling I was making a difference.

I didn't even know, though, if sports journalism was my calling anymore. As a fan, the pros were starting to disinterest me. Part of it seemed superficial, especially in the wake of 9/11 and other real world problems. Owners seemed sleazy. Players, doing their jobs, were labeled heroic and gritty. They weren't content just earning a living, instead grabbing every last penny and flaunting it with fancy cars. The whole sporting world seemed petty and mean, and had little connection to my life. I even lost interest in my favorite team, the New York Yankees. As recently as the late 1990s, I lived and died by them. But by 2003, it was ho hum, they just keep buying players, it's too easy. And when the hated Boston Red Sox beat the Yankees in 2004, I wasn't as devastated like I would have been at some other point in my life.

Every once in a while, I'd think about the Irish players, grown men who battle the daily tedium and soul-crushing days that we all go through. They show up bruised to work, put in a long day and then beat the crap out of each other for the honor of representing their people. In American pro sports, the players want a check. In the Irish sporting world, players want a jersey. No wonder the Irish people felt more of a connection with their sporting heroes than I did mine. They lived in the same communities, shopped at the same places. There was an electric authenticity to their world.

One time I carried that vibe. I thought back to when I played on my high school's freshman football team as an undersized 110-pounder. I was the fifth-string strong safety, and so low on the depth chart as a receiver, I can't remember my place. I hardly got playing time, unless it was a blowout. My moment of glory came when the coaches inserted me on the kickoff team in a rout. The runner came right at me—I briefly thought about digging a tunnel to escape—but held my ground and wrapped him up with both arms. He fell on top of me, and I got up with my glasses crooked and not sure where I was. Unfortunately, there was a penalty on the play so we had to re-kick off and I didn't earn a tackle in the official stats. My sideline, though, was howling that a stick-like figure with shoulder pads—me—contributed the best way he could. Even though I wasn't a NFL prospect, I was still part of the team and practiced hard.

It was that combination of fun and effort and dedication that I wanted to recapture. I thought I might find "it" by going back to Ireland to see what drives their athletes. Then, I'd snap out of my Irish daydream and say, Who am I kidding? Not only did I not know anyone there, I knew nothing, absolutely nothing about the GAA scene—not when and how long the season lasted, not even who the top teams were. Planning an extended move to Ireland didn't seem realistic. But there was something gnawing at me. So in the spring of 2004, I started peeking at Irish newspapers and GAA Web sites. I wanted to just quit my job, tell the boss to shove it, take my lifesavings and go overseas. Ah, how romantic, but also a pipe dream.

Then I read about the 2004 All-Ireland hurling quarterfinal between Kilkenny and Clare in late July. Midway through the second half, a butt of a stick suddenly smashed through Kilkenny star Henry Shefflin's facemask near his right eye. Blood streamed down his nose as the red-haired twenty-four-year-old left the game with a severed tear duct. He needed surgery that evening to restore his blurred vision. Shefflin was lucky—if he got hit a hair over he would have lost the eye. All week there were questions in the media and on fan Internet message boards whether the 2002 Player of the Year would play that Sunday in the semifinal. But Shefflin didn't have much time for recuperating and relaxing. He had Monday off for a bank holiday, but Tuesday his livelihood beckoned. Shefflin returned to his job handling finance for the Southeast region tractor sales for a subsidiary of the Bank of Ireland. One hitch—he remained office-bound because he wasn't able to drive to meet customers.

He did play in the semifinal, risking further injury to lead Kilkenny to a win. So this is Irish sports, I thought, a world where a superstar gets bashed in the eye on national TV on a Saturday, is sewed up that evening and doesn't miss a day of work despite a shining purple face—and his co-workers barely flinch.

Something clicked in me. I wanted to experience that passion. I woke up one day and said I'm going to do it. I had enough of the daily grind and thought maybe joining the Irish time warp, where everything seemed simpler, would wake me up out of my funk. The time was ripe for an adventure. I recently turned thirty and didn't have a wife, 2.5 kids or pets to tend to, just some fantasy sports teams and an occasional beard to mind. I hoped that by entering this foreign world and looking at it as a wide-eyed outsider, I'd be excited again and feel like I did as a ninth grader.

I devised a plan, where each month I'd go to a different place with a different theme. Unlike the U.S. pro sports setup, there isn't one league culminating with the playoffs and championship. Gaelic football and hurling have inter-county leagues from February to May followed by the more important All-Ireland tournament running from May to September. Then there is the competitive club scene. I wanted to experience all of these aspects. During my research I discovered that the GAA connects people from bustling cities to picturesque villages, from rolling green hills to messy riot-torn neighborhoods. All of Ireland is covered. Pride is based on where you're from, fostered by the snugness of the country. Dramatically, the Republic is six times smaller than California. It takes only three hours to drive from Dublin on the East Coast to Galway on the West on a perfect day. The island's 5.7 million people are divided into four provinces and thirty-two counties—which includes the six counties of Northern Ireland that are part of the United Kingdom. The country is compact enough to have All-Ireland competitions in everything from butter making to fiddle playing, and of course, its native games.

I didn't want to write a travelogue and detail all my misadventures. I was thinking more a *Friday Night Lights* than Bill Bryson. This would be a look at Irish culture and a sports book where I tell the athletes' stories purely through third-person narrative. But after a month of travel, I came to realize nothing revealed more about my subjects than my own first-hand experiences. I decided to weave in my encounters to help bring out the people's personalities.

I called a handful of team officials to let them know I was coming. Other places, I just showed up. I had many kinks to work out, and a few imminent problems loomed. I needed an extended visa to stay in Ireland for more than ninety days. I explained my plan over the phone to an immigration officer in County Clare, the site of my first stop. He didn't guarantee anything, but told me to meet with him after I arrived and to bring bank statements and a travel insurance card. Like everything else, I worried about deportation later and bought a plane ticket for an eight-month stay.

When I landed at Shannon Airport on the last weekend of January 2005, it didn't go smoothly. A custom official asked each passenger his length of stay.

"Two weeks"

"Three days"

"A week"

Then me.

"Uh, I plan on applying for an extended visa and staying until October to write a book about Gaelic football and hurling."

A long stare, then "What?!?"

He directed me to a bench as the other passengers whisked through. Aye. This would be a pretty short book, *My 25 Minutes in an Irish Airport*. He finally motioned me over. I calmly explained my intentions to the agent's perplexed face. *Oh no, don't tell me he's a soccer fan.* He then asked if I had a newspaper ID card or any proof that I was a journalist. The reason—anyone could say they're writing a book as a way to enter the country. *Damn, that guy was a soccer fan.* He finally stamped my passport for a month. *Soccer, please, he probably has GAA underwear*. I still needed to meet with the other immigration officer so I went about my business until he could see me three weeks later. No problem—I showed my documents and received an extended visa until October 10. I thought then that while I might get thrown out at some point, at least it wouldn't be for remaining illegally.

Problem No. 2: the manager of the first team I wanted to follow didn't know that I was coming. I had no idea if he would mind me hanging around. It all depended on his personality. If he was like a paranoid NFL coach, he might put his players off-limits. I nervously came up with another alternative title, *My Week in West Ireland*. Luckily, he didn't send me packing and offered great access.

Problem No. 3: I waited to book a room at the small parish's lone bed and breakfast until a few days before I left. If there was a cow handler convention in town that month I'd be screwed. Fortunately, not only did they have space but it was owned by one of the player's parents.

I was lucky at the start, and that luck stayed with me for the next eight months. I arrived with the All-Ireland club championship concluding and left in early October, shortly after the inter-county All-Ireland tournament.

The result is part travel book, part history book, part current events and part narrative-driven. One theme connects every signpost: the people's love of sports and willingness to compete no matter what the situation or obstacles they face. I was hoping that by observing them, it would awaken something that was going dead in me.

Hurling & Gaelic Football Primer

I'm expecting that many people reading this book will be fans and players of the GAA. But hopefully newcomers will also take a peek. What follows is a brief explanation of the rules and history of Gaelic football and hurling.

Pre-GAA

They don't compete today, but the Firbolgs were winners of an important hurling match that kicked-off a doubleheader ... in 1272 BC. The fearsome tribe then killed its opponents. Unfortunately for the Firbolgs, they didn't fare as well in the nightcap and lost the Battle of Moytura to the invading Tuatha Dé Danann.

Ireland's native games are still part of the country's folklore, despite tamer victory celebrations. Even before Christ, legendary warriors like Setanta—who took the name Cúchulainn after killing a savage hound by driving a sliotar (hurling ball) down its throat—used hurling in their training regimen. The Brehon Laws, the legal system beginning in approximately the seventh century, provided for compensation for hurling injuries.

Not even invaders and cultural cleansing attempts could stop play. In 1366, the Normans (which arrived in the late 12th century) banned hurling in the Statue of Kilkenny, afraid that their own settlers were losing allegiance to the king by adopting Irish customs. Hurling survived, but was again banned in the 1537 Statue of Galway, which contained the first mention of Gaelic football.

By the mid-1880s, hurling and football were disappearing, weakened by the Great Famine and English landowners withdrawing support because of the increasing Irish nationalism. Enter the GAA, originally called the Gaelic Athletic Association for the Preservation and Cultivation of our National Pastimes. The four original GAA sports are hurling, Gaelic football, handball and rounders. The first two are by far the most popular and my focus.

Hurling

A coach called hurling the "Riverdance of sport" and it's been labeled the fastest game in the world. The concept is simple. Drive the ball—a tad smaller and softer than a baseball—into the net (for three points) or over the crossbar and through the H-shaped goal posts (for one point). Players use a curved stick—called a hurley—that's between thirty-two and thirty-six inches long with a flat end. It'd be too easy to merely run from end to end carrying the ball—a sliotar—so only four steps are allowed at a time.

Enter the magic of the sport. After the steps, players place the sliotar (pronounced slitter) on the flat end of their hurley while running with it, usually using one hand. The move, called a solo, takes balance, quickness, fearlessness and concentration as opponents attempt to knock it away—either with their stick or body. Tackling like in American football is illegal, but hard shoulder-to-shoulder contact is permitted. While running, a player can tap the ball from his stick back into his hands twice. Again, rules are in place to show off the athletes' skill and finesse in the face of adversity.

To pass, a runner tosses the ball slightly in the air and strikes it with both hands griping the hurley. The motion resembles a vicious tennis forehand, home run shot or mammoth golf drive. He can also pass it with his hand, but it must be in a striking motion like an underhanded volleyball serve. Throwing the ball is illegal.

Defenders come in at close range to block the sliotar. Sticks smack and frightening noises are common. I still haven't figured out how more jaws aren't shattered. Most of the players, though, have been playing since they were in single-digits and know just the right angle to come in and when to pull away.

On high 50-50 balls from the goalie or a pass, players jump in the air, with sticks and hands flying up to catch the ball or to swat it to a teammate. Timing and guts are everything. On the ground, players can't directly pick up a loose ball. Instead, they must scoop it up with their stick either by jabbing at it, or by rolling it backwards onto the hurley.

After a penalty, a player is awarded a free shot from where the foul occurred. Meaning, no defender can stand directly in front to block it—consider it like a long foul shot in basketball. It's performed by either striking the ball from the ground, or lifting it up with the hurley before taking your whack. If the defense hits the ball out of bounds past the goal line, a free is awarded from 65 meters (71 yards). Accurately hitting balls a hundred yards approaching a hundred miles per hour is the norm.

If the ball goes out of bounds, the player gets a sideline cut, in which he chips it back into play directly from the ground. The movement resembles a 9-iron shot in golf. Hitting the ball is called a "puck."

Gaelic Football

In Gaelic football, men run with a ball (heavier, yet slightly smaller than a soccer ball) while twirling it from feet to hand. You score the same way as in hurling: into the net for a goal (three points) or over the bar (one point).

The two sports have similar rules with a major difference, of course: a foot replaces the hurley. Like in hurling, a runner is allowed four steps before displaying skills honed by years of practice. A solo run occurs when he kicks the ball back to himself in a toe-tap. It takes concentration and slickness as defenders try to thwart you with hard contact (throwing someone down is illegal). A player could also bounce the ball like a basketball, but not twice in a row—again too easy.

Defenders stand in the way. They throw a shoulder into you or knock the ball away with an open palm. Pushing and pulling is illegal, although there are gray areas. Different referees allow different degrees of contact, much like baseball umpires' strike zones differ. Action is physical—bloody knees, elbows, lips and muddy jerseys are the norm. So is an occasional elbow or punch when the referee isn't looking. I was surprised at how players jump into the air to win loose balls, which leads to violent collisions. Picking the ball up directly from the ground is a foul—he must use a foot in scooping it up.

Football has the same free kick system as in hurling. But instead of getting a 65-meter shot, players get a 45-meter kick (49 yards). He kicks it either straight from the ground or can toss it to his foot, like a punter, depending on personal style.

Different teams favor different strategies, which have evolved through the years. Long passes via kicks downfield used to be en vogue. Recently, a more possession-oriented game consisting of shorter hand passes and kicks have become popular.

Goals are hard to get—some games don't have any—and exciting as players quickly drop the ball near the net for a dead-on shot. Fisting the ball over the bar for a point is fine, but throwing it is illegal.

Overlapping Rules & Regulations

Positions: Both sports have fifteen players broken into a goalie, six defensive players, two midfielders and six offensive players. The offensive and defensive players are divided into two lines of three. Most teams use man-to-man defenses.

Equipment: None required. Helmets are optional in hurling (but a recent rule change made it mandatory for players under-21). The helmets are similar to those worn in ice hockey. Some have face guards, others are open. Footballers may wear thin gloves that help in catching.

Field size: Fields range from 142 to 158 yards long and 87 to 98 yards wide. (In comparison, an American football field is 120 yards long and 53 yards wide. An international soccer field is between 110-120 yards long and 70-80 yards wide.)

Goal posts: The posts are 21 feet apart. The crossbar is 8 feet above the ground. (The NFL posts are 18 feet apart and 10 feet above the ground. Soccer goal posts are 24 feet apart and 8 feet above the ground.)

Game time: Inter-county games have two thirty-five minute halves. Club games, two thirty minute halves.

Substitutions allowed per game: Five.

If it's tied: There is no sudden death overtime or shootouts. An entire game is replayed after a tie, including All-Ireland finals. A famous example was in the first round of the 1991 Leinster provincial football championship, in which Meath tied Dublin three times before finally winning the fourth game by a point. Injury time is commonly added, usually at least two minutes worth, but it could be several more based on the referee's discretion.

After a score: The goalkeeper booms the ball down field. In hurling, he sends it with a whack of his stick. In football, a long kick.

Score line: Goals are listed first, then points. For example, in the 2007 All-Ireland hurling championship, Kilkenny beat Limerick 2-19 to1-15 (25 to 18), and in the football final, Kerry demolished Cork 3-13 to 1-09 (22-12). For clarity sake, I sometimes listed the score by adding the total points, like in baseball or basketball.

Officials: Maintaining order is a referee, one linesman on each sideline to mark where the ball went out and four umpires (two on each side of the net) to signal scores and to assist the referee and linesmen. Umpires wear long white coats, resembling a lab jacket. They wave a green flag for a goal, a white flag for a point and both arms if the ball goes wide.

Jerseys: No lucky numbers need apply. A player gets a digit based on his position, from 1 to 15. Managers wear a shirt with the term Bainisteoir across the chest—the Irish word for manager. Player names aren't displayed on the back.

Team names: Many clubs don't have a nickname and go simply by the parish or local church. Some clubs are nicknamed for Irish patriots. The inter-county teams go by the county.

All-Ireland Tournament format: Teams first play in the four provincial tournaments—Connacht (upper west coast), Leinster (east coast), Munster (southwest) and Ulster (northwest and the six counties of Northern Ireland). In the past, it resembled the NCAA basketball tournament: one loss and you're out. The four provincial winners advanced to the All-Ireland semifinals. Now, there's a back-door system in which teams are guaranteed two games up to the All-Ireland quarterfinals. Provincial winners get automatic berths to the quarterfinals. The hurling format changed in 1997, and Gaelic football followed in 2001. The debate is similar to having the wild card in baseball. Purists hate it, while others love it because teams have a second chance. The provincial clashes, though, are like a tournament within a tournament. They still have great meaning and tradition and are taken seriously.

Chapter 1
Hoosier's, Irish-style

February: Kilmurry-Ibrickane, County Clare

It wasn't raining on this February evening along Ireland's West Coast, and the wind didn't make your hair break dance, so it counted as a mild night. Still, the cool breeze splashed against your face and the Atlantic Ocean purred in the background. Sensible people were curled in front of a fire, sipping tea and munching on muffins and homemade jam. On a dimly lit field, though, Johnnie Daly and twenty of his teammates ran out one by one wearing shorts and wool knit hats to keep their ears white. They were capping a long afternoon with a night of pain in preparation for the upcoming Gaelic football national club semifinal.

Daly, a star forward, already had a difficult day. His three-month-old daughter, Sophie, kept him and his girlfriend up most of the night with her first cold. By the time he got to his job in the government's motor tax office, thankfully there were no bags under his engaging dark green eyes and he looked smooth in a crisp button-down shirt and corduroy pants. During his ten-hour shift, Daly renewed licenses and eased customer concerns as two lingering injuries—a tender hamstring and a sore back—forced him to stand instead of sit at a stool. It was all a juggling act with sports vs. real life. Today, real life was winning.

After work, the twenty-seven-year-old hustled out the door like he does on the field, his physique neither doughy nor ripped but perfectly spread along his five-foot-eleven frame. He grabbed a slice of pizza and hopped in his car for the thirty-minute drive straight to training—a full dinner and hugging Sophie would have to wait a couple more hours. Other players hurried from their jobs as plasterers, electricians and construction workers.

"One of the guys said for the next few weeks everything else comes second—football has to come first," Daly said later, wanting to believe it. "But how can you put your little daughter second?"

Unfortunately, his teammates, too, were having trouble juggling their lives with the biggest game of their careers. Their small parish team, Kilmurry-Ibrickane, had emerged from a Christmas break flat. So now, a white-bearded man who could double as a fit Santa Claus was trying to get Kilmurry out of their funk before it was too late. He barked instructions, his voice oozing urgency.

"C'mon lads," he repeated. "I don't care if you run yourself into the ground to stay with your man. Do not allow him to have a free reign of the downfield."

This was the wrong time to be in the doldrums. Already, few thought Kilmurry could compete with the Ballina Stephenites, a powerhouse squad from a town six times bigger. An upset would advance Kilmurry to the championship on St. Patrick's Day at Croke Park, the hallowed 82,000-seat national stadium in Dublin where young boys dreamed of one day playing. Daly, like all his teammates, had bought into that dream. For most of the players, it was their one shot at national glory, a kind of Irish *Hoosiers* in which villages of a handful of thousands faced off against large towns and cities. As night fell over the Atlantic and the Kilmurry footballers, the grand stage was up for grabs.

My journey started at the most romantic level. Clubs were the salt of the organization. Here, superstars—while on loan from the high-profile inter-county team—played alongside their buddies they grew up with and on the same field graced by their father and grandfather, which was cut by their neighbor. Everyone felt a sense of ownership. The senior team competed in the county championship through the summer. In the fall, the winner advanced to one of the four provincial tournaments, which determined the All-Ireland semifinalists the following February. The final Daly hoped to lead Kilmurry to on St. Patrick's Day would shape into one of those Cinderella moments in a tournament where an unknown small team occasionally broke through.

Kilmurry-Ibrickane (pronounced I-Brick-In) was this year's golden girl after winning its fifth County Clare title, then bucking 150/1 odds to capture the Munster provincial crown. The parish of 1,800 consisted of two small villages—Mullagh and Quilty—and tiny Coore, too small for village status. The sprawling landscape featured a backdrop of mountains on one side and rocky beaches leading to the Atlantic Ocean on the other. The next city to the west was New York.

"If we didn't have the GAA, even though it's an amateur organization, there wouldn't be much else for young kids to do, especially in a place like west Clare," midfielder Odhran O'Dwyer, Kilmurry's captain, told me later in the month. "It's different when you're in the cities and you got all the boxing clubs. You've got the soccer, you've got hurling, you've got different things. But in west Clare, you know, everything seems to revolve around the GAA and obviously the pub culture—but the two sort of go hand in hand."

With the semifinal approaching, the normally sleepy seaside parish was coming alive like Brigadoon on Market Fair Day. Red and green flags flew from windows, just like they would in any small American town, say in West Virginia or Texas, in support of its high school football team. Someone wrote "KIB Munster Kings 2004" in white chalk across the main two-lane road near the team's field in Quilty. Kilmurry, occasionally shortened to KIB, was football-mad, no doubt, but the community center in Mullagh also burned with activity. Locals were practicing for a production of *The Field,* a play by legendary Irish writer John B. Keane about a man's obsession and attachment over his land in rural Ireland. Other nights, a teenaged team of Irish step dancers prepared for a national competition.

People generated the action, not shopping malls, stadium-style movie theaters or Internet cafes. The parish provided just the basics—eight pubs, five elementary schools, three churches, two food/hardware stores and two gas stations. For other amenities, residents must drive ten minutes up the coast to Miltown Malbay, offering a clothing store, a florist, a Chinese restaurant and a bookmaker—what more do you need?

Kilmurry's team had its personality shaped by that self-sufficiency and its surroundings, notably a refusal to succumb when things looked bleak. Among the parish's proudest moments was a heroic rescue at sea in 1907. About thirty Kilmurry men jumped into boats and risked their lives against strong winds to save a crew of twenty-two from a French ship that had crashed off the coast. Rescuers salvaged the ship's bell, placing it in the Quilty church named the "Star of the Sea."

Their sons and grandsons carried that same DNA, and in 2004, Kilmurry had a chance to display that grit. Trailing by seven points at intermission on county championship day, Kilmurry rallied for a late lead, only to have its opponent, Éire Óg, score right before the whistle for a tie. In an American sport, the winner would have been decided in overtime. Instead, the teams needed to play again from the beginning a week later—consider it a massive do-over. In that contest on the last Monday in October, Kilmurry led by five points at the half, squandered its lead, but won on two late Daly scores to advance to the Munster tournament.

The moments to make your knuckle hair turn gray were just beginning, especially for Daly. As the quarterfinal against Drom-Broadford of County Limerick approached, his mind wasn't just consumed with strategy. In a case of poor timing, Davina, Johnnie's girlfriend, was due to deliver their baby the day of the quarterfinal. He couldn't miss his child being born. No way. Then again, getting to this provincial elimination game had consumed him for the last year. Davina and her football-obsessed family were confident that the baby knew to wait. She felt good that morning and instructed a relieved Daly to play. Davina, though, decided to stay away after having a scary dream: she went into labor while in the stands.

So on a surprisingly calm afternoon on the final day of October, Daly cleared his mind and was ready to go. Kilmurry started slow, but rallied from a four-point halftime deficit for a tie late in the game. A replay seemed necessary. But with the referee checking his watch deep into injury time—a few extra minutes were usually added to make up for various stoppages throughout the contest—Drom-Broadford fouled Kilmurry and Daly had a free kick from the left side, thirty-two yards away. The damp grass from the previous night's rain gave the ball a greasy feel, but Daly gripped it with all his might. He seized up the needed slant, took his usual seven steps back and two steps to the side and struck the ball at the sweet spot. Daly's calculations proved correct. The ball sailed through the middle of the uprights for the one-point lead. No time for celebrating, just yet. Kilmurry dropped back on defense and the referee allowed Drom-Broadford one final flurry. Drom did get a kick off but it fell just short of the crossbar. As his mates exhaled and celebrated, Daly's mother handed him her cell phone to speak with Davina. She was fine, if not nervous from listening on the radio, and a healthy Sophie was born at nine the next night.

The semifinal three weeks later featured less dramatics—no babies, no down-to-the-wire kicks, just a solid five-point win as Kilmurry reached the provincial final on December 6. What else, but a tense tie. The videotape showed their opponents, Stradbally of County Waterford, scored a point that the umpire ruled wide. Luck happens. In the replay a week later, a Kilmurry player received two yellow cards and was automatically ejected, meaning it had to play a man down for the final twenty-five minutes. Stradbally had the wind in its backs, a boon for accurate kicks, but fired eight nerve-racking shots wide. Kilmurry held on for a one-point win, keyed by five points from Daly, the Man of the Match.

Now, few experts were giving them a chance in the semifinal against the Ballina Stephenites from County Mayo, a large club that breezed through the Connacht regional with a superstar lineup. The drama was set for the next month. I wanted to see how ordinary people embraced the sporting moment of their life. I didn't speak with the manager before I arrived, so I was hoping he wouldn't mind me hanging around.

After the practice, I pitched my idea for writing about the team. There were no PR people or agents to convince. I went to Santa himself, the manager Patrick O'Dwyer, who was worrying about a thousand other things. We arranged to meet for lunch later in the week at The Quilty Tavern, better known as Cooney's, a nod to the owner. Because Kilmurry didn't have a clubhouse attached to its field like bigger or richer clubs, the players ate team meals at Cooney's.

The cozy pub welcomed you with a fire burning to the left of the entrance. All around, black and white pictures of legendary local heroes decorated the walls. American police badges and license plates stood past the bar counter. At noon, the pub had few customers giving us quiet. We sat on the far side behind a large world map. O'Dwyer immediately controlled the conversation. What angle was I taking? Who was my audience? Why would they be interested? Did I bring any of my newspaper articles with me? (I barely remembered my passport, let alone clippings.) Where could he read them on the Internet? O'Dwyer had every possibility covered. But I couldn't blame him. Here, I just barely got off the plane and wanted inside information. For all he knew, I could've been a spy for the opposing team. That thoroughness was part of his personality. I noticed he usually carried a small notepad, jotting down ideas and inspiration.

"He prides himself on seeing the little things," veteran midfielder Aiden Moloney told me. "He's got a lot of good ideas on how to play it. That's his strength."

O'Dwyer wasn't honeymooning in his retirement after twenty-nine years as a high school English teacher. Instead, he was raising cattle on his family's farm in Mullagh. For fun, he was building a bird sanctuary around a lake. I couldn't miss the scratches and cuts that rippled across his meaty hands from hauling trees and guiding stubborn calves. He didn't exactly plan on coaching. In 2002, O'Dwyer stepped down after leading Kilmurry to the county title, but could only stay away for a season. Now his days were spent worrying if the midfielders would step up or about the nagging injuries to a handful of players, or, most of all, if they could regain the intensity that carried them earlier in the season. A free weekend didn't exist, and he even canceled an overseas trip to the Lewis and Clark trail in Oregon.

O'Dwyer reflected on the long campaign between bites of pork chops and carrots and parsnips. Preseason practice began in the winter. Kilmurry then competed in the county league and the county tournament, advancing from the group qualifying stages to the single-elimination quarterfinals to the championship to winning the six-team Munster tournament, consisting of teams in the Southwest. That earned a three-week respite right before Christmas, until practice resumed in early January.

"It was necessary," O'Dwyer explained. "I don't think we could have continued—it was too intense. See you're talking about amateur guys. They all have to go to jobs. They have families. If they're young, they're going to college."

O'Dwyer's broad knowledge kept things in perspective. When I got him talking about history, he didn't throw out stats about GAA championships in the 1950s. He told me instead how he became "utterly riveted" by Ken Burns' nine-part series on the Civil War while channel surfing one day. That began a fascination with the topic—understandable, maybe, given Ireland's tortured history of infighting. A few years ago, he traveled through Yankee and Confederate country for three weeks. First stop—Ford's Theatre in Washington because of his admiration for Lincoln. Then on to Gettysburg and Richmond, soaking up every detail and making park rangers earn their living by answering his questions, follow-up questions and then more grilling. His wife remained in Ireland—someone less obsessed would be bored.

O'Dwyer looked like he could be an older cousin of Honest Abe with his tall frame and his white beard, hair balding on top. It was easy to get him going about Lincoln and his other idols.

"Churchill, I mean even though Irish people don't generally admire English people, but I admire him hugely. I think his courage and his *unbelievable* self-belief, you know, was fantastic. I admire Lee, I think he …"

O'Dwyer couldn't finish the sentence as his excitement jumped to another hero. The smattering of freckles sprinkling his forehead seemingly vibrated.

"I admire Grant, oh god I admire Grant. I think Grant was wonderful. Grant was utterly fearless. He was not afraid of his own carcass. He was completely and utterly fearless."

Gratefully, O'Dwyer refrained from making those inevitable lame comparisons between war and sports. He was smarter than that. But he did draw inspiration from real people who never gave in, his curiosity going all over. On a bus ride to a scrimmage, he chatted about volcanoes, historic graves and the latest popular nonfiction reads.

"I just love English and I am fascinated with words and I am fascinated with the possibility of words," said O'Dwyer, again starting to burst. "And I'm particularly fascinated by history because I think we are a lot poorer as a generation and as a people if we don't understand it. Someone preceded us and great sacrifices preceded us. And if we have a nice time now, there were people in the past who didn't have that through a variety of reasons, either through war or through social circumstances. So I'm always mindful of *that* kind of background."

For all of O'Dwyer's philosophizing, though, he was also a pragmatist and giving everything to ensure that Kilmurry was ready. Depending on the situation, he'd offer encouragement or tough leadership like chiding players for text messaging while studying a tape of an opponent.

"He commands a lot of respect being a school teacher," Moloney, the midfielder, told me. "He's got his thirty students here, you know. He's a good coach and he's a good communicator."

People agreed that his strong points were coaching and implementing strategies. His weakness? Making adjustments during a game. He'd often ask the opinion of veteran players and his assistants. Heck, even Grant had his advisors. O'Dwyer, though, was adamant in demanding that his players carry discipline and make sacrifices. But you better be careful if you call him a disciplinarian.

"I wouldn't want the word to be confused with autocratic," he cautioned near the end of lunch.

No, O'Dwyer could be open-minded. So he let me hang around despite wanting to protect his players. As the month developed, he never shooed me away from anything.

I stayed at a bed and breakfast owned by Johnnie Daly's parents, a mile from the sparkling coastline. In the distance, the 700-foot Cliffs of Moher loomed close enough to see their imposing, ragged charm. Also noticeable was Mutton Island, split from Kilmurry's mainland by a tidal wave in 804. The ocean's moods still determined the beach landscape. One day the jolly water looked calm blue and the sand smooth with a littering of rocks; the next, the sea turned livid and violent white waves surfed in. A few days later, the beach returned with everything rearranged. A dead seal with its eyeballs ripped out laid near crows chirping away on rotting seaweed. They had a menu. One variety was tan, the other was slippery black and similar to an ice rink. There was sleabhacan, the seaweed known as fisherman's cabbage: slow boil and you've got yourself a meal. During World War II, tins of beans and other goods washed on shore from torpedoed ships. Parents often brought their sick children out here to inhale the fresh sea breezes, a natural form of penicillin. To the far left, steam billowed out of the Moneypoint energy plant.

The Dalys were a living library, always helpful and a GAA family to the core. Johnnie's twin older brothers and father, John, all played for the parish at one time. Dad later coached and served in administrative roles. He was currently on the lotto committee, the financial lifeblood of most GAA clubs as people try to pick the right numbers for a couple bucks. I'd go with the elder Daly before the draw and help sort numbers. It was mandatory to conduct GAA business in the Irish language (sometimes called Gaelic), so I signed the book Andrias O'Mendlo—two weeks in and I had an Irish name. I met locals there, but my ear needed to become adjusted to the thick Irish accent. People made sure to speak slowly to me, but to each other they might as well have been speaking French. If I didn't understand something, I just nodded my head and smiled. Accents differed throughout parts of Ireland just like they do in the United States. By the end of the year, my ear was nearly pitch-perfect.

In-between lotto draws, I developed a routine of sorts. On Tuesdays and Thursdays, I'd walk an hour past the beaches and nine-hole golf course at Spanish Point, to the library in Miltown Malbay to use the Internet, attend Kilmurry's evening practice there (Kilmurry's field was too choppy after the long season) and catch a ride back. I didn't mind the walk. I appreciated the open land and quiet of the countryside, and the absence of strip malls and billboards. But my departure always encountered an obstacle. The Dalys had three friendly dogs, which would sooner lick you to death than bite you. The problem was, I couldn't leave the house without being engulfed and followed. So it became a game. I'd wait until the dogs were on the other side of the yard. Then I'd quickly bolt out. Sometimes, they came charging toward me with their tongues swaying and I would have to retreat indoors and try again later. When I did get free, down the road, past a cemetery, a white dog would be waiting, bouncing near the top of a fence, barking and scaring the heck out of me. Next to him was a horse that seemed capable of leaping over any second. I simply made a shushing sound and quickly tiptoed away. The roadway itself was just as nerve-racking. The narrow, two-lane roads featured few sidewalks. Every time a car whizzed by, I needed to jump onto the raised grass or rocks. Thorns were always a nice surprise. Chewing cows and new dogs—beefy Dog Vader-types—watched me pass. The dogs strolled to the front of their driveway and barked, while slowly inching toward me to make sure I wouldn't be stepping onto their digs. As a result, I could never totally relax despite the glorious ocean scenery. It'd be a constant ruff, ruff, ruff … moo, moo, moo … hop, hop, hop. Fortunately, there was no bah, bah, bah because few sheep lived in the area due to the wet terrain. At least twice, I turned around and walked an extra forty-five minutes to avoid dogs.

My fears weren't totally paranoid. In mid-March, the county council proposed a rule that banned dogs, even leashed, from beaches during eleven in the morning to six at night. Newspapers reported there had been various attacks on people. One included an elderly man falling and breaking his hip. If it was open season by the Fidos of Clare on its senior citizens, I didn't stand a chance. Beach goers rallied against the proposed ban, including author Nuala O'Faolain. You can't compete with writers in the island of Joyce, Yeats and Wilde. The proposal was tabled, but eventually passed the following January.

Now, I'd hate to paint the area as the Wild West with foaming cujos roaming freely along with buffaloes and humans dueling each other at high noon. In fairness, I'd been to parts of rural America with even scarier pups. In Kilmurry-Ibrickane, there simply were a few dogs not on leashes. Couple that with a cat person who values quiet, and you could see that we were perhaps better off without each other.

One night, I avoided the route by the graveyard. The other way, though, wasn't any less frightening, especially with the wind ripping and howling in the distance. Johnnie Daly happened to be driving home from work and scooped me up. He saved me just like he's rescued Kilmurry as the team's free taker, the player designated to take an open kick for a point after a foul or when the defense knocks the ball out past the goal line. The distances and angles vary. Daly must assess the situation and apply just the right power and touch to sail the ball over the bar and through the uprights with his right foot.

His was a high profile and high-pressure position. Unlike a field goal kicker in American football, a free taker wasn't a specialist. Daly primarily played at forward, running all game, trying to score any way he could. Throw in tired legs, wind, mud and the pressure of everyone watching with the game's outcome in his hands, and a free wasn't always a give-me.

The role suited the laid-back Daly to a tee. One teammate described him as "cool as the breeze."

"He never gets rattled," Patrick O'Dwyer agreed. "You never see him involved in fighting and he never gets overexcited."

Daly had short stints on Clare's county team, battling injuries and never finding a permanent spot. Now, he was peaking after his best season for Kilmurry and has started receiving national exposure. Fans held yellow Johnny 3:07 posters—3:07 being a wishful score line of three goals and seven points. It was a play on a sign spotted at GAA games promoting a religious scripture. (It didn't bother Daly that his first name was often spelled with a y instead of an ie.)

The cheering Daly received on weekends was levered by a quick wit that made him a favorite among his teammates despite his star status. His delivery was so perfect, it took a moment to register. One night I remarked that soccer wasn't as popular in America as I watched an English game with the team at dinner at Cooney's after practice.

"Neither is Gaelic football."

On a Saturday morning, Kilmurry arrived in rural County Kerry for a scrimmage after several wrong turns down tight roads with narrow bridges. Patches of hilly dairy farms surrounded the field. I must have appeared jittery at one point.

"This is Knocknagoshel. I haven't been here either."

At another dinner, a teammate hogged the rolls and was eager to gobble more before the vegetable soup arrived.

"Quick, hide the butter."

When I asked if I could go to an award dinner with him, he said yes if I didn't bring the "hairy jacket" referring to my big, ragged tan coat.

Daly's life was more than one-liners, though, evident by a mature look. There was no denying the gray edge of his hairline, the whiteness spreading to the top and back. A quick glance, and one might think Daly was in his forties. I tentatively brought that up one day.

"What's your point?" he responded, trying to sound tough before smiling.

Heredity likely caused it. His recent schedule wasn't helping either. Sophie's cold just meant his long hours were even longer. And at least once a week, he worked late and went straight to the 7:30 practice. Those nights he didn't see his family until around ten.

So there's a big game? We need you in the office.

Two weeks before the semifinal, he was invited to two award dinners. The *Irish Independent,* the country's highest circulated newspaper, sponsored the first event. The paper had selected Daly as its sports star of the week following the Munster final. At the celebrity-filled banquet in Dublin honoring the weekly winners, Daly sat with the daughter of Irish President Mary McAleese and retired Gaelic football legend Mick O'Connell.

A few days later, Daly missed three hours of overtime to attend the Clare Community & Sports Awards banquet. Area luminaries delivered speeches and the message was clear: local heroes matter. Like Daly, who collected numerous good luck wishes along with the Gaelic football Player of the Year award and a statue with an eagle on top of a man. Unlike the other reception, attendees rolled up their sleeves for the festive music and dancing after dinner. Daly lithely moved from the electronic train to the old-time waltz to the Siege of Ennis, a popular Irish wedding dance. It looked dangerous and dizzying to an outsider—in, out, over, back, twirl. But a sweaty Daly held his own.

The hobnobbing was nice, but work beckoned. I went with Daly to see what a day was like in the week before the game. Even the dogs were staying in their sheds on this particular nasty morning. Gaelic football players, though, didn't have that luxury. So Daly rolled out of bed despite the driving rain at 8:20 with just twenty-five minutes before he needed to leave, meaning there was no time for food. A shower and out the door it was. He kissed Sophie one last time and left their house less than a couple hundred yards from the Atlantic Ocean, today harsh. The curvy stretch of roads through the countryside lacked traffic, so he didn't have to speed during the half-hour commute to Ennis (the county's largest town).

When he got to his office, Daly poured a glass of water. He normally drank five or six pints a day to stay hydrated. The fluids would help him motor through a practice later that evening. The morning's first customer was a woman paying her annual tax and requesting an address change. Her two little girls, dressed in pink as he one day expects Sophie to be, motored around the empty office, marching and laughing, then each hugging one of their mom's legs.

Daly smiled.

"Did you feed them Weetabix?" he joked, referring to Europe's version of Wheaties, which promise to bestow nutritional powers and generate energy, which the girls definitely possessed.

The foul weather had evidently kept people indoors, so Daly used the slow morning to catch up on paperwork at his desk behind the front counter. He took a break at 11 a.m. to eat three pieces of brown bread and gulp a glass of water—breakfast. He joked with his co-workers, who needled him for using a dish for cookies, obviously for my benefit. After everyone returned to work, Daly washed the cups and plates.

"We don't have any maids," he told me while moving the cloth in a circular motion. "It's not glamorous here."

For the day, he made seventy-one transactions dealing with approximately forty customers. The beginning and end of the month were busier as customers rush to renew their licenses and make payment deadlines. Daly could service 200 people a day, stamping and filing forms, easing concerns. Some of the work makes an accountant seem like a flame-thrower, but it could be worse.

"As jobs go it's not so bad," said Daly, his dimples winning fans like a baby's smile would. "There are times in the summer when I look out and the sun is shining and think I'd like to be outside today, but there are more wet days than dry days in Ireland. A lot more, so I'm thankful to be inside a lot of times."

Fifteen minutes before he was about to leave, a *Clare Champion* reporter surprised Daly on his cell phone after a teammate dished out his number. On the car ride home, through boggy land that wasn't fertile for farming like in the country's flat middle, Daly shrugged off the attention he received for his scoring prowess.

"A lot of times I don't get fouled for the free but I'm still taking them. So the person who gets fouled should get the credit. Of course it always looks better for the person that's actually scoring. I guess I get the glory. You also get the criticism when you miss."

Like when he shanked a shot in the provincial final three months ago that would have put his team up by three points instead of two late in the game.

"A lot of lads were asking me after—even though we won—what happened with that …"

Suddenly, Daly stopped his red sports car after passing a white van advertising Munster Food Distributors, glanced back, and hit reverse to meet it on an empty two-lane road near the parish. The windows opened and a mutual nod of heads followed.

"Ooh, I thought that was you," said Daly, reaching to a folder on the back seat. "That's the form. Have a good look at it."

It was a big man known simply as Butcher—who got the moniker from his father. Nicknames were passed from old man to son like a large nose or high blood pressure. The team also had a Horse and a Rabbit, whose brother went by Moose. Daly had so far avoided acquiring an heirloom nickname. Butcher, either lucky or not so lucky depending on one's point of view, was a rabid fan and a neighbor of Daly's.

"You'll see me later—or hear me," Butcher promised.

A few hours earlier, Butcher called Daly asking him to bring a tax form home for him. The night before, Daly received a similar request from another neighbor.

"Everybody calls me," Daly said with a shrug. "It's just a favor. You do favors for people and you sometimes get a favor in return."

Daly dropped off the second document, went home for a quick dinner and was soon off for the 7:30 practice, his day not yet done.

Now, the same guy who tidied up after his co-workers and fetched forms for his neighbors would soon be playing for a chance at a national championship. The game meant everything to him, but he had his priorities in check. A baby's cry and love of his lady came first. But make no mistake—if Kilmurry lost, Daly said he'd be "gutted."

Kilmurry faced just one problem: things still weren't clicking. Team management thought a trip to picturesque Killarney in County Kerry two weekends before the game could be the solution. Bing Crosby sang *Christmas in Killarney* in honor of the town's beautiful mountains and lakes. This wasn't a sightseeing trek, though. It was forty-five hours designed for fine-tuning and confidence gaining.

Players sacrificed their weekend by leaving Saturday morning at 9:19 a.m. A comfortable chartered bus traveled up the West Coast, through the Kerry ferry where you could spot dolphins on a warm day, through Listowel in Kerry, the hometown of the writer John B. Keane and Gort in Galway, which surprisingly had a large Brazilian population.

The team first stopped in eastern Kerry near County Limerick for a scrimmage with Kerry's under-21 team. Farms and cows surrounded the field, which didn't have a locker room. Players dressed off to the side near a decaying building. At one point, people passed by on horses. It was a windy day, and with it, Kilmurry's crispness was returning. They won loose balls and hustled like they had an All-Ireland semifinal in two weeks. Most of the players sported a bloody knee or a thigh covered in mud. Every time someone took a tumble, though, breaths were held.

If it looked serious, Odhran O'Dwyer, a winner possessing trophy ears with a slight curl, quickly followed, delicately probing the bones and joints for the extent of the injury. O'Dwyer conveniently ran a sports medicine and acupuncture practice in Ennis. Kilmurry's captain was moving gingerly himself, picking his spots to push it. A specialist recently recommended surgery for a torn groin. O'Dwyer—with little thought needed—decided to wait until the season was over. By now, he knew how to deal with injuries. He had a similar operation nine years earlier, once broke his left hand, endured gashes over his eyes and had suffered concussions. Gaelic football was physical and with the players not wearing pads, trouble followed. Hard shoulder-to-shoulder contact led to violent collisions. Heads banged and bodies got slammed to the ground.

"Probably lost a few brain cells along the way," O'Dwyer said like it was no big deal. "You just get on with these things, you know. It's a physical game and there's no point complaining. You just take the knocks and the bangs and the good and the bad all together."

Now was no time to worry about pain.

After the game, the opponent's coach Charlie Nelligan—a famous retired goalkeeper for Kerry—addressed the wide-eyed Kilmurry players.

"You're as good as anybody out there," he said generously, merely trying to help out a fellow Munster provincial team.

Next up was a practice session with a coach who guided a Killarney club to the 1992 All-Ireland title. He offered tips and encouragement as the fire was starting to return. Outside voices were always best heard.

Before dinner at the hotel, another Kerry legend gave a motivational speech. Eoin "Bomber" Liston, a big, bearded man the size of Mark McGwire, reinforced the message that Kilmurry could win; all they had to do was to stay focused. When the Bomber talked, people tended to listen.

Most of the advice came through sincere clichés, but the positive reinforcements were working. I could just feel the players' confidence rebounding. After they watched a tape of Ballina in the County Mayo tournament, it was back. Their opponents looked good, but not great, and very beatable. When Kilmurry finished dissecting the tape at eleven o'clock after an hour, I asked Odhran O'Dwyer if he could chat for a few minutes. He obliged and plopped into a chair to the side as his teammates walked out. Before the season started, O'Dwyer told them that they would win the Munster title.

"I think some of the guys were laughing," he said now.

O'Dwyer's confidence came from experience. The thirty-one-year-old played for Clare since he was nineteen and for Ireland against Australia in the annual challenge series two years ago. The professional Australian Football League (AFL) was similar to Gaelic football, but with more tackling. The associations tweaked a few rules to please everyone, and all-star teams played two games before large crowds in October. It was the closest thing to the Olympics a Gaelic football player could hope for. The Irish coaches selected O'Dwyer for the 2003 team, which split with host Australia before 100,000 fans.

The Australians earned several hundred thousand a year. O'Dwyer? Well, as a Gaelic football player, he could lose €200 or €300 in lost patient fees a couple nights a week when he leaves work early for practice during the summer.

"I've never estimated how much because I'll only upset myself," said O'Dwyer, who had deep lines that extended from the bottom of his nose to his chin.

It didn't take much for him to justify his choices. The GAA, after all, measured success differently. Putting on your parish jersey meant something. That explained why O'Dwyer was here on a Saturday night, willing to put off surgery, playing through pain.

"When you're representing your country, obviously it's a higher grade and you want to get out there and do your best," O'Dwyer continued. "But competitions like this, it's with guys you've been playing with since you were ten, twelve years of age and the whole way along. Especially in a small parish like Kilmurry it's a close bond. Everybody knows each other. And to win with people that you're really close with is a great feeling."

Bloodlines ran deep. A family reunion could easily break into a game. The O'Dwyers, with father Patrick and the four brothers/teammates—Odhran, Michael, Peter and Robert—were Kilmurry's current first family. The clan claimed football as their birthright, kicking in their backyard since they were little. Flowerbeds and pretty Georgian-style windowpanes didn't stand a chance.

"I can't say that every window was broken," Dad recalled, "but definitely 50 percent of them were. You'd hear the smash and the culprit would disappear. Sometimes, in fact, I came home and there would be total silence and I would be steered away from the area where the window had been broken.... Sometimes they even repaired the windows and if you saw the botched job—well, I could only laugh then at that stage."

Football taught various lessons—competitiveness, loyalty, forgiveness.

"We were always there and egging each other on," said Odhran, often the instigator as the oldest. "At the end of the day you're there and you're going to back each other up if something happens."

Odhran, appropriately, was named after Saint Patrick's chariot driver who martyred himself to save his boss during an ambush. As a boy, this Odhran grew up shy and was still a bit of a loner, rarely stopping at the pubs en masse with his teammates. Doing his own thing led him around the world in his mid-twenties. The plan was to stay six months. He returned two years later after traveling through Australia, Chicago, Canada and Fiji. He went from fighting the cold on Lake Shore Drive to playing rugby on the beach off the South Pacific Ocean.

As O'Dwyer was telling me this, I looked at my phone's clock—midnight, and now I felt guilty keeping him this long.

"Hey, we could talk all night, but I should let you go."

"No, that's okay."

O'Dwyer felt revitalized and sensed the long day had provided the needed boost.

"After watching the tape, guys said 'Jeez, you know we could beat these guys,'" he said with newfound energy. "When they left there was like a buzz in the room."

Wear and tear eventually punished joints and ligaments. For perspective, most careers end in their early thirties at the highest level. Going until thirty-five was pushing it. Playing past your forties was almost unheard of.

"It's like living to 130," Gerard Talty, one of the assistant coaches, told me.

Aiden Moloney was not ready for the glue factory just yet. The forty-year-old—known by everyone as Horse—still plugged along, hoping to break into the lineup one more time. Lately, though, he had been more a mascot than a thoroughbred, only occasionally coming off the bench. In his prime, Horse was like a Triple-Crown contender. He played on the 1992 Clare team that brought home the Munster title for the first time in seventy-five years, and narrowly lost to Dublin in the All-Ireland semifinal. It was a special moment for Clare football. After the Munster final, the team paraded the trophy throughout the county, stopping at each player's parish.

"That's where we made our reputations," Horse said of his calling card. "Whatever we do, we'll always be remembered for that."

Another day he'd never forget took place in May 1994, when he was twenty-eight and in his prime. Horse's left foot got tangled in the turf and he crumbled, followed by a crashing opponent. The resulting broken ankle and torn ligaments needed six operations. The outcome: a cast for seven weeks and a playing career in jeopardy.

He ran with a limp and lost speed. But his skills and savvy remained, enough for him to contribute at the club level. Horse still distributed the ball like a point guard and rarely dropped passes. He could read and anticipate the action, which compensated for a loss in physical prowess. So, he wasn't hanging around to chase past glory. Football was just what he did.

"We all know once you reach a certain age it's all over and all you have left are your memories," said Patrick O'Dwyer of every player's nightmare. "So a lot of guys try to extend their playing time span as long as they possibly can because when it's over, it's over forever."

Sometimes, Horse looked out of place as younger players sported Fcuk jackets and nifty hairdos, messy in the right spots. He'd often wear a white hat, but not in the fashionable crooked or backward way, with graying sides, resembling a coach or dad. He showed me a picture taken after Kilmurry won the 1993 county title with two little mop haired kids—who were now his current teammates.

The father figure role was fine with him.

"They wouldn't discuss music with me now," said Horse, laughing briefly at the thought. "Ah, I get on well with them. They slag me for being so old. I played at a good level, so when I do take the mickey a little bit they still respect me."

So the Horse continued on, or, as he put it, "hanging in there with my fingernails, just hanging on."

His arms had a far reach. The more information you got about him, the more interesting he became. Like he once ran a marathon when he was seventeen. And for the last few years, he had trained caddies part-time at nearby Doonbeg Golf Club, which featured a course designed by Greg Norman along 1.5 miles of beaches and dunes. He lugged nine-irons for politicians and celebrities including Hugh Grant.

Oh, and he once saved somebody's life.

A certificate from the Comhairle Na Mire Gaile (the council to recognize deeds of bravery) with flowery heliographic lettering was proudly mounted in the front hallway of his Quilty house. A few years ago on Christmas Eve, Horse and three co-workers were driving home when they saw a car veer off the pier into the darkness of the ocean. The furthest Horse ever swam was the length of a pool. Still, in an act of exceptional courage he jumped into the freezing water and dragged the man back while holding onto a life buoy.

He wasn't exactly Superman.

"I gave it a good thought," he said with a laugh.

Horse's life almost took a different turn. At eighteen, he moved to Chicago and drove a forklift because jobs were scarce in Clare. A friend set up an interview at De Beers diamonds near Shannon Airport and Horse returned. Between working on machines that grind industrial diamonds, there was football.

Now, old Horse was getting one last chance. Ballina's powerful midfield duo of David Brady and Ronan McGarrity concerned the Kilmurry coaches. The strong inter-county stars helped Mayo reach the All-Ireland final last year and were skillful at winning 50-50 balls. Horse, at six-foot-one, 196 pounds, resembled a solid slab of limestone plinth and wouldn't be pushed around. Plus, he carried invaluable experience. So the coaches decided to move Odhran O'Dwyer from midfield to forward and insert Horse. His first start of the season was coming in the biggest game.

"I know my limitations now," said Horse, offering honesty a week before the semifinal. "I know physically I'm struggling a little bit. I'm actually in good shape for my age. I know I can last a game, but some of these guys we're playing against are as close as you'll get to professionals. They have some of the top players in the country playing for them."

Already, fans were whispering that the old Horse couldn't last. He recalled a conversation he had with his brother-in-law after the news leaked.

"You're playing Sunday, I hear."

"I am."

"Congratulations, but believe me they're talking already. If things go bad and you play bad you'll be blamed for losing the game—they should have never played you. This will be a taint on your playing days."

Some in the team's peanut gallery thought saving Horse as a reserve was safer. That way, Kilmurry wouldn't blow one of its five substitutions if Horse was out of gas. Sixty minutes of physical play might be too much with all the miles he's already logged. Even Horse admitted he felt the pressure. Right now, the 1992 Munster championship meant nothing. If he played poorly in the semifinal, Horse could be remembered as the goat in Kilmurry's biggest game. Lasting memories were sometimes strongest.

Usually, only the *Clare Champion,* the weekly county newspaper, covered Kilmurry. During the Munster tournament, though, national papers started calling. Reporters played up the underdog angle, calling Kilmurry "minnows."

An article in the *Irish Star* featured a punchy tabloid lead, "Kilmurry-Ibrickane have proven that even seemingly impossible dreams still come true in sport. Chances are, this time last year you would have got better odds on Michael Jackson launching a Childline concert in Baghdad than you would have of Kilmurry-Ibrickane winning a Munster senior football title."

Ouch.

Supporters were optimistic, but some quietly worried if Kilmurry could even keep it close. Publicly, everyone gave reinforcements. They referenced Caltra, a tiny parish in Galway that stunned people in winning the All-Ireland club title last year. Kilmurry native Marty Morrissey, a well-known RTÉ sports announcer, showed up one night to offer inspiration.

Their fans shouldn't have been on edge. The players had emerged from their weekend in Kerry convinced of a victory. That opponents helped to instill confidence wasn't unusual in the GAA. Éire Óg, the team that Kilmurry beat in October for the county championship, displayed a sign at its field wishing them luck. Another Clare team donated blue and white practice jerseys so that Kilmurry could get used to those colors. (Since Kilmurry and Ballina both have red and green jerseys, each team had to wear its provincial colors.) Miltown Malbay offered its sand-based field after the Christmas break because it drained better than Kilmurry's. Usually, bitter rivals weren't exactly rolling out the red carpet for each other. But exceptions were made in times of inter-county competitions.

"It helps to boost morale in the area, in the county," said Miltown coach Martin Flynn, just glad that a Clare team was still alive. "It gives people something to talk about and something to smile about if your team is doing well. Everybody feels good."

A local musician recorded a song, *The Men Behind The Dwyer,* a play on words from the Irish Republican song *The Men Behind The Wire* that was popular in the 1970s and 1980s. The Kilmurry tune featured lyrics with the players' names. Butcher, also a youth coach, even got a shout out. Clare FM aired it countless times in the build-up as the team tried to stay grounded.

"I don't know in Grecian times whether they had a god of sport or not, but I believe the present god has got an agent for sport," Patrick O'Dwyer told me, once again going into his philosopher's mode. "And that agent is pretty merciless. So the moment he sees people that are too high up he's ready to pull the carpet directly from under them. So I'm mindful of that all the time."

The night before the game, Kilmurry's fourteen-to sixteen-year-old step dance team won the All-Ireland title. Kilmurry tradition dictated that residents greet winning teams by lighting bonfires, banging drums, honking horns and flying flags near the outskirts of the parish where five roads lead outward called the Hand. That Friday night, Kilmurry chairman T.J. O'Loughlin scooped me up at the Dalys, and we drove around the parish as he passed out tickets to the game. We joined a dozen others at the Hand near midnight on a cold evening. A small fire burned on the side, a flicker of what the football team's celebrations were like. The joyous teenagers soon returned, displaying their medals for their winning footwork and precision stomping, and posed for pictures under a light rain.

Everyone converged at a small pub in Coore, brightened by an open fire. Friends, relatives and admirers passed the oversized championship cup filled with soda around the packed bar, pausing to take sips and then looking up with a smile and a carbonated mustache. In an extra room, the dancers performed a victory jig well into early morning on a night where no one seemed tired.

"It's a good omen for the weekend," someone hoped.

The following morning, many of the players went to Cooney's for breakfast. Well-wishers drove by exploding horns and waving checkered red and green Kilmurry flags. The priest in Mullagh moved mass up an hour to accommodate the fans. Yes, it was an important game.

Players joked on the way down, keeping things loose. I sat up front on the chartered bus to not distract anyone, but starting midfielder Peter O'Dwyer plopped down next to me, chatting away.

"You want to stay relaxed," he said before putting new laces in his worn black cleats halfway to the game. "You'll worry if you think about it too soon."

Kilmurry arrived at a college to run through drills because each team was only allotted ten minutes to warm up on the playing field before the whistle. A little boy and his father were kicking a ball under the gray sky, but moved to the side when Kilmurry showed up. Dad pointed to Kilmurry's players—they had tickets for the game—as the boy twirled the ball in his small hands in awe. The players kept their normal routine, stretching out and running in lines, practicing hand passes and booming kicks downfield. Michael O'Dwyer kept asking me what time it was. The laughter on the bus had disappeared.

As I watched, an official from the college asked if I was with the team. I stammered something like, "Huh, I'm an American, who's not really with the team, but I'm following them for a book I'm writing. So I came down with them and, yeah but not officially with them."

His response—"So, you're the mascot."

I suppose I'd accept that.

It was soon time. The bus received an escort to Pearse Stadium near downtown Galway. The white and yellow police car charged ahead, blue lights flashing as the bus driver tried to keep pace. Assistant coach Gerard Talty took a picture with his cell phone camera and players marveled as the bus raced down the two-lane road, ignoring red lights and narrowly avoiding cars on the side through curves. Their nerves didn't need this.

"Ahhhhhhh"

"Jesus Christ"

"This is something," Patrick O'Dwyer said to no one in particular, with thoughts of crashing racing through his mind.

The police car then turned right but the bus continued straight. In a second, team Kilmurry went from the fantasy of being world leaders to the butt of a Keystone Kops plot. A wide U-turn later, the bus met the retreating police car and the escort was back on.

The players entered the stadium through a back door near the ramp of the locker room. It was big enough to fit four or five of the Miltown dressing rooms, but was still no-frills with drab cement walls. Patrick O'Dwyer, wearing knee-high dark Wellington boots, a black jacket and a light tweed cap with a brown border, looked like he was preparing for a hunt or a long day out on the farm. He had his pregame speech ready—short and with no words wasted.

"Play. With. Fire," O'Dwyer roared, his voice rising with each word. "Every ounce of blood that you have in you, you're going to give and that's the way ..."

"C'mon boys, c'mon" drowned the ending, as the blood started to boil. A minute or two remained from sprinting onto the field. Some leaned against the wall, stretching out their calves. Others threw a ball back and forth. Most bounced and buzzed, leaping up and down, ready to go.

They charged out. I followed meekly. Earlier, I had asked O'Loughlin about getting credentials. He said come on the bus, carry a bag into the stadium and everything should work out. Sure. So when we arrived, I grabbed a bunch of balls and walked past the security guards. I tried looking official, but suddenly felt like I should be wearing a dog costume. I made it into the near-empty dugout along with the team's secretary Gillian Talty, assistant coach Frankie Frawley's wife and one of their sons. But that was it. The players sat in the stands because of a GAA rule that attempts to clean the clutter from the sideline.

Early in the first half, I lowered my head to scribble something. I heard "ohhh" and the ball came flying in from the action and hit me in the back of the head. Ouch! It was harder than a soccer ball. I looked up and saw a photographer laughing at me. Bastard. I rubbed my head and tried to play cool. After that, I didn't take my eyes off the action the rest of the game. I had learned my lesson—Gaelic football could be a fast and dangerous game, especially if you're watching it with your head down, just yards away from the action. Good thing it wasn't hurling. I don't even want to think about a flying stick. (Mental note: check to see if they use pine tar.)

Kilmurry took a surprising three-point lead in the first ten minutes before 8,500 fans—decent attendance on a cold day for a game that was supposed to be a rout. They remained sharp, going right after Ballina's stars, trying to gain a physical advantage. The lead could have been greater, but Stephenites goalie John Healy swatted away a dead-on shot in the eighteenth minute. From that point on, Ballina changed momentum by breaking through the clogged middle, and took a two-point lead into halftime.

Games developed in different ways. Some were free flowing with smooth hand passes and short and long kicks. Players moved the ball upfield with ease. Scoring attempts were plentiful, with balls getting sucked to the goal. A rhythm and an order made it fun to watch. Other games turned physical. Defenders used their bodies and threw elbows. The opponents pushed back. Players fell in pain away from the ball and no one knew exactly what happened. Officials called constant fouls, stopping action while the quality of the football suffered.

This game exemplified the second type. It seemed more like pro wrestling than Gaelic football, more a picture drawn with crayons than a Picasso. What did I know? The newspapers the next day confirmed my suspicions. Eamonn Sweeney of the *Irish Examiner* called the game "a nadir in modern Gaelic football." The *Irish Times*' Keith Duggan said it was a "fascinatingly poor All-Ireland contest."

But Horse was right in there with Ballina star David Brady, struggling for territory and holding his own. True, the papers showed pictures the following day of Horse shoving Brady. The Ballina faithful complained, convinced that Horse's rough play was over the line. But he did his job, again turning time away. He wouldn't be blamed for this one. With things so physical, though, the match seemed to be getting out of hand. Kilmurry unraveled first. Two young players were ejected for attempting head-butts during skirmishes. The discipline that Patrick O'Dwyer swore by failed him. Kilmurry had to play the final ten minutes down two players. In the stands, supporters shouted at one another and a scuffle broke out with the police rushing to break it up. In America, fights in stands fueled by alcohol rage weren't newsworthy (unless, of course, fans started fighting with players). And it wasn't shocking in English soccer where hooligans famously brawl. In the GAA, though, it was extremely rare for fans to fight. Seating wasn't segregated along team colors like in some soccer stadiums, and fans took pride in peacefully co-existing.

With everything spinning out of control, Kilmurry wouldn't go away. At the end of regulation, Ballina led by two points, but two minutes of injury time was added. There was still a chance. With 30 seconds left, Daly curled the ball through the uprights on a free kick to cut the deficit to one point. The Ballina goalkeeper would now kick the ball downfield. Kilmurry had a chance to tie—or win—right before the final whistle. That would open up a new chapter in Gaelic football lore—or at least be remembered as an improbable upset. But then, the clock struck midnight. Ballina regained possession and quickly kicked the ball through the uprights with seconds left. Their fans raced onto the field to celebrate the 10-8 win. Hugs and smiles for Ballina. Tears and pats on the back for Kilmurry, their Cinderella season over. I squirmed and jimmied my way around, noticing Johnnie Daly, Horse—with blood on the tip of his nose—and Patrick O'Dwyer holding themselves accountable by answering reporters' questions. A picture in Monday's *Irish Independent* showed Daly squatting, head down. Players looked grim, fans cried, offering support. Someone called to Daly, "You have nothing to be ashamed of."

"I know," said Daly, trying to force a smile then biting his lip and turning his head. "So near."

In the locker room, somber players stood or sat saying nothing. Others tried to put a positive, almost a pissed off "We'll be back next year" spin on it. Either way, it hurt.

Eventually, Patrick O'Dwyer, his ashen face not showing any comfort, slowly walked to the center. The showers weren't yet whistling off to the right. Players still had sweat matted on their foreheads. Many kept their muddy blue shirts on, not wanting to take off their jersey for a final time because that would make it more official. A background chatter filled the room, but heads remained down and arms slowly fell past jelly-like calves to untie cleats. The defeat was sinking in.

O'Dwyer took in the scene and corralled his team's attention. Some looked up, some inched closer. O'Dwyer, as leader, had to give a catharsis, even for those who didn't want to hear it.

"I mean this from the bottom of my heart," O'Dwyer spoke up, standing straight, his eyes doubling as a pat on the back. "I am so proud of the way you played today. Tremendous guts and courage. I have to say that. I just applaud you for that. You gave it every ounce and I would not ask for more from a team other than that. We asked for it at halftime, we asked before the game and you gave it. You gave every single thing you had."

He couldn't avoid all of the ugly details.

"I am not blaming," he continued with a combination of compassion and regret. "I am not going to blame anyone. Any guys who got sent off or anything like that they know the reasons why. And I am not going to blame. It's a thing you have to learn when you do things like that."

Nothing he could say would take back the defeat, but O'Dwyer knew they could at least leave the locker room proud.

"Hold your heads high, lads. You take it from here. I want to say finally lads, anybody that I hurt over the course of the year or anything that I did that offended players I apologize for it now unreservedly. It's my last time ever with a football team. I had great times. I have enjoyed it wholeheartedly. And I want to thank particularly my fellow selectors for what they've done. I want to thank T.J. O'Loughlin for tremendous support and for everyone involved with the team. It was a fantastic year and we'll look back at it with pride. And the best of luck to everyone in the future, and I hope you have a tremendous future in football, lads."

The team clapped. It was over. Death of a dream.

Callers besieged Clare FM radio praising Kilmurry's effort and an unlikely request was played—Queen's *We Are The Champions* roared as the players boarded the bus. This time there were no police escorts. Just slow moving traffic, allowing ample time to silently sulk. They couldn't get home fast enough. The radio then cut to the game report. The announcer noted the turning point occurred when Kilmurry lost discipline. Michael Hogan, one of the players ejected, was in the midst of a text message on his cell phone. His head remained down, no expression on his face. That evening, Hogan hung with his teammates. After all, they were friends first.

In a few weeks, the team would begin training again with hopes of defending its county and provincial titles. Horse took over as the temporary coach. (Patrick O'Dwyer eventually came out of retirement—again—to lead Kilmurry for a final season.) Horse's local legend remained intact.

"I felt like I did as good as expected," he said a week later, after arriving home from a twelve-hour work shift. "There was a lot of pressure on me to play. Obviously, it could have really turned bad for me, as such. Obviously, I could have been steamrolled by this guy. I could have been taken off after twenty minutes. It wouldn't have been a good way to finish."

He wasn't sure about his future plans.

"I don't think we make a big announcement and say 'Hey I'm finished.' There's no press conference—you just fade away."

The losing hangover carried for weeks afterwards with *what ifs*. Disappointed fans repeatedly told players they were proud, but everyone knew it was a missed opportunity. Key moments were replayed and agonized over. One remedy was a vacation to the Canary Islands, quickly put together for the middle of March. Assistant coach Gerard Talty had made preliminary inquires, found a flight, but needed to go to Dublin for work. Since Johnnie Daly worked in Ennis, he was enlisted to finalize the last-minute arrangements with the town's travel agency.

Daly obliged, as always, but faced a problem despite leaving early—the travel agency didn't open until 9:30, the time that Daly was needed in the motor tax office. He waited—his football mates came first. He greeted the agent as her co-workers strolled in.

"I'm going to get sacked," said Daly, half-joking and half-serious as he watched her check the computer.

Bad news. Most of the seats on the flight Daly wanted were sold overnight.

"The trip is in ten days," the agent said. "Lanzarote is popular now."

"We were in an All-Ireland semifinal. We didn't know until last week."

The agent worked the phones, bouncing between two lines, desperately seeing if there were any group flights from nearby Shannon Airport. If not, half the team would have to travel from Cork or another group destination would quickly be needed. Daly checked his watch on his left wrist, wondering what his boss would say. It didn't look good.

As the agent clutched the phone, a sparkle suddenly sprouted in her eyes—extra seats were found. Other passengers would get bumped. Kilmurry had its holiday. See, sometimes favors do get returned, just like Johnnie Daly had told me. And while a trip in the sunshine spent scuba diving and sun tanning didn't make up for a moment of passed glory, it was a sign of life going on.

Chapter 2
End of a Hex?

March: Ballina, County Mayo

A week after the semifinal, I left for Ballina, Mayo, to follow the Stephenites in their quest for the All-Ireland club championship. Part of me felt like a traitor after ditching Kilmurry. I enjoyed the people, saw their hurt after the loss and now I was heading to the enemy.

I knew, however, I had to experience the entire country as part of my journey. So I arrived with divided loyalties, not quite sure what to expect. I got lucky—there was the full complex of pain, anguish, despair, agony, sorrow, panic. A happy bonus, at least for a writer.

The fans in Ireland's uppermost western county, though, were praying their sporting misery would end. They were long sufferers, Irish cousins of the Boston Red Sox and Chicago Cubs. Like those cursed baseball teams, Mayo fans had witnessed freaky heartbreak. The last senior inter-county All-Ireland title came in 1951. Since then, they squandered away leads and sure wins and dependably underachieved whenever the spotlight turned on them. Forget hold the Mayo jokes, it was hold the All-Irelands. Mayoitis. Mayo, God help us. A hoodoo—pick a name to call it.

Last season, a double blow. Mayo lost in both the senior All-Ireland and the under-21 finals. Just picture the frustrated fans banging their heads against the television: Not again. Not again. Not again. Not again.

The Ballina Stephenites, a large club in an area known for nature and salmon fishing, had sent hundreds of players to the Mayo team through the generations, and their clubmen knew the heartache of the drought. Recently, Ballina had been battling its own ghost, a crushing loss in the 1999 club All-Ireland final with seventeen wide shots. A monkey wearing shades might not miss that many, given enough chances. It was a bad day. Crossmaglen, the Ulster provincial champs from the Northwest, took its first lead in the final minutes to win by one.

The poster boy for all this torture was David Brady, a star for both Mayo and Ballina. The powerful thirty-year-old had lost eight All-Ireland finals at various levels—reaching one or two was a career highlight for many. Playing in eight was almost unheard of. So was losing them all. Now, Brady and the fans would get yet another chance to reverse the curse on St. Patrick's Day.

It wouldn't be easy. Ballina lost two key players to injuries and were the underdogs. The town's St. Patrick's Day parade was postponed from Thursday to Sunday. Would it also be a victory parade?

"You have to go up there and take a right," Brady said while leaning out of his seat in the front and peering through the window. "It's left actually."

Two weekends before the final, Ballina traveled to Dublin for a scrimmage followed by a short practice at Croke Park. Brady had no problem helping guide the bus driver to the famous stadium that hosts most of the national championship games. He knew the way with his All-Ireland finals résumé—the senior level losses in 1996, 1997, 2004; the under-21 defeats in 1994, 1995; and the 1999 club loss with Ballina. That roster included replay losses in 1995 and 1996 after draws. Perhaps the most famous was in 1996 when Mayo blew a huge first half lead against County Meath. In the final seconds, a Meath player took a desperation kick—along the lines of a half court shot or a Doug Flutie pass—which bounced before the goalie and over the bar for a point to tie the game. It stopped short of hitting the floodlights, sailing against a vending machine, off the bathroom door and into the goal. Meath won the much-anticipated rematch two weeks later.

Suicide watch, anyone?

No, that wasn't Brady's style. Losing didn't make him go around kicking cats.

"I have a good attitude in life," Brady made clear. "As I said after we lost the [2004] All-Ireland final, I put it in perspective—no one died. We lost a game of football. You don't make life-altering changes because of it.... At the end of the day, I won't change whether I win or lose. I'll still be the same."

Brady never swayed from his convictions, which often included clashing with Mayo manager John Maughan. Their controversies—like when Brady quit the team in 2003 because Maughan wouldn't allow him to play rugby in the off-season—made great bait for headline-starved journalists. Brady returned in 2004, but lost his starting midfield job late in the season.

This year, the butting of heads had already started. Brady wasn't practicing with Mayo in its preseason inter-county training to focus on the club tournament for Ballina (the top players moonlight between playing for their county and club teams). But for the inter-county National League opener in early February, Maughan put Brady in the starting lineup despite not telling him. The manager claimed to have called Brady several times, while Brady denied receiving any calls (no phone records were subpoenaed for this hour-long dramatic episode). Big egos, strong-willed men, showing who's boss—not a good way to make nice. So the standoff continued with the media and fans wondering if Brady would play for Mayo this season.

Brady has remained tight-lipped. During Ballina's media night two weeks before the game, he popped in to show his face, but quickly ducked out before the reporters found him. And thank goodness for caller ID.

"Oh, you have phone calls nonstop," Brady said shaking his head. "You just don't answer the phone. If you don't know the number, you don't answer the phone. It's as simple as that."

But I was less interested in Brady-and-Maughan's swordplay than in the issue of Brady's mentality before the final. All that losing must wear on him. Were the doubts starting to creep into his head? He agreed to speak with me two nights before the game.

Earlier in the afternoon, Brady got his lucky haircut as he always does two days before each championship. Nothing fancy—short on the sides, just a tad off the top of his high forehead. Later that night, his superstitions included spreading out his gear and making sure the *Rocky* CD he listens to before warm-ups was nearby. A lucky white T-shirt couldn't be forgotten. This particular one was a relative newcomer to the pregame routine.

"I've kind of thrown out one or two lucky T-shirts over the years," Brady explained with a laugh, like he does after many statements. "I lost so many finals. I decided they're unlucky so I got rid of them and started wearing a new one again."

After the team's final practice, Brady drove me to his place in The Quay village a mile from downtown. In another 45 minutes, he must leave to present awards to a youth team an hour and a half away.

"You can't say no to those things," Brady explained.

I didn't have much time to waste. But I had to be delicate. I couldn't blurt out, "How much does it suck losing so many times?" Luckily, Brady brought it up on the short drive.

"For me, this is a big game. This is a big game. This is my ninth All-Ireland final. I don't know of too many players that ever played in nine All-Ireland finals. I know no one has ever played in nine and lost. That's a record in itself."

We walked into his fashionable townhouse. To the left, a fireplace mantle in the living room displayed a row of good luck cards from friends and students. Brady, who worked for the Bank of Ireland for seven years, had been coaching football at Ballina's elementary schools for the past six months. Another card from a well-wisher sat on the coffee table in the middle of the room. To the right of the fireplace was a congo drum from a trip to Tunisia with the Mayo team. A cabinet overflowed with awards and player of the month trophies. Past the white leather couch and down the hall was the kitchen, where a green scratch-off New York lottery ticket sat on the white counter courtesy of a friend from Queens, N.Y. Individual beer coolers or stubbies, souvenirs from his travels to the warm climates of Australia, New Zealand and South Africa, surrounded the television against the far wall.

He offered me an Elite Chocolate Kimberley mallow cookie and a drink.

"Do you want coffee or tea?" he asked trying to be nice, before deciding for me. "You're not getting coffee in this house."

No matter where he went, Brady always returned to the tea, but never iced. The Irish snicker at the concept.

Now, given the green light, I asked Brady about the losing past. The baggage must haunt him after a while. Are you sure you don't kick cats I wanted to ask him. But I didn't quite put it in those terms, though.

"There's a small difference between winning and losing," Brady said calmly as he cupped a mug with both hands on a chair in his living room. "As they say, a pat on the back is six inches away from a kick in the arse. So you know, it's funny.... You try to learn from them. Definitely learn from them, but never, never remember them. If I was carrying baggage, I would have given up football long ago. It's been a great career but there's one more step I want to go."

How important is it to win an All-Ireland?

"For me, besides family, definitely the most important thing in my life is football. Just one [more] for me—that's the football finish for me. I won't play again. Ever. I'll retire happy. I came, I saw and I conquered if we win."

What if you lose?

"Draw or lose, no—same thing. I'm not playing. All I know is what I'm doing after Thursday and that's coming home Friday. But no, I'm not going to play again."

I nearly choked on my tea—did he just say that? Suddenly, the ante was up for Brady. This could be his last shot at an All-Ireland title, unless he pulls a Michael Jordan or a Sugar Ray Leonard or a Richard Nixon and comes backs multiple times. Brady knew the deal and didn't wince when I brought up his record. He left the sugarcoating to the cookies.

"I don't really get mad at it because it's a fact and I don't hide from facts," Brady said matter-of-factly.

And this was the hard truth—Brady's legacy depended on the outcome. A loss, and he was a nice guy who couldn't win the big one. An Adlai Stevenson. An Ernie Banks. A bridesmaid. A Charlie Brown. A Jim Kelly. An answer to a trivia question. A nine-time loser. Cruel, but the truth.

"I wouldn't be a happy man if we lose," Brady continued. "It probably would be the most disappointing point in my career if we lost. But, and I go back to it again, I played in so many finals, I know that I can say without a shadow of a doubt, heart and soul, that we're going to win this one. If we fucking crash the bus going up and there's ten guys injured we still win it. I just know it. I know it. And I just can't wait. Can't wait."

Just how bad did Brady want the win?

"I'd give fucking the right leg," he answered quickly. "I'd hop around on one leg."

Brady carried a saying in his wallet that he found on a calendar two years ago. *Success is a matter of luck. Ask any failure.*

Brady refused to quit in his quest for an All-Ireland medal, convinced his work would eventually pay off. After he left the Mayo team in 2003, Brady took off around the world and bagged Gaelic football titles with teams in Chicago, Australia and then the Mayo county title with Ballina—after the club flew him home for the game. That loyalty meant something to Brady. After Mayo lost the All-Ireland final in September 2004, he planned on returning to Australia and hanging on a soft beach under the hot sun. Ballina's coach asked him to stay for the upcoming county championship. Brady agreed, they won, the beer coolers were never packed.

He couldn't really complain, especially with his friends and family nearby. His twin younger brothers were stars in their own right. Liam, one half of the twenty-five-year-olds, was the team's top scorer as the free taker. Ger played on the forward line behind Liam, and often fed him the ball. Brother helping brother. David manned the midfield. Three Bradys, all different. The Brady bunch. Pick your favorite.

Interestingly, both Ger and Liam had battled serious injuries. For Ger, it ended his professional rugby career. He had a two-year developmental contract with Connacht, a provincial team. Rugby, though, could be a rough sport and five years ago Brady suffered two broken vertebrae in his back after an opponent fell on him. Only twenty, his contract wasn't renewed. Enter a career selling pensions and insurance. When his back healed, he resumed playing Gaelic football and club rugby.

Liam was the sleekest of the three, with his prematurely graying hair and dapper three-piece suits—in his other life he was an auctioneer evaluating property. On the field, and off, he always found his way to the center of attention. In 2003, he spent the summer in Chicago and played Gaelic football with David.

"I thought we would have killed each other," said Liam, who lived with his parents and Ger just around the corner from David's place.

Instead, they made lifelong friends and enjoyed each other's company. A good summer, though, ended in pain. Liam broke his right foot during a game and needed six months off from work to heal. One thing drove him while rehabilitating—a return to the Stephenites.

I asked assistant coach Paddy Ruane about the three brothers. He had that wise man look to him, with a full head of silver hair and a wealth of experience. Ruane saw them quite specifically. About Liam: "He questions things. There is that little bit more abrasiveness about him.... He's demanding enough, too. He will look for things and he won't kind of hesitate and say 'I want this' or 'I want that.'"

About Ger: "Ger, I'd say of them all, is the most introverted. He's quieter, but that being said, he will stand up and be counted too. But he's not as forward or as pushy as the other two boys."

About David: "David loves attention. He thrives on it. You know, can't get enough of it. Laps it up. And the other boys, I'd say they live in his shadow. But they still enjoy his shadow."

Pick a Brady. Pick your favorite.

In my first week in Ballina, I flipped through the three local newspapers, reading them cover to cover. I did a double-take when I got to the Country Diary column of the *Connaught Telegraph*.

"The great tits are staking out their territories"

Tits? Ah, I knew there was a reason that I came to Ireland.

Then I read on.

"Ornthithologist Ludwig Koch recorded sixty-eight different calls from the great tits he met ..."

Oh, the article was about birds that blossomed and multiplied in the spring, while making sweet music. Damn. It did remind me that sometimes you couldn't believe everything you read in Ireland, which was full of tales involving the supernatural, Leprechauns, myths and fables.

"Coming from Ireland you hear stories of giants and Fionn Mac Cumhaill and mystical monsters," said Ger Brady, taking pride in the uniqueness of his homeland. "And people, I suppose, they have creative imaginations ... it's just the way things developed from this particular part of the country."

Little kids grow up learning about Fionn Mac Cumhaill (pronounced Fin McCool), a giant warrior who led the Fianna soldiers in protecting Ireland in the third century. He nearly reached the clouds, had the strength of 500 warriors, wrote poetry and could see the future when he sucked his thumb. All in all, a typical giant. The latter power came courtesy of the Salmon of Knowledge. The elusive fish held wisdom, and whoever took a bite became a genius. The poet Finegas finally caught it, and instructed his student Fionn, to cook the salmon but, no matter what, not to taste it. Fionn obeyed his master, but oil splashed on his thumb and he licked it to soothe the burning. Talk about a technicality, but it counted. Fionn used those brains to defeat his enemies. One rival was a fellow warrior from Scotland named Benandonner. Fionn heaved large pieces of Ireland into the ocean, making a bridge so he could challenge his opponent in a sort of WarriorMania pay-per-view event. (One errant toss reportedly became the Isle of Man. And the Giants Causeway, a series of rocks and interlocking columns off the Northwest coast in County Antrim, supposedly formed because of the throws.) Fionn eventually tired from the Earth shot-putting which allowed his nemesis to show up first. Fionn didn't panic, he merely put that salmon mind of his to work and dressed up as a baby. When the Scottish warrior came around, Fionn's wife said he wasn't home, but told the visitor to be sure to say hi to their toddler. Benandonner sprinted out figuring if the baby was that big, then Fionn must be a GIANT.

Mayo had its share of lore. The county was where Saint Patrick supposedly drove out all the snakes of Ireland in 441 A.D. He fasted for forty days on the summit of a 2,500-foot mountain now called Croagh Patrick, which is still an important religious pilgrimage. One story said that black birds turned into satanic serpents, but St. Patrick protected himself with a bell. The serpents were driven out and Ireland was saved from the demons.

Another tale involved a man named Maughan (no word if he was a Gaelic football coach, too). Maughan raised a boy named Cuimín, after he washed ashore as an infant. Cuimín became a religious hermit and built a small church. After his death, his family inherited a flagstone called the Leac Chuimín. The superstitious stone supposedly cursed evildoers and slanderers. People of all clans arrived from miles for the privilege of payback. To activate the stone, you needed to fast for fifteen days, walk around Cuimín's well and then have whatever Maughan family member currently in charge of the stone turn it. The sea roared for days resulting in death or madness to the bad person. The family was apparently capitalists and charged a hefty fee. Win-win for nearly everyone. Power like that, though, never lasts. Another family who married into the Maughans claimed a right to use the stone. Feuds ensued between the different factions. One tale had someone named Waldron obliterating the stone into little pieces because the fighting over it was giving the area a bad reputation. Another had Waldron himself cursed with madness, and then avenged by a friend who smashed the stone. Either way, people rushed to collect the little pieces. Dean Lyons, the administrator of Ballina cathedral, emerged to quell the chaos that followed and built an altar with the little pieces. End of that. (Hmm, the Ballina manager's name was Tommy Lyons. This coaches' connection was eerie.)

It only made sense that a snippet of folklore would extend to the playing fields. Mayo people were constantly reminded of their football woes as it was.

"There is a comical element to it, a fun element to it," Ger Brady said with a sarcastic twinkle in his eye. "You could be in Dublin and somebody asks you where you're from and you say 'I'm from Mayo' and they'll go 'Mayo God help us.' I would think it would come from the fact that we never win bloody All-Irelands."

His reaction?

"You've heard it all your life so it doesn't bother you. It puts a smile on your face. It gives you an identity as well. Probably not a great one, but it gives you an identity."

I wondered if the team was actually cursed like the Red Sox or the Cubs. I went on to explain to David Brady how Boston's Curse of the Bambino started when Red Sox owner Harry Frazee sold star Babe Ruth to the rival New York Yankees in 1920 to finance the play *No, No, Nanette* and how Ruth, the Bambino, led the Yankees to several World Series wins while the hapless Red Sox didn't claim a world championship for eighty-six years. In that span, the Red Sox always, always, always found a way to lose, no matter how sure the win appeared. Brady just listened, politely smiling. Chicago's hex began in 1945 when pub owner William Sianis brought his pet goat to a World Series game. Despite having a ticket and being a Cubs fan, the goat was booted. An angry Sianis naturally placed a curse on the Cubs, which hadn't won a World Series since 1908. I didn't tell Brady this last fact. I figured there was already enough pressure.

On the GAA side, a witch/wise lady named Biddy Early supposedly cursed the Clare hurling team. Eighty-four years passed before Clare won its first All-Ireland title in 1995.

Initially, nobody knew about a Mayo story. I read that *The Quiet Man* starring John Wayne and Maureen O'Hara was filmed in southern Mayo and released in 1952, a year after Mayo's last win. The curse of the Duke? Nothing. Then someone mentioned hearing something about a priest cursing Mayo. So I asked around and discovered three versions. One—a priest was mad that Mayo football players left church early for a game. Two—mad that a Mayo football player got a woman pregnant in the early 1900s and bolted to America leaving her to fend for herself. Three—mad that Mayo football players didn't give him a ride after his car broke down in an early example of road rage. The priest might have been legendary local Father Joseph Foy. Residents told tales of Father Foy walking on the River Moy—without getting his feet wet—to answer sick calls. People still prayed and left flowers at his grave. Since Ballina occasionally represented Mayo in national competitions in the early 1900s, they, too, might also be cursed. I asked David Brady for his take.

"It probably never existed," he responded with a loud laugh. "But it's only piseogs, piseogs. I wouldn't believe it. You have to start making up stories once you start losing so many. Looking for excuses."

Piseog is an Irish word for a superstition or old wives tale. Brady then paused for a second.

"If something happens on Thursday," he said shaking his head, "I'll start thinking about it."

So why did all this affect the Ballina Stephenites Gaelic football team in 2005? They weren't the county team, they hadn't stranded any priests and they didn't bring goats to games. And it wasn't like a dark cloud had been blanketing the area. The town produced Ireland's first woman president, Mary Robinson, who served in office from 1990-1997 and later was the U.N. High Commissioner for Human Rights. The Moy featured fantastic salmon fishing. Eye catching St. Muredach's Cathedral overlooked the river. A street and arts festival drew thousands every July.

Still, the hurt of the 1999 All-Ireland loss remained.

"Aye, you were gutted like," veteran defender James Devenney told me. "I just couldn't talk to anyone. I couldn't face anyone. I just wanted the fucking ground to open up and swallow me up."

It affected everyone. Remember, the Stephenites *were* the town, not hired millionaires. Little kids got coached by the star. Former players became the fans. Contrast that to the Red Sox. After finally breaking their curse in 2004, beloved players bolted for more money and other cities. Through the years, past tortured Red Sox players eventually won the World Series with other teams including Hall of Fame third baseman Wade Boggs and pitching great Roger Clemens. In a twist, they captured rings for the Red Sox' biggest rival, the New York Yankees. In Ireland, you couldn't leave town so quickly—let alone don the colors of your enemies. You merely suffered and tried again.

One man who eases pain for a living was the team's patron, Father Gerry Courell. His grandfather, Thomas, was the club's first president in 1886, and his dad, Gerald, was a star player and longtime officer. Father Gerry, now based outside Liverpool, England, found a fill-in so he could attend the final and stay for the weekend. If necessary, he would have flown in the morning of the match and left that evening. See, Father Gerry was a gentle, loving man, always putting others and his duty to the church first. When it came to the Ballina Stephenites, though, oh my.

"Oh, I bleed," the good Father said. "I bleed. When we lost the last All-Ireland I didn't get over it for—I've never gotten over it. There's many lads here who didn't get over it. Six years ago and we still haven't got over it. We're heartbroken. Because you can lose games but we just didn't lose that game, we just threw it away. It was just, oh, the most sickening experience I've ever had in my life as regards to football and sport. The most devastatingly, sickening, disappointing, ah, just to have it in the bag and to throw it away. It was a dream and the dream was shattered."

You figure the Ballina players would have gotten drunk in the days after the game to escape.

"We didn't even drink much to be honest," veteran forward Brian McStay remembered. "The drink didn't even taste good. You were just so disappointed. You just wish you had that hour back."

The red-haired McStay knew a little about the Stephenites and curses. As a chubby adolescent, he grew up watching his brothers play for Ballina. With the Irish economy poor, McStay emigrated to Boston to work in a bar near Fenway Park. He played football with other Irish ex-pats and had his mother place the radio to the phone so he could listen to Stephenites' games. In 1998, McStay couldn't take it any longer and moved home for the summer to play for the Stephenites. By then he was lean and fit, and helped them win the county title. But McStay needed to return to Boston during the provincial and All-Ireland tournaments in the fall and winter. The solution—he flew back and forth eight times for games (the club paid on one occasion).

"Ah, it was something that I wanted to do personally. I didn't want money or anything like that," said McStay, surprised that I was impressed. "A childhood ambition I suppose. As you get older, you always think that time might run out and you don't want any regrets."

The loss in the 1999 All-Ireland final, though, haunted him as he remained in Boston. In 2003, it burned so deeply, McStay moved back to Ballina and found work in a sporting goods store. Now at thirty-four, he was the oldest player on the team and desperate to erase that one last regret.

Naturally being near Fenway, McStay learned about the Curse of the Bambino.

"I wouldn't have believed that either, with the whole trading Babe Ruth thing," he told me, refusing to acknowledge the paranormal. "I just don't buy that."

As for Mayo's curse?

"You know, when people get drink in them they can make up some hairy stories," McStay logically explained.

Ballina had a bustling feel with the River Moy swimming through it on the outskirts of downtown. Most of the shops were on two streets that intersected like a T. The week before the game, nearly all of them displayed a Stephenites picture and good luck sign as men hung bunting for the St. Patrick's Day parade.

The Stephenites hub was their clubhouse next to the field that included a bar, squash and handball courts and meeting and banquet rooms. Pictures were displayed with trophies and cups earned through the years. Deceased members live forever here. The current generation could relax after a game and exchange war stories. You got a sense of how the GAA both created and reflected a community. Even in a town like Ballina, which was the second largest in the county with nearly 10,000 residents—big for this part of the country.

As the final approached, the nights grew busier as fans waited to get their tickets. Many just needed to release nervous energy. *Who's coming back for the game? How are you getting to the game? How will the boys do?* People like Michael Kilkenny, a former club official and player, gave me a Ballina tutorial. Tradesmen and laborers formed the club in 1886—one of the oldest in the country—after another Ballina club banned manual workers. The name Stephenites honored James Stephens, the founder of a secret society seeking independence from Britain through armed revolt. The British placed a £1,000 reward for his whereabouts. The club displayed that blue collar, fearless attitude from the beginning with a county championship in 1889 and titles from 1904-1916. Currently, they owned the most Mayo titles with thirty-four.

A GAA fan, though, had two loyalties—his club team and the inter-county squad. A Ballina Stephenites supporter often cringed when rooting for Mayo. Sure, every once in a while Mayo would win an All-Ireland title at another level: women, under-21, under-18 (called minors), club and junior (a lower skill level that features a mix of young guns gaining experience, veterans winding up a career and players not good enough or too busy to make a commitment to the senior team). But the senior men's All-Ireland meant the most, and the drought was going on fifty-four years now.

What was a fan to do?

"We'll keep supporting them anyway," said Gerry Kenny, a former Ballina player who now sponsors the Stephenites through his sports store. "That's part of the religion, we say. It's like a religion. We support them for ever more."

But once that losing was embedded, you needed quite a razor to shave it from the mind. First-year Stephenites manager Tommy Lyons had that task. The former player was an assistant coach for the 1999 team so he was looking for redemption as much as anyone. Lyons—who was sometimes confused with an ex-Dublin manager with the same name—worked in the police department as a Juvenile Liaison Officer.

"I'm J-Lo for short," Lyons told me in his office. "Jennifer Lopez. If you remember that, then you know who I am."

Not a bad comparison and a naturally easy way to remember Tommy Lyons.

J-Lo A: Jennifer Lopez, a sexy star, with flowing hair that oozed coolness.

J-Lo B: Tommy Lyons, a non-imposing balding man, with some locks remaining in the middle, but barely enough for a comb-over.

Dig deeper, though, and similarities could be found. Both targeted the important teenage demographic. Lyons dealt with youth crime, mainly in drug and alcohol cases.

"If you get them past that period, you know they're straightening out in life and they're going on to jobs or third-level education," said Lyons, whose four brothers were also police officers. "We try to make sure they stay on the right side of the law."

Like the female J-Lo, Lyons must hit the right notes, in his case getting the Stephenites mentally ready. And like the singer, Lyons traveled with an entourage. In early January, he brought in John O'Mahony as an advisor. O'Mahony coached Galway to two All-Ireland titles in 1998 and 2001. In 1994, he led tiny Leitrim to its first Connacht provincial championship in sixty-seven years. You couldn't help but look at O'Mahony and think winner. He gave pep talks citing Michael Jordan's fearlessness, displayed a Muhammad Ali poster with a quote about the will to win and offered tips on strategy. He oozed wisdom. Lyons knew O'Mahony, a Mayo resident, for twenty years through football. He was available after recently resigning as Galway's manager. For some, bringing in a bigger name would be an ego blow. Many managers sought the glory for themselves. Lyons simply wanted any available advantage. In that sense, Lyons differed from the other J-Lo in that he wasn't on that kind of a trip.

I noticed a calendar hanging on the far wall of his office, right behind his desk, that displayed a shot of the towering Canadian Rockies. It showed the October 2004 page—five months ago. Lyons had more important things to worry about than office decorations, and the past.

"I just don't look behind me anymore," Lyons declared. "I keep looking in front."

Things, though, weren't going perfect. Ballina defender Kenny Golden broke his left wrist in the semifinal against Kilmurry. Golden lived and worked in Belfast, but during the weekend made the cross-country drive for practices or games. Dedication like that was found on nearly every GAA team. Another player, Shane Sweeney, flew back from his job as a lawyer in London practically every weekend for a five-month stretch.

Unfortunately, Golden wasn't the only defender injured. The speedy Enda Devenney tore knee ligaments during the scrimmage in Dublin two weekends before the game. The twenty-two-year-old college student was named the club championship's Connacht Player of the Year for his stellar defensive performances. He optimistically postponed surgery, clinging to a slim chance of playing in the final.

Ironically, his older brother now got to start. James Devenney, a stud defender in his own right, couldn't fight the travel bug last year. He took his life savings and a leave of absence from his electrician job to go with his girlfriend to see Earth. They flew into South America visiting Argentina, Chile and Peru, and then to Southeast Asia—Singapore, Thailand and Vietnam. The bald-by-choice globe trekker next went to Australia for three months where he exchanged e-mails with Lyons and worked out with a Gaelic football team in Sydney. He took out a €5,000 loan to continue his travels in September, but eventually ran out of money. He returned to the Stephenites in mid-January, bicycling to work and practice on his blue Raleigh because he couldn't afford car insurance. Devenney didn't play in the semifinal win, but could now be the team's lifesaver.

The injuries also ensured a spot for Eanna Casey, a versatile substitute who started at forward in the semifinal. The curly-haired Casey always had potential. He was a sub for Mayo in the under-21 All-Ireland championship in 2001. The loss continued the great Mayo M.O.

"It was gut-wrenching, like unbelievable," he recalled. "I don't know how anyone can go through that six or seven times. I'd just give up football. I'd take up, I don't know, boxing where I could hit someone. It was such an anticlimax losing."

Now, he got another chance. The only thing better would be if his father could be in the crowd. Willie Casey was a teenage substitute on the 1951 Mayo All-Ireland champions, later captaining Ballina for thirteen years. Willie was known as a hardnosed player with a beautiful voice, whose rendition of Al Jolson songs, often with a young Eanna bouncing on his knee, could bring listeners to tears. Casey inherited the voice and football skills. Willie naturally followed Eanna's progress during the season, but two weeks ago he suffered chest pains. He was now in a Mayo hospital awaiting a triple bypass surgery to be performed when space opens in a Dublin hospital.

"He's assured me I'll have enough to think about," said Eanna, who is a quantity surveyor overseeing construction projects in Dublin. "He gave me his blessing. He goes, 'Get your head together and sort yourself out. Do what you have to do to be in the best shape you can be.'"

Ballina had plenty of inspiration. Paddy Ruane, whose son Brian was the team's captain and another son Fergal was the team doctor, battled prostate cancer in 2004. Radical surgery killed the tumors, but he was in the hospital for five weeks and out of work for five months. Ironically, Ruane pledged to give up smoking if Ballina won the county title in 2003. That he did; but instead of feeling better, Ruane felt worse. Maybe it was withdrawal, but something wasn't right. So Fergal sent him for tests, which confirmed cancer in March 2004. That fall, a weakened Ruane returned to the sidelines. In the wild All-Ireland semifinal win over Kilmurry-Ibrickane, he even strolled onto the field during a skirmish.

"I wouldn't have backed down," he said. "Put it that way."

With that kind of attitude, Enda Devenney returned for the final practice with his right leg braced. He sported a Boston Red Sox cap that James had bought him on his travels. He wore it backwards, as good a symbol as any for breaking the curse. Before 2004 when Boston was still cursed, it would have been like walking under a ladder holding a hanger in an electrical storm. In 2005, it was an omen.

Every little thing would help. Their opponents, Portlaoise (pronounced Port-Leash), were the bookies favorite and the pick by most of the national media. Observers weren't impressed with Ballina's hard win over Kilmurry, but were with Portlaoise's nail-biter over powerhouse Crossmaglen in the other semifinal. Plus, Portlaoise was injury-free and experienced. The County Laois club had won seven Leinster provincial titles, a record for the region that covers parts of southeastern and eastern Ireland, and the 1983 All-Ireland.

Ballina's J-Lo was pleased his team were the underdogs—no pressure. But the motivational ploys weren't finished. The night before the game, he showed the Stephenites a tape of season highlights with Kenny Golden passionately talking about how much the final meant to him. Lyons had filmed it on Ballina's field earlier in the week.

On the bus ride to the game, Lyons played a song from popular Irish band the Saw Doctors called, *To Win Just Once* about hometown heroes getting it done for their people.

St. Patrick's Day in Ireland is an important day, with most of the country getting off from work. This year happened to be an unseasonably warm, shiny day, with people out in droves all over. A parade ripped through Dublin's streets. Gamblers were tuned to the annual horse racing festival from Cheltenham in the southwest of England. Rugby supporters packed the provincial high school championships. GAA fans feasted on the All-Ireland club championship doubleheader, with football following the hurling final.

One fan chose not to enter Croke Park. Mary Brady—David, Ger and Liam's mother—usually found watching too painful. During the semifinal, the slender woman prayed at Knock, the famous Mayo site where an apparition supposedly occurred in 1879 when Our Lady, St. Joseph and St. John the Evangelist appeared on a rainy August night. For this game, she paced up and down the sidewalk outside the stadium on Jones Road.

For myself, I couldn't wait to find my seat. I didn't get the same access that I received for the semifinal. There would be no getting hit in the head with a ball while in the dugout. I couldn't really complain. I appeared out of nowhere, and the Ballina people had been great to me, offering insight and letting me travel with them to Croke Park for their scrimmage a couple weeks ago. I listened in on team meetings and got an insider's view. But for the final, I was on my own. So I sampled the fans' frustrations firsthand. I sat in a section brimming with green and red. Next to me was a vocal man in his forties, who I gathered had seen it all.

From the beginning, he was nervous. Ballina missed two scoring opportunities with wide kicks in the opening minutes.

"That's fucking typical," he yelled out.

The fans stayed on edge throughout. The game ebbed back and forth as the contest differed from the ugly semifinal win, possessing a pleasing flow. One team would score, and the other blinked temporarily and hurried right back.

Ballina faced adversity near halftime when defender Shane Melia hobbled off. Eanna Casey moved from forward to defender and young Patrick McHale went in at Casey's position. Once again, Ballina adjusted but needed a comeback. Portlaoise led by two points at halftime before 31,236 fans, a slightly disappointing crowd when 50,000 was expected.

Thirty minutes remained before another crushing loss. But there was time. During the intermission, Tommy Lyons showed his team an All-Ireland club medal—but he kept the owner's identity a secret—as motivation. The hardware had an impact. If that wasn't enough, David Brady spoke up. Unscripted. The words were wrapped in tears. The emotion flowed. He literally cried. He pointed at John O'Mahony, a walking trophy. Few could recall his speech verbatim, but it hit everyone. Brady said "not today" and that he wasn't leaving Croke Park a loser—again.

The Westlife contingent—younger players jokingly named after the Irish boy band because of their fashion choices and slick hair—didn't let Brady down. Five minutes into the second half, a small rabbit of a forward named Stephen Hughes broke free from his defender, received a hand pass from McHale and kicked the ball past the keeper. The goal gave Ballina a 1-8 (11 points) to 1-6 (9 points) lead. To my left, the fan was on the floor after jumping on a friend (good thing they were friends). Martin Wynne, another Westlifer, successfully defended Portlaoise star Colm Parkinson, limiting his impact. But Portlaoise took a two-point lead at 2-8 (14) to 1-9 (12) with just over half the game remaining. Remember, this was a team from Mayo.

"They're throwing away their chances," my neighbor yelled. "C'mon Ballina, we want a good night tonight. Put them in their coffin."

Enda Devenney, looking mean in his mohawk, provided inspiration by entering with eighteen minutes remaining. With nine minutes left, Patrick Harte tied the game for Ballina with a strike over the bar. The outcome, though, was still very much in doubt. Both teams continued to run, neither one backing down. This would go down to the wire, once again. I looked to my left, and the fan appeared on the verge of passing out.

David Brady was doing everything he could, and with three minutes left he lined a kick toward the net. A defender crashed into him and was called for a foul—illegal contact. Enter brother Liam, who took the free kick from fifty-five yards out. David Brady walked over and wanted to know if little bro was going to make it. Yes, Liam said, and David got in a Hail Mary just in case. The ball made it through to give Ballina a one-point lead. Maybe those priests responsible for the curse decided enough was enough.

Portlaoise mounted one last attack in the final minute. Ballina goalkeeper John Healy charged out of the net, but Portlaoise's Peter McNulty juked him out of position. McNulty now had a quick decision to make at close range. What to do—go for the lead with a goal or for a tie with a kick over the bar? He seemed caught in the middle and went for the three points with a somewhat weak, but dead-on, shot. Defender Aidan Tighe instinctively ran back to the goal line and caught the ball to save the game.

Two minutes of the traditional injury time was added. Two minutes from heaven or a sad, sad St. Patrick's Day. Ballina passed the ball around, keeping it away like a massive monkey in the middle game. In all, there were twenty-two passes beyond the reach of the desperate Portlaoise players in the final minute. With the clock ticking down, David Brady held the ball and was clipped by an opponent near the sideline. Ger Brady ran over with advice: *stay down, let more time tick.* Seconds later the whistle blew and David Brady popped up with a roar. He yelped to the crowd raising both arms and joined his teammates in celebration. Liam and Ger rushed over and the three hugged. Brady moved to the sideline again giving an underhand salute to the roaring fans. Despite pleas from the loudspeaker, people ran onto the field. Finally, security didn't bother. Little kids engulfed Brady, as a man tried to whisk him away for a television interview. Thousands of fans in red and green, waving flags, covered the field. Mary Brady heard the cheers and came running back in. Soon, she was in the mob. I had no idea what happened to the guy to my left.

The players climbed the famous steps of the Hogan Stand to accept the winning cup. Brian Ruane praised his teammates in the traditional captain's victory speech and led them in the club's rallying song with the key verse of "forward to the goal of victory" now taking on new meaning. When they finished, a voice from the loudspeakers told the fans to exit. Yeah right. It was a sunny day and nobody wanted to leave. Everyone milled around, soaking up the moment. One delirious fan started walking to the train station, but never got there.

"I turned around," he said in a daze, as he rejoined friends. "I had the train ticket and I stopped. I'm not going home. I don't know where I'm staying."

He said the final two sentences with glee and amusement, ready for an adventure and a night to remember. After all, he earned it. This night belonged to the fans as much as it did to the players. Many exchanged hugs and handshakes and congratulations.

"I had 130 text messages after the game because I suppose they knew how much it meant to me," David Brady told me a week later. "Within an hour, I had text messages from Australia, Shanghai, Amsterdam, London—it was amazing how far and how wide people were able to watch the game or get the news. People were listening on the Internet, they were watching it on TV, they were listening on the radio. It was just fantastic."

Yes, Shanghai. Two Ballina men on a business trip fought through jet lag to listen on the Internet. Brady received cards from people he didn't know, including from Crossmaglen—the team that beat Ballina in that now forgotten 1999 final, when after leading the entire match, victory was snatched away from them in the final seconds.

Later that evening, the team had a banquet and celebration at the upscale Citywest hotel outside Dublin. But first, the Stephenites needed to make a stop. They visited Willie Casey, now in a Dublin hospital awaiting his triple bypass, which would be a success.

At the hotel, the players mixed with the fans, then went into a large room for dinner. Club officials, Tommy Lyons and captain Brian Ruane lauded the team and offered thanks to just about anyone connected with the squad in speeches, and the partying continued late into the night.

The next day, the win turned into a countywide bash. People from opposing parishes—Mayo fans desperate for any reason to celebrate—lit bonfires and waved Mayo flags as Ballina's bus drove by. The players got out several times to thank their new supporters.

Back home, about 3,000 fanatics mobbed the team's parking lot, with their vocal chords somehow still working. Music blared in a festive atmosphere. Club officials made repeated calls for fans to create space for the bus near the entrance. The bus, though, was nowhere to be found. It broke down along the way and a replacement had to be found. Finally, the heroes arrived.

They joined various politicians, team officials and representatives from the Mayo and Connacht GAA boards on a stage set up in the parking lot. The players wore dark, pinstriped suits, threads they remained in for most of the week. Impromptu chants of "Brady, Brady, Brady" filled the air. Later, there were more "Brady, Brady, Brady" chants. David Brady obliged, taking the microphone, looking casual chic with no tie. He proclaimed it a team effort and joked about the Westlife crew and the Devenneys' cycling habit. Between cheers and foghorns, Brady spoke to the point.

"I think any young person out there, you know, you've got to realize we're club players," he said to his people. "Whatever you want to do while you're young, you can always be a club player. You might not be a county [player]. But the thirty guys that are up here are honored. We are from Ballina. And we're always going to be from Ballina. Thanks very much."

During the next two weeks, they hit schools, hospitals, receptions, all while carrying the championship cup everywhere. Each player signed countless autographs, decorating kids' jerseys. At one signing session, a little girl, as tall as the thighs of many of the players, pinballed around getting her Stephenites jersey signed.

"This is what it's all about," proclaimed Aidan Tighe, the defender who made the key stop, and now more than happy to please the fans. "This is why we don't get paid. It's class."

Sunday, the bender continued with the St. Patrick's Day parade past Ballina's brightly colored buildings. It included a Prince Charles and Camilla wedding float—featuring a man with a blond wig as the bride—and a float with a pint of Guinness and a cigarette bemoaning their break-up, a bow to Ireland's strict no smoking in the pubs law. The players earned a spot in the parade with the win. First, they went through the route on a double-decker bus. Later, they returned, walking through town spraying champagne.

This time, the stout tasted sweeter. Brian McStay compared Enda Devenney playing to Curt Schilling pitching with blood on his sock during the American League Championship series when Boston finally beat the Yankees in 2004.

"There was a ghost there since the loss," McStay said of the 1999 defeat. "I think winning does kind of kill him."

For David Brady, the win made the pain of the other eight defeats all worth it. He told me, "I will never come down, why would I? When you're up in a cloud you never come down. There's no better feeling than knowing you're a winner."

Brady still had a question to answer. Everyone—fans, newspapers, radio—speculated whether he would play for Mayo in the upcoming inter-county season. Two weeks after the game, Ballina played in a charity exhibition to benefit a hospice. On the way, Brady read in a newspaper that he hadn't made a decision yet and was out of the country.

"I wish I was fucking out of the country," Brady said looking up in disbelief.

That day, he finally gave the scoop to the *Irish Star*. The tabloid ran a two-page spread, and Brady spoke about his career and the previous defeats. A few days later, Brady sat in his parents' living room with me as he vented. He never raised his voice, but spoke forcefully, his points clear and laced in triumph.

"It's been going for the last six or seven months and it's sickening," said Brady, getting it all off his chest. "... For the last year, the pressure has been tremendous because I've been in the limelight leading up to the [inter-county] All-Ireland final and then, all of a sudden, now in the club final. I suppose people will say I made headlines. I made headlines for what I wanted to do. That was to win an All-Ireland final.... The headlines were made for the right reasons. Now I just want to get away from football."

Brady's memories would always remain. Among the most poignant was when the team arrived at the hotel after the game. Fans stuffed the elegant lobby like meat in an oversized sandwich, only leaving a slim walkway for the players to squirm by. It was the proper setting for royalty. Chandeliers hung from the low ceiling with a fireplace to the right and statues near the steps. The mob extended up a staircase that veered off into additional steps on each side. Cheers and pats met each player, as they made their way from the bus. Brady received the loudest cheers and was lifted high on shoulders, as he pumped his fist to the heavens. They were his family, friends, teammates, drinking partners, people he fought with, people he grew up with, classmates, students, churchgoers, neighbors and coaches.

Now all of them roared.

NOTE: David Brady retired from the inter-county team for the 2005 season. But with a new manager in 2006, Brady came back—Roger Clemens anyone? Mayo rallied to stun Dublin in the All-Ireland semifinal. Next up was Kerry in the final. Fans finally thought the county's fifty-five year championship drought would be broken. Did Ballina's championship break the jinx? No. Kerry demolished Mayo handing Brady another loss. But no one could take his All-Ireland medal away from him, and it just made Ballina's win that much more meaningful.

Chapter 3
From Hell to Riches

April to early May: County Leitrim

April, like in baseball, was a time to wax poetic. Clubs began their county leagues. Inter-county teams prepared for the All-Ireland tournament beginning in May. Everyone was undefeated. Everyone was on the verge of a breakthrough season. Visions of glory sprouted up along daisies on hard, muddy fields across Ireland.

Perhaps that was why I went to County Leitrim, the least populated of the thirty-two counties and not known as a bastion of optimism. A national newspaper summed up that perception in a review of a television show featuring an undercover cop, "And boy is it dark—it's darker than Leitrim on a dirty winter night mid-power cut." Yes, Leitrim was always good for a punch line, kind of like Cleveland never fails to be boring no matter how many hall of fames it builds. Leitrim's rep was its hardship. The darkness came not in its beauty along the River Shannon, but in its barren land and remoteness. The soil was so damp that the running joke had been the farmland wasn't sold by the acre, but by the gallon. Another common phrase: there were more Leitrim people living outside the county than actually in it because of the high emigration rates. Leitrim was part of the Connacht province, the upper western area that Oliver Cromwell compared to hell as he attempted to cleanse Ireland of Catholics in the mid-1600s.

On the field, Leitrim (pronounced Lee-trim) was the ultimate small-market team struggling against competition drawn from populations double, triple and even twenty times its size. Every year, they were like a No. 16 seed on the first day of March Madness. What often counted as a successful season was winning just one game in the provincial tournament and then not getting embarrassed. This season, Leitrim faced 500/1 odds to win the All-Ireland. And there were no quick fixes. The front office couldn't dangle millions to lure free agents, and a wealthy tycoon looking for a hobby couldn't buy the franchise. While every county was in the same position, Leitrim was always hit among the hardest with its population hovering around 25,000.

So, I was expecting to find a defeatist attitude in the Ireland left behind by the Celtic Tiger, the catchy name for the country's economic revival. I was anticipating wallow, just hours from fancy homes and BMWs. What I found surprised me. Something more in tune with the country ditty *Lovely Leitrim* that celebrated the county's hills, deep valleys, lofty mountains and lakes perfect for sailing and salmon fishing. And yes, the people even smiled. Why wouldn't they? They had an outstretched energy for life and were now finally getting financial opportunities in a thriving Irish economy. That zeal extended to the playing fields. Leitrim's GAA Web site bragged it had more Gaelic football clubs per person—one team for every forty-two males of normal playing age—than anywhere else in Ireland. Players made huge sacrifices, seemingly unaware they were supposed to lose. In the end, I found the things that kept them going weren't crazy at all.

My first acquaintance with a Leitrim man took place thanks to the affable and white-haired Ballina assistant coach Jim McGarry. Luckily for me, McGarry was a native of the small Leitrim parish of Annaduff located in the southern tip of the county. He helped organize a charity exhibition between the clubs shortly after Ballina won the All-Ireland title. After the game, McGarry introduced me to the right people. As word spread that I knew Jim, I realized a vouch goes a long way in the GAA. Annaduff coach Eugene Cox invited me to the parish, a place on my radar because it won the county championship last fall for the first time in seventy-six years. I wanted to see why the drought lasted so long, and what propelled them to the title—especially in the context of playing in the smallest county.

As I was getting ready to leave Mayo, I called Cox to see if there was a nearby bed and breakfast.

"Don't worry, we'll take care of you."

It sounded kind of sketchy, but I figured I'd worry about it later. At the Ballina bus station, I asked the woman at the counter how much the fare to Annaduff cost.

"We don't go there."

I happened to be clutching the time sheet, so I glanced down, tracing my finger to the small print.

"It's at the church, two stops down from Carrick-on-Shannon."

She lowered her head for an investigation.

"Oh."

The bus driver gave me the same double-take. *Annaduff?* Apparently it wasn't a hub of activity. Then again, Carrick-on-Shannon, Leitrim's largest town with a population of 3,500, wasn't exactly a metropolis.

A busy Cox picked me up in front of Annaduff Church at 7 p.m. He was scurrying about, trying to find a papal flag for an upcoming memorial service honoring Pope John Paul II, who had died over the weekend. At the team's weightlifting workout later that evening, assistant coach Donal Fox filled me in on the scene with his encyclopedic knowledge of nearly everything. At one point, I wondered to myself where I was going to sleep. The players trickled out of the gym/community center and soon Cox, Fox and I stood in the empty gym. They had a discussion—who was going to get the stranded American. I kept my distance, certain I'd be sleeping in a cowshed. Fox agreed to take me in, though I didn't know if he owed Cox a favor or had lost a quick rock, paper and scissors game.

Cox—dressed in his normal attire of black jeans, wool knit hat in which his white sideburns snuck out and a sleeveless vest over a sweater—gave me my bags from his car in the dark parking lot and I left with my new ride. Fox now lived half an hour outside the parish, and as he drove through narrow back roads, snow suddenly started shooting down. He peered out into the thick whiteness as he called his wife to warn her company was coming—always good to hear at eleven at night. They set me up in an extra bedroom and offered seasoned eggs in the morning along with friendly conversation. At night, I got a Gaelic football lesson from their elementary school-age son (his skills negated my size advantage). After catching my breath, Fox provided me with my first taste of Bushmills whiskey, and we sipped the malt blend diluted with water over football talk.

For two days, I went to Fox's office in Drumshanbo where he worked for an organization helping unemployed and disadvantaged people (no wonder he was so kind to me). It was great to catch up on transcribing my interviews, but I needed to get closer to Annaduff. Enter two nights at the parish's lone bed and breakfast. It was full, however, for the weekend with excited fans attending a car rally in Carrick. Homeless once again, a cowshed seemed like a real possibility. But the Annaduff faithful wasn't going to let me freeze. Thanks Jim. Cox had a plan all along and spoke to me after Friday's practice.

"Do you mind staying alone?"

"Um, no."

He just happened to have an extra house available. Sure. Some people have an extra piece of gum or a pen to spare. He had a house lying around. It turned out that he was building a new home for his family near their current one. Their move in was planned for June, and now it was about three-quarters finished—a perfect place for a stray American. The outside resembled, well a house under construction. The front yard had dirt, rocks and high, uncut grass. Three packages of brown bricks stood on the grass near the front door. The backyard doubled as a hardware store with more bricks and long pieces of wood on the mostly dirt ground. Inside, there were only a few eyesores—some soil in the hallway and a rolled-up carpet. Underneath the stairwell, I saw more pieces of wood (the house could have been a tree cemetery) and unfolded cardboard boxes. The living room had a forty-two-inch television and a fireplace that doubled as a garbage can. A smooth leather recliner sat on nice red carpeting, and a long glass table in the kitchen made it a perfect writer's retreat. I sensed a future spread for an Irish architectural magazine. My finished room included a warm electric shower. It was home.

I asked Cox several times, Are you sure you don't mind me staying?

"I don't give a shit."

Well, that was good enough for me.

Initially, I had company. He let a friend having family problems stay a few nights. Basically, it was a halfway house for poor visiting writers and buddies in marital transition.

By the third night, I was on my own and soon heard a drip in the ceiling. The wind crashed into the windows. A dog was barking. And suddenly the thought of Irish witches and ghost stories churned in my head. It was time for bed. Upstairs, I heard a creaky noise as if the doorknob was about to turn. The dog still howled. So I did what any thirty-one-year-old would—I turned off all the lights, pulled down the shades and went to bed clutching the blanket and wishing my mommy was there.

Each night I became braver, and ended up staying about a month—free of charge. Because of Cox's generosity, I didn't have to worry about running out of money later in the year and resorting to eating cheap potatoes and beans. Not only did I have my own mini-mansion, but I got VIP treatment whenever I went over to the Coxes. Eugene's wife Olive had a way of making a sandwich or breaded chicken cutlet and fries materialize without my ever asking. One morning I went for a walk as Olive was leaving. She said to go into their empty house and to help myself to a bowl of cereal. I was in awe of their generosity. In fact, everyone went out of their way to help me throughout my eight months in Ireland. For all they knew, I could have been Jack the Ripper, but I was welcomed in home after home. I couldn't see this happening in the U.S. The Irish reputation for hospitality was legit.

Annaduff became my Leitrim base. The spread out, but sparsely populated parish near the County Roscommon border consisted of two villages—Dromod and Drumsna—and several small areas called townlands. There was nothing cosmopolitan about Annaduff. For the most part, it was a nondescript Irish parish with plenty of small farms dotting the countryside as well as the ubiquitous well-placed pub and variety shop. A sign leading to Dromod bragged of its silver medal in the recent national tidy towns competition. Drumsna got a dollop of recognition because it was the birthplace of Robert Strawbridge, a pioneer of the Methodist church in the United States in the 1760s after he emigrated to Maryland. The village's cemetery held the remains of Thomas Hazel Parke, a surgeon who accompanied Henry Morton Stanley on his expedition to the African Congo in the late 1800s. (Stanley's famous line was "Dr. Livingstone, I presume?") The people went about their business, doors were often left unlocked and neighbor knew neighbor's family history.

That didn't mean Annaduff was stuck in the 1950s. A steady stream of smoke puffed from Drumsna's Masonite factory, an outpost of the American company that makes door fronts. The major N4 highway ran through the parish, connecting the West to Dublin. Annaduff was no longer isolated, but maintained its country roots. It was a perfect parish to examine where old, backwater Ireland under British rule met the trendy Ireland dotted with multinational companies and designer boutiques.

You begin with the past. So I sought out longtime resident Tommy Daly, now 102 and the last surviving member of the legendary 1928 Annaduff team that captured the county championship. He wasn't hard to locate. Tommy lived in the same house he grew up in, that had been in his family now for seven generations in the townland of Moheraven.

I had a peaceful walk over in the late afternoon, and the only rush hour was the cows moving with the sun. His daughter-in-law took me to Tommy in the living room, one of several additions to the house. In Tommy's day there was a straw thatch roof, a kitchen doubling as a family room and two other bedrooms. (Annaduff didn't get full electrical power until the early 1950s.) She gave us cookies and tea and left us to talk. He was dressed impeccably—a dapper blue sports coat, a red sweater and a blue tie. His full head of neat, white hair gave him a distinguished aura. Tommy—a widower—lived with his son George (in his early fifties) and daughter-in-law Anne. One grandson, Barry, played for Annaduff. When I spoke with Anne later on, she peeked at her cell phone to see if a daughter visiting Australia had texted her.

I was here to get perspective from Tommy, and I thought how much times had changed. For Tommy, a text message and a cell phone were the same thing—a stroll for a chat with a neighbor. Organic food wasn't trendy, it was the only choice. Teenagers dreamed of owning a convertible, though in the form of a horse and buggy. Bricks of peat warmed homes and stoves. The Internet probably had something to do with fishing.

One thing that didn't change was the GAA's importance to the parish. I knew from my research that Tommy's uncle was the secretary of the first GAA club formed in Drumsna in 1889. A couple months later, the Annaduff Parnellites were founded, named after Charles Stewart Parnell—the Irish Parliamentary Party leader who fought for home rule and land reform. The GAA was closely tied to Irish nationalism and survival of clubs depended on the country's political and economic health, which often seemed ill. A graveyard of failed Annaduff GAA teams would include these epitaphs:

> 1889-1893, Cause of death: The Parnell Split—after Parnell had an affair with Katharine "Kitty" O'Shea, the wife of another politician in 1890—which led to a division between his followers.

> 1904-1906, Cause of death: Political feuding stemming from the Parnell Split and the death of a club leader.

> 1917-early 1920s, Cause of death: The outbreak of the Irish Civil War after some people weren't pleased with the treaty that split Ireland into the twenty-six county Irish Free State and the six-county Northern Ireland after the War of Independence with England.

> Mid-1920s-late 1920s, Cause of death: A lack of numbers caused mainly by emigration.

The GAA, though, kept coming back from the dead as an indefatigable social outlet. Fans would walk ten miles to attend games after long, hard days working on their farms, or between curfews imposed by the Black and Tans, the British paramilitary group that terrorized locals, and between shootouts in the parish during the Civil War.

"The times was bad," said Tommy, his mind still working in the twenty-first century, even if it took some prodding to get him going. "The people was poor. Money was very scarce. We had a great team. Then America used to play hell with it. Six left and went to America. Ahhhh, they used to rob every team in the county. The better player he was, he was the first they'd lose."

Missing men were common as a stream of bodies fled across the pond in search of work. Seven of Tommy's siblings emigrated to America and England. He remained with two sisters and his parents to run the family's cattle farm.

"The rest of the family was gone," Tommy recalled. "They promised me that I'd have more money than I'd be able to spend, and they sent me a good amount of money for the first year, but it went down very low later on."

Times were tough all over. The coherent and sharp Tommy filled me in. There were a few technical difficulties with his hearing aid not picking up my accent, but truthfully, I tend to mumble as it is. Half the people I met in Ireland probably thought my name was Eddie instead of Andy, so Tommy was off the hook there. He would, however, ask what county I was from.

"New Jersey in America."

Five minutes later: "What county and parish are you from?"

"Ah, New Jersey in America."

Ten minutes later: "What county are you from?"

Considering he was just telling stories from 1919, I'd give him a break. And they were well cherished, like a breathing volume of history. I learned he raised cattle until they were two then sold them at a fair to slaughter. Sometimes, farmers bought the cows needing to first fatten them up. He also sold milk to a creamery.

"Some years you do well," Tommy said. "You were dependent on the English market for everything ... They didn't give us fair play at all, and there was no opposition. They'd give you very little for it. Ah, we had to take it. England was the boss. She got away with murder. Of course it was tough, shipping cattle. Ah, they was hard times."

He remembered seeing cows from other counties that were bigger and "round as a top" because they ate off of green land over rich soil. Leitrim had wet and rocky soil.

"We had bad land in Leitrim," said Tommy, then recalling what a neighbor told him. "He said if you were out in the states and working as hard as you are here, you'd make a fortune. And I often thought of it."

Instead, Tommy had to scrap by like his neighbors, barely making a living. The Economic War from 1932-1938 didn't help. Irish Prime Minister Eamon de Valera refused to pay England land annuities—money the British government had loaned to Irish farmers to buy land before Ireland won its independence. England responded by instituting quotas and tariffs on Irish imports, mainly cattle and dairy products. The whole economy suffered. Four of Tommy's six children emigrated to America, England or Australia. They didn't have much of a choice. One daughter stayed, as did son George, who took over the family business of raising cattle. Tommy didn't exactly retire, doing as much as he could well into his seventies and eighties and always taking an interest.

He even went missing for a few seconds toward the end of my visit while I chatted with Anne. We spotted him outside the window, motoring around with his walker along the peaceful country lane. Both hands were navigating, with skin smoother than you'd expect for a century old farmer. She could only laugh, and I thought I should be that lucky.

He once displayed that guile on the field. But with men constantly leaving, it was a struggle to field teams. Tommy captained a re-formed Drumsna squad in 1932 that wore four different uniforms acquired from the participating parishes. Whoever was around, played. Leitrim always had high emigration rates and the population fell from 55,907 residents in 1926 to 30,572 in 1966 to 25,799 in 2002.

Gaelic football survived in Annaduff fueled by youth teams coached by Father Sean Manning. An adult team came back for good in 1958, and the parish captured under-14 county championships in 1961 and 1964. A year later, the adult team earned promotion to the top division in the county league after winning the junior title. Annaduff needed to play on its neighbor Bornacoola's field because it didn't have one, and emigration continued in the 1970s and 1980s. Things, though, were getting better.

One of those men forced to leave in the 1980s was Annaduff's current coach Eugene Cox, once a member of the under-14 county champions. At that time, a construction worker in Annaduff was an oxymoron. So Cox took off for London, flying back every few weekends to see his family, longing to return permanently.

Events were in motion that gave people like Cox hope. In 1973, Ireland joined the European Union (then called the European Economic Community), allowing it access to new markets while lessening Ireland's dependence on England. The EU paid billions in support, money that went into Irish infrastructure projects such as road improvement and business development. The government lowered corporate taxes—now the lowest in Europe at 12.5 percent—thus giving attractive investment incentives. By the mid-1990s, these components merged together, causing a boom called the Celtic Tiger, coined after Asia's resurgence in the preceding decades.

Ireland transformed into a cyberspace hub and its murderer's row of satellite offices and European headquarters included Apple, Dell, IBM, Intel, Gateway, Google and Microsoft. Top medical product and pharmaceutical companies also opened shops in Ireland. The boom slowed in 2001, only to blast off again. In 2005, *The Economist* named unlikely Ireland the best country to live in using several quality of life criteria such as low unemployment, stable family life and gross domestic product.

Most of the new money, though, was concentrated in Dublin and the East Coast. Some claimed the Tiger got drowned in the River Shannon. Eventually, as Cox told me, "The country boys caught on quick enough." Masonite opened in Drumsna in 1994 and MBNA credit card lenders opened in Carrick-on-Shannon in 2001. In the last five years, Carrick's population had increased 31.6 percent and now included forty nationalities. The ten-minute drive from Annaduff to Carrick regularly featured construction cranes fanning across the countryside for necessities to support the boom from houses to supermarkets.

Leitrim didn't suddenly become the Silicon Valley of Ireland. (Although it did get its first set of traffic lights two years ago in Carrick.) The hardship reputation still lingered, and Leitrim's poverty level still ranked near the country's highest. But the government made an effort to spread the wealth. In the last five years, Leitrim received millions in projects ranging from vital services like childcare facilities to quality of life amenities such as an arts center in Carrick and broadband Internet networks. A rural renewal scheme provided tax relief in new home and business construction or refurbishing. The growth aided the GAA in subtle ways. For example, a decentralization plan was bringing government offices to Carrick. As Leitrim GAA chairman Gerry McGovern told me, "People will be coming from different parts of the country to work here. So it will create more employment and hopefully we get a few footballers out of it as well."

More importantly, people like the Eugene Coxes were now able to remain. Cox moved back in 1993 and slowly found construction business. Five years ago, he joined forces with two nephews. They had nine employees and enough work for six months. Now, they had sixty-five workers and enough jobs for two and a half years, and they were turning down projects. Most of their labor went to building homes for first time owners within a twenty-mile radius of the parish.

Cox—who had been known to work through bank holidays saying, "Do I work for a bank?"—was an anti-Donald Trump. The fifty-five-year-old still helped on construction jobs, whether he was up on a roof, driving machinery or bouncing around with his cell phone solving problems. Cox exemplified the type of person that made the amateur GAA succeed—someone who was conscious of the parish, willing to give back and not wanting any thanks. He told me, "If somebody needed a bit of help and you can give it to them, why the hell wouldn't you give it to them?"

On the field, Cox coached various youth squads, with kids piling in his van to travel to games. He took over the adult team in 2001, guiding them to the county's second division championship. In 2002, Annaduff played in the county's first division and in 2003 reached the "B" final for teams that didn't qualify for the elimination round of the county tournament. In 2004, Annaduff upset its way to the Leitrim title, even presenting Tommy Daly with a medal.

One night as we spoke, Cox showed me a framed article. Respected *Irish Independent* columnist Eugene McGee visited the parish months after Annaduff's 2004 win to celebrate the GAA's impact on small areas in a column titled "Where parish pride runs deep, runs free." McGee told how the Gaelic football team helped give the parish of 350 homes and 1,100 people an identity and, "As we head into another GAA playing season the Annaduff story is probably more indicative of the power for good that the GAA can be than any of the major events that will hog the national headlines in 2005."

Indeed, Cox's most memorable image was seeing grown men, those he knew nearly all his life, thank him with tears streaming down their weathered faces following the county final. The team's talent went a long way, sure, but there was something else that former players didn't have.

"For the first time we've had people about," Donal Fox explained. "You know, we had numbers. We never used to have numbers. None of the clubs in Leitrim had. Back in the 1980s for example, everybody was away. They were all emigrating or they were in Dublin. There were very few football players about. Several of the clubs in Leitrim used to say we've got a better team in New York than we have at home.... So really for the first time, this is the first generation of young Annaduff men that has had the opportunity to stay at home, to work at home and to make some money and to really plan their futures living here—which is a wonderful thing."

About ten years ago, Annaduff would field six to ten players for a mid-week practice because few lived nearby. Now, Annaduff could have fifteen to twenty-five players show up at a Tuesday or Wednesday practice. More players present meant more team bonding and cohesiveness. Not every Leitrim club held full practice sessions with many players still living and working in Dublin, and then coming home for the weekend. But there were opportunities, and Annaduff's players took advantage of them, whether they worked as brick masons or lawyers. Only a handful lived beyond a half-hour drive from the parish (excluding the students away at college).

At one weightlifting session, I chatted with two players in their early thirties. In the past, both would have been elsewhere. One was Cox's nephew Gerry (there were eleven Coxes in all on the team). In the late 1980s, he worked in a local meat plant, which closed, then found a job in construction.

"You'd get a job alright, but you wouldn't get money," Gerry explained. "Work wasn't here."

He left for England in 1991 and easily found good money sweating as a laborer. But his wife and daughter remained in Leitrim. Gerry was finally able to return eight years later. He drove a truck transporting cattle feed, and now drives a truck for a local hardware store.

"If it was the same as it is now, I wouldn't have left," said Cox, who looked like he could be a cousin of John Travolta. "Ireland was just starting to become good at that time."

As I headed to the adjacent locker room to talk with goalkeeper Kevin Ludlow, I dodged a flying Gaelic football. A basketball hoop hung near the front door in the left corner of the building. Between grunts, players shot or kicked the ball through the hoop, with amazing accuracy. But that was about the only extra perk. The room lacked mirrors or TVs, just folded tables against the wall. The building doubled as a community center used by groups ranging from farm associations to disease awareness organizations. A floor upstairs had just enough space for three stationary bikes, rowing machines and treadmills. Downstairs, near the back wall, were three machines for bench presses, leg press, dips and other muscle building lifts. It wasn't fancy, but it worked. Members built the complex in 2001 next to the field, which opened in 1983. Both projects required intensive fundraising. For the community center, members wheeled a player resting on a bed around a 300-mile radius. People did double-takes, laughed and contributed money for Annaduff's cause. In the early 1980s, parish members pushed a football made of timber the size of a room from Leitrim to Dublin while collecting donations. How could you say no to things like that?

I found Ludlow on a bench in the locker room. Love took him to Annaduff. The native of County Meath, near Dublin, dated a Drumsna woman while attending college. After he graduated in 1993, Ludlow accepted an engineering job with IBM in Dublin, but often spent the weekend in Drumsna.

"The train would be full to the gills with people going back up to Dublin to work," said Ludlow, remembering his return trips. "But now the transit has turned around. Leitrim is certainly a really happening place. Like you see ads in all the Sunday papers about apartments for sale, houses for sale. It's a real place to go invest. Certainly the last five years it's turned around. I see it anyway. You can see the wealth around Carrick-on-Shannon."

After he became engaged in 2001, he and his fiancée settled in Drumsna. Ludlow decided to switch teams instead of driving back to Meath every weekend. Word leaked to Annaduff players, and Ludlow had his GAA transfer papers signed before his wedding license. He found a job working as a sales/account manager out of his home. In the years before cyber commuting, he said moving to Annaduff wouldn't have been an option.

Ludlow and Gerry Cox are just two valuable players that Annaduff would have lost through the decades because of a poor economy. People were a team's greatest currency, and when their lives flourished, so did the result on the field.

My time in Annaduff coincided with the beginning of the county league, and I watched three games before I left. The season-opener on April 9 drew extra interest because it was against neighbor Bornacoola. The club formed in 1889 and, like Annaduff, often struggled to fill teams. Now, the fully revived squads competed in backyard brawls. Last season, Annaduff won the league and county title, but lost to Bornacoola in the opener. Both teams had something to brag about. (The county league was an entirely different competition than the county tournament. The latter awarded the winner that competed in the provincial tournament and was considered more important.)

I observed another local derby. Elbows. Headbutts. Tackles. Shoving. Cursing. Simply, it was neighbors beating the crap out of one another before shaking hands and earning local pub bragging rights. Football donnybrooks on green Gaelic fields were a staple of the GAA. It didn't matter that most of Ireland couldn't care less about the outcome. Here, it was everything. The few hundred fans lined the fence to cheer, whine and call the referee blind. The play was sloppy, but intense. Yellow cards flew to match the budding dandelions.

No Annaduff player sat during the entire game. Everyone stood as close to the edge of the field as allowed, cheering on their teammates, yelling at the opponent. In the second half, Bornacoola scored a few points in a row and cruised to a surprising seven-point victory. In the whole scheme of things, it didn't mean much. This was still April, after all, and things wouldn't heat up until June when the championship started. But the Bornacoola players celebrated like they had just won an All-Ireland, while the Annaduff side spoke a little softer. The coaches focused on the big picture.

"I'm not worried," declared Cox, holding his head high and really meaning it.

In the following week's game, Annaduff easily won to soothe some of their wounded pride. The last weekend of April, though, provided a test against Gortletteragh, a squad expected to contend. Annaduff played without four starters—the county suspended one for a head-butt in the Bornacoola game—and trailed by six points at halftime. In the second half, Annaduff missed several shots and just seemed a step behind. Cox paced the sidelines trying to inspire his players, but words didn't help. Gortletteragh even scored a fluke point that bounced over Ludlow as he came out of the net, and won by three. That summed up the season. As the defending champs, everybody wanted to take Annaduff out. Fox told the players he thought they got "mentally soft" and they needed to readjust their attitude. Cox still wasn't overly concerned.

The slide, though, was just beginning.

Annaduff's season of high hopes turned into a disaster. It finished 4-5 in the league and tied for fifth place out of ten teams. In the county championship, Annaduff failed to advance to the single elimination quarterfinals despite a 2-1-1 record. They didn't play horribly, but there was no room for error. Simply, the tie and a loss off a late score did Annaduff in. It was a crushing blow following the championship year. Annaduff rebounded to win the "B" tournament for squads losing in the main draw. But the celebrations just weren't the same.

Cox had hit the wall. He put in five years and genuinely felt the team needed a fresh voice. It wasn't like he received pressure to quit after the poor season. In fact, the players wanted him back. But the GAA coaching lifespan was often short. Business and family needed time, too. The *Leitrim Observer* reported on November 18 that Cox had retired. Of course, he'd still be active on various committees—just no more sideline pacing. But Annaduff had trouble finding a replacement for whatever reason. Cox couldn't desert his beloved club, and he volunteered to return for another season, no matter what he had going on in his personal life.

"I would always help the club," Cox told me.

It meant too much not to.

I hated to bail on Annaduff, but six months and more stories remained in my travels. So I headed to north Leitrim, split from the south by the Lough Allen (lough means lake in the Irish language). You needed to briefly sway into County Roscommon before re-entering Leitrim. Up north, people felt more of a kinship with neighboring County Sligo to the left and County Donegal to the right. I wanted to see if Leitrim's growth had extended to other parts of the county.

The Melvin Gaels GAA club, based in the village of Kinlough, sat two miles from a beachside town in Donegal called Bundoran. It had two surf shops, arcades where you could win real money, amusement rides, an indoor water park, a wide boardwalk and a golf course along the Atlantic seaboard. Kinlough didn't quite attract the same number of tourists, but anglers came to outwit four species of trout—brown, ferox, gilaroo and sonaghan—that swam in the Lough Melvin. To illustrate the importance of nature in these parts, the local GAA club was named for the lake instead of an Irish patriot or church. The nearby townland of Tullaghan contained Leitrim's two miles of coastline.

A new housing development greeted visitors to Kinlough from the Bundoran side. If you continued past the post office, down the main street by a somewhat pricey restaurant, a pub, a supermarket and an elementary school, you saw more cranes. Joe McCarron, a club official who had lived in the village for thirty years, filled me in.

"A lot of American people come here and they expect to still see the little thatch cottage without electricity and this type of thing, but Ireland has moved on," McCarron explained. "I have relations of me own who's been away for years and years and they come back and they can't believe it. They didn't like it. They wanted the green grass and the little cottages—that's gone. Some people think it's sad that that's gone but I don't, really. I mean you have to move."

Sad in the sense that the close-knit community would disappear, and a little village of friendly faces transforms into aloof, busy strangers.

"This is where the GAA comes in, in a big way," said McCarron, whose two sons play for the Gaels.

Kinlough had retained its homeliness despite major activity. Its population in 2006 stood at 864 people, an increase of 73.5 percent from 2002. McCarron mentioned that in the last twenty years the local elementary school has added two extensions and doubled its enrollment to about 200 pupils. In the last few weeks, a laundromat opened and there was an application to build a hotel.

The growth probably saved the ailing Melvin Gaels. On its thirtieth anniversary in 1984, the Gaels played only three games and couldn't enter a team in the county championship. Morale was exceedingly low and there were real concerns for the club's existence. As recent as the early 1990s, there weren't enough players to form an adult team.

So the club instead focused on its youth squads, with the hope that jobs in the area would rebound. It worked. The Gaels' children teams won several county championships in the mid-1980s to early 1990s. In 1988, the adult team formed again and captured two low-level championships.

Jobs were becoming available in Bundoran, Sligo city and Donegal city, thus keeping those young studs nearby. Presto—the Gaels earned a promotion to the highest county division in 1993, and won the championship in 1998 for the first time in thirty-three years. Now, recognized contenders, only about half a dozen players didn't live within thirty minutes of town. The management also improved.

"There's more work put into coaching now," explained Michael McGowan, a well-known member of the club who just finished a stint as the Leitrim GAA chairman. "In the '70s, there was little work put into coaching because basically the manpower wasn't available to do it."

McGowan cited two factors that permitted the players to stay local: the government's offering of free high school education for every resident in the late 1960s and technology. In the past, many Irish who emigrated could only get jobs as laborers in poor conditions. Thus, the well-known folk song, *Paddy Works On The Railway*.

"People are more educated now and they saw they didn't have to do slave work for a living," he told me. "That they could get employment using their head, and then of course they used their heads very sensibly."

McGowan, now in his late sixties, was one of those dedicated members that helped keep the club alive in the lean times. As a young man, he taught high school math in Galway, but continued to play for the Melvin Gaels and Leitrim at the inter-county level. He spurned an offer to play for a more successful Galway club.

"I wasn't interested in All-Irelands," he told me on the edge of the club's field as a youth team practiced. "I was much more interested in playing for my local club. There was one fella, and he spent an hour and a half trying to give me every reason why I should play for them. He could still be trying, but I wouldn't play for them."

There was one problem: his principal wouldn't let him make the 100-mile trip back to Leitrim with fears his teaching duties could suffer. McGowan went anyway, but used the monikers of Michael Kelly or Michael Smith just in case anyone checked.

Even when he retired, McGowan couldn't fully get away. In 1972, when attending a Leitrim game as a fan, the thirty-four-year-old wound up playing when someone didn't show up. Then, the Melvin Gaels needed a player—in 1997. After an injury, they stuck the sixty-one-year-old McGowan in goal.

"I didn't make any spectacular saves," said McGowan, only able to chuckle at the memory. "There were more spectacular goals scored on me. It was a long night."

But he was a body. Now, the club didn't need to use senior citizens on the field. That was one thing everyone hoped for, whether it was in Kinlough or Annaduff.

"You'll never see bad times in Ireland again like we did in the late '60s, '70s," Eugene Cox confidently proclaimed. "We'll never see times like that again. Nobody would want to."

The club teams only told half of Leitrim's GAA story. The other was the intercounty squad that played in national competitions. Since you couldn't bring in free agents, the player pool was important. Size-wise, Leitrim was a wristwatch trying to compete with Big Bens. The slim pickings always made them an underdog. Success, consequently, got measured in different ways. In the recently completed National League, for example, Leitrim finished with a win over nearby rival Roscommon causing a celebration afterward in an otherwise meaningless game.

"In Leitrim, you don't have that expectation of winning an All-Ireland," Gerry McGovern, the county GAA chairman, told me. "But you like to be progressing, at least."

The county didn't have a lighted field, so the team rented time at either a GAA club or a rugby club in County Longford, to the southeast of Leitrim. The location was central for players hustling to practice after work. Of the twenty-eight players, thirteen worked outside the county, seven in Leitrim and eight attended college outside the county.

I checked out a typical training session in early May. Leitrim goalkeeper Gareth Phelan arrived after his one-and-a-half-hour drive from the northern part of the county. Defender John McKeon scooted the same distance from Galway on the West Coast, while forward Dara McKiernan was stuck in traffic from rainy Dublin on the East Coast. Eventually, after three hours, he arrived as his teammates were already on the field. Were they nuts? No one expected Leitrim to contend for the All-Ireland title and they were put at 33/1 odds to win the Connacht championship. You were better off throwing your money into a wishing well. If Leitrim could beat County Sligo in the first round—a toss-up game—then it should get pounded against Galway. Not a close game. Pounded. Yet, those three players and their twenty-five teammates were here.

"The traveling is tortuous," Phelan said a few days later, soon adding a laugh. "And I never get used to it. I hate it. I get stiff. I got back from Longford the other night and my arse was so sore. My arse was in knots after driving after the training session. It was a hard training session and I just jumped in the car and drove an hour and a half."

The obvious question was why do it? It made sense to give that commitment to a power team that expected to make a deep run. But for Leitrim? So, you got a jersey. You got to play at the highest level. Maybe women threw some extra attention your way. But you weren't getting paid. You were achy at work the next day. Relationships and family life become interrupted. Chances were certain know-it-all fans would criticize you during the season. Undoubtedly, they'd be some smart put-down in the newspaper just to remind you of your place on the food chain. For example, the *Irish Star's* preview asked, "Who are you?" to every team.

The answer: "We're Leitrim, the last county in the country to get traffic lights. Unfortunately, on the football field we've been driving down cul-de-sacs for way too long now."

You might as well just play for your club and forget about the county team. Phelan, McKeon and McKiernan had their reasons, and their answers revealed much about the soul of the GAA.

Phelan actually quit before the season. It wasn't a knock on Leitrim. Rather, the real world beckoned. Phelan recently built an office for his physical therapy practice, and was now working on a house. He always seemed to be doing something, including coaching his club team, the Melvin Gaels. That would never go. His father and his two brothers played there and the club meant a great deal. With everything colliding, the twenty-nine-year-old decided to retire from the county team after seven seasons.

"When I was in college I didn't think twice about other commitments," said Phelan, remembering those carefree days. "Football was my main priority, but now it's definitely different. In fact, the last couple of weeks have been pretty stressful … when I have 101 other things I should probably be at."

When a substitute goalkeeper got injured, though, Phelan said the Leitrim coaches persuaded him to return. He couldn't resist, even if he wasn't guaranteed a starting spot. Phelan, who shaved his head a few years ago, today had neck-length wavy hair. The natural way worked for him. Phelan was living in a mobile home with his girlfriend in the middle of nowhere until his house was ready. They kept roosters as pets and had an envious view of a high mountain. The brightest—and only—double rainbow I ever saw was by Phelan's trailer. He had a philosopher's aura to him, which extended to football.

"I got to a stage where I'm very conscious of our capabilities and what we are capable of on any day," he explained one afternoon at his brother's pub in Kinlough. "Everyone has potential. So if you get a group of guys and you train them for a specific purpose for nine months of the year and if you're fit to mentally get them prepared, then I don't see any good reason why you shouldn't be fit to compete with any other team. I used to use the weaker county thing. I used to use that as a motivator but now I don't because it's an illusionary thing. The realistic part of it is, it's fifteen against fifteen and that's the way I like to keep it. Just to keep it as real as possible."

Keeping it real. They kick, you kick. They run, you run. Same thing.

Sometimes, things weren't complex.

"I'm not going to be fit to do this in a few years time, so I'm using whatever energy I have in my body to contribute to the county while I can," Phelan continued. "There's a certain vitality to it as well, the life energy of it. There's an energy existence, I think, around the team and I find it appealing to be a part of that."

Before, during and after a Leitrim practice, a steady stream of spikes strolled into the physical trainer Brian Beirne's room. Players dropped in to get their ankles taped or hamstrings loosened and the banter flowed. The varied topics included politics, current events, celebrities, gossip about other players—it was like a barbershop. At the rugby club, Beirne manned a table set up on the edge of the dining room that acted as a makeshift treatment area. The barroom was just beyond and the TV showed the Liverpool-Chelsea semifinal of the UEFA Champions League, a prestigious soccer tournament involving the best professional teams in the world.

McKeon stopped for a few minutes after getting his hamstrings massaged. He worked for Boston Scientific, a medical device company, as a quality engineer for heart monitors. When it came to sports, he didn't even think of transferring to Galway—which won two All-Ireland titles in the last eight years.

"No," McKeon said as quickly as it took to breathe. "It's part of the pride, pride of your own—representing your family and friends.... If you go to Galway you know no one there, like you're an outsider."

In transient professional sports, the city often wasn't as important to the athlete compared to how much money he was getting. You still wanted to win, but New York, Chicago, San Francisco, Liverpool, Chelsea—what was the difference? You followed the paycheck. In the GAA, it was the opposite.

"It's tough when we're playing against bigger teams, better teams, it's hard to keep going all the time," McKeon agonized. "It's tough, like when you're up against counties that have such big populations, such a pick. It's tough after getting beaten. Ah, it's the pride of the county."

Like most of his teammates, McKeon grew up in this world. Both his father and mother played for his club. Putting on the Leitrim jersey extended his family.

"In some ways Leitrim represents us all," Annaduff's Donal Fox told me, before outlining an unofficial social contract a fan had with his county team. Since the squad represented *him*, he had a right to be critical of the players if they were struggling. He also, however, was entitled to share in the victories like he had won himself.

"It's not like supporting Manchester United or the New York Jets or whatever," Fox continued. "You don't really have a choice. This is your team because it's your team. It's because of who you are."

That was why McKeon didn't blink in putting on the green and yellow jersey of Leitrim. It was an honor.

Then you had McKiernan.

Let's face it—rush-hour traffic from Dublin was a bitch. Especially when the pouring rain only lengthened McKiernan's already annoying two-and-a-half-hour commute. When he finally arrived, over three hours after setting off, he rushed to get his tender hamstrings treated, which had definitely not been helped by sitting in a car for so long. He'd like to live in Leitrim, but his IT career took him elsewhere, specifically to the Bank of Ireland.

"In IT most of the work is in Dublin," McKiernan told me while lying on his stomach as Beirne applied some sort of electric treatment. "So there wouldn't be very many IT opportunities down here, you know."

Beirne heard this, and offered a one-liner. After all, this was his barbershop.

"That's where all the big cash is. Big bucks in Dublin."

That drew a laugh from McKiernan, who continued.

"The high skilled jobs will mostly be in Dublin. You have to get experience up there first anyway, you know. Bigger companies would be there and that's where you get your experience. And once you have good experiences, there would be opportunities down in the country, but it's all about getting the initial experience. I'd love to move down home again."

Instead, for now, he makes the long round trip on practice nights, figuring out how to function on way reduced sleep.

"Why do it?" said McKiernan, repeating my question. "I don't know, it's just...."

Beirne couldn't resist another quip.

"Money."

"Yeaaah," McKiernan said in a sarcastic tone, now laughing harder. "Noooo."

In the background, the TV could be heard with fans chanting. Now, that was money. Chelsea and Liverpool, both English teams, imported stars from around the world and paid them millions.

McKiernan got paid in other ways.

"Just you want to play for your county," he said of *his* compensation. "You dream about it. From when I was able to walk, I've been playing football. Kicking since I was about three or four. My father played for Leitrim. It's something you do and you want to be the best at what you do. Inter-county football is as high as it gets with GAA. And you know, if you can represent your family, your club—it means a lot to most people as well."

Beirne moved closer to the TV, while McKiernan answered my questions, occasionally grimacing as the treatment took effect. When the inter-county season was over, McKiernan also commuted for club practices. Again, switching squads was taboo.

"Oh never," he said with a nod. "I wouldn't transfer clubs, either. You don't do that. It's a no-go. You don't do it. I mean sometimes you change clubs, but it would have to be outside the county and it would only be out of total necessity, like you really have no other choice."

So McKiernan's fate was to play for Leitrim, which likely meant never winning an All-Ireland. This underdog thing was only sexy to an extent.

"I'd rather not be an underdog," a practical McKiernan said. "But everyone has goals and you measure success in different ways playing for a smaller county. You know, you just try and do your best, you win a couple games and people are satisfied. I think the gap is closing between a lot of teams now, anyway and will more so as time goes on."

McKiernan pointed to Fermanagh, another small county that recently stunned opponents by advancing to the All-Ireland semifinal.

If Fermanagh could win, why not Leitrim?

"They came from nowhere. We used to beat Fermanagh all the time. It's amazing what can happen. It only takes a few players."

So possibilities remain. Like in that magical summer, 1994, when Leitrim won the Connacht provincial championship for the second time, eventually losing to Dublin in the All-Ireland semifinal. Everything came together—a run of good players and first-rate coaching. Leitrim again reached the Connacht final in 2000, but the momentum couldn't be sustained. At least 1994 gave everyone hope.

"It was a brilliant year for Leitrim, the year that everyone looks back on and thinks about," Gerry McGovern reflected. "You'd certainly like to try to relive it again. You never know—we might just get the break."

And that was also why they play.

Chapter 4
Northern Ireland

Mid-May to late June: More Than a Game

How could a bed and breakfast go on vacation? Talk about a bizarro world. That was like cows milking humans, I thought, as I found myself in a mild panic. My stay in Leitrim had extended into early May, and I desperately needed to leave or my plan of a new place every month would be in jeopardy. My next destination: Northern Ireland, with the first stop at Crossmaglen, a small village near the border. I confidently—or more like in an absent-minded moment—waited to call Murtagh's B&B a few days before I was planning to arrive from Kinlough, Leitrim. The owner told me that his family was going away for a week—that's what happens when you leave things to the last minute. With no others in town, I quickly called teams in different areas and got in touch with the bar manager at the Sean Dolans GAA clubhouse in Derry. He said sure, come, and he'd introduce me to the right people. So Derry it was.

The city of just under 85,000 was the second biggest in the North, and County Derry extended toward the top of the Irish map on the Northwest Coast. A nonstop flight to Dublin took roughly the same time—just under an hour—as it did to Glasgow or Liverpool. Derry, it turned out, was a good starting point for a Northern Ireland journey, partly for bad reasons. The hilly, walled city sat on the banks of the River Foyle where unrest, then hope, flowed through the generations. Many of the flashpoints during the Troubles—the conflict from the late 1960s to the late 1990s that involved the police, the British Army and paramilitary groups as Catholics sought civil rights and political freedom from England—happened on this soil. People expressed themselves in different ways, but blood inevitably spilled from generations of hatred in a dispute dating back to the twelfth century. It was a history pockmarked by martyr-like hunger strikes and peaceful marches, bombings, arrests and chronic unrest.

Right in the middle was the Gaelic Athletic Association, a nice afternoon diversion, a way of expressing local pride, a means to let off a little stress. Sure, the games were fun. They were also intensely representative as a symbol for the oppressed, and as a jab at the mighty. Gaelic football and hurling were Irish games, and that identity meant everything to Catholics, most of whom considered themselves to be under British occupation. In essence, sport became another weapon in their arsenal.

The recent problems went back to the early 1920s. After Ireland's War of Independence against England, leaders of both countries partitioned Ireland to gain peace. Of the thirty-two counties, twenty-six became the Irish Free State—changed to the Republic of Ireland in 1948—and held a large majority of Catholics. Six counties in the Ulster province became part of the United Kingdom, which featured a 2-1 Protestant majority, and it was named Northern Ireland. Many of those Catholics, or nationalists as they were known, wanted to unite with Ireland in one country. (Republicans was the term often used for the more militant faction.) Many Protestants or unionists, as they were called, sought to remain a part of the UK. (Loyalists were known as the hard-liners.) Some saw the dispute as a religious conflict. Others viewed it as a quarrel over land. Either way, it was impossible to seal those bitter feelings off from the sports world. Sectarian attacks were carried out on athletes and officials, still to this day.

While not perfect, peace continued to move incrementally forward. Both sides realized that the other wasn't going to leave, and the violence led to talks and power-sharing agreements. Northern Ireland now owned one of the world's lowest crime rates and many bullet-ridden areas were prettied. I had decided to come to Derry—and later to Crossmaglen and two large cities, Belfast and Lisburn—to see for myself how sport was intersecting the problems of the past and the hope for the future.

Derry

Before I left, Leitrim folk sincerely told me to be careful of where I am in the North and to whom I mention the GAA, such as asking directions to clubs.

"People have been shot before for asking," one told me.

But the two-hour bus ride into Derry mirrored the rest of Ireland's countryside. Mountains, hills, green grass, sheep, cows, no 7-Elevens or gas stations and no check point at the border—just a straight shot into another part of the country. Then I noticed "Free Seamus Doherty" scribbled on a wall. I spotted the United Kingdom's red and blue Union Jack flag flying. The currency changed from euros to pounds—each Northern Ireland bank printed its own bills, but you were guaranteed to see Queen Elizabeth II on English coins.

Because I was rushing, I didn't book a place to stay. My only concern was that I'd get stuck in an expensive hotel. I asked a taxi driver near the bus station if he had any ideas, and he called a reasonably priced bed and breakfast, which had room for me.

"This is the Bogside," he said after we passed through downtown.

"What's the Bogside?"

"You don't know much about Derry's history."

I played it cool, "Oh the BOGside, yeah, yeah, yeah."

"Did you hear of Bloody Sunday?" he asked, stunned that someone wouldn't know such a poignant part of the city's history. "This is where it happened."

A large, five-pointed white block that read "You Are Now Entering Free Derry" greeted visitors. To its right, large murals telling the history of the Troubles covered whole sides of buildings with triangular roofs. Many were in black and gray, reflecting a somber tone, portraying murder victims, civil rights leaders and skirmishes with British authorities. One mural called the "Saturday Matinee" featured a man, back turned, glaring at a tank with smoke in the air and debris on the ground. Riots in the early 1970s were as common as going to the movies. Fed-up citizens on the edge threw stones, bottles, nail bombs and petrol bombs at the police, who shot back rubber bullets and CS tear gas.

Nearby sat the B&B, right in the heart of where historic and horrible violence had occurred. I quickly learned the Bogside was a Catholic ghetto where Protestant politicians gerrymandered residents to ensure an overwhelming Protestant majority in elections. A pro-Ireland and anti-British, anti-authority sentiment was still found from the graffiti decorating dozens of walls. If you made a right past Bull Park and walked a bit, you'd get to the Creggan Estates, another Catholic ghetto and the location of the Sean Dolans Gaelic Athletic Club.

The club's bar manager suggested that I stop by the next day to catch the team before it left for an away game. On my walk over, I thought how it was hard to imagine what the area was like thirty-five years ago when barricades and tanks were the norm. This was a no-go area, where the police didn't even dare enter.

Now, I was observing a sunny, T-shirt wearing type of day in mid-May. There were no bullets or bloodshed, just footballs and smiles as I entered the club's grounds. Kids were bouncing up and down on an inflatable playground. Parents relaxed in the sunshine when not scurrying after them. Others sipped pints on the patio while watching a youth Gaelic football game out on the field. Creggan Estates sat on a hill, offering a postcard view of Derry city to the left. I noticed horses in a fenced-in area past the right corner of the field. There were hills beyond and an open blue sky. It was tranquil. It was a picnic. It was somewhere in the middle of America in the fifth inning of a little league game.

As I took in the atmosphere, Sean Dolans coach Hugh Hegarty asked me if I was the Yank and directed me into a car with players leaving for their game out in the country. I barely had time to introduce myself as I squeezed into the middle back seat. The four players seemed unfazed they had a visitor and chatted away about the team and what they were doing that night. After we arrived an hour later, Hegarty gave me a hand motion to follow him into the locker room. There, he introduced me to the team as the Yank, grabbed my shoulders and playfully—somewhat—dragged me into the middle of the room. I didn't understand everything he said because of the thicker brogue found in the North, but I made out something about hanging me. I wasn't about to argue. Fortunately, everyone laughed. Upon release, I stood to the side but Hegarty swooped his right index finger up and commanded me to "blend in." Before I knew it, I was filling water bottles and chasing balls during the warm-up, muddying my shoes. I couldn't have asked for better access.

Dolans won an important county league game in an unexpected rout. If anything, I was seen as good luck. My co-passengers were more talkative to me on the ride back. Their facilities were top notch for a GAA club including locker rooms, an upstairs room, and a snooker room—a game that I had never heard of, but learned it was similar to pool and popular in Ireland. It was during our celebratory pint that Hegarty asked what exactly was I doing, and he introduced me to several people. That night, I stayed for a birthday party entertained by a rocking live band.

In the next few weeks, I found out just how much Sean Dolans meant to the people. The GAA selected it as the club of the year in 2000, an honor not based on wins or losses, but for a club's impact on the community and its promotion of Gaelic games. Even its name was unique to the city. Dolans formed in 1942 in the Waterside area across the river and honored an Irish republican/football player/GAA city board official. Sean Dolan was arrested in 1940 under the Special Powers Act, which allowed for arrest on suspicion of a crime and the act denied trial by jury and suspended other civil liberties (the law would affect the club in the 1970s). He spent time on a prison ship and in a jail, dying at twenty-eight in 1941.

Back then, the GAA with its seventeen clubs was a thriving force in the city. Eventually, all but Dolans folded, and they moved across the River Foyle to the Creggan Estates in 1972 to join the majority Catholic population. All they had there was a raggedy field that would fill with puddles, goalposts made from telephone poles and an Irish tricolor flag displaying orange, green and white. (A 1954 law essentially banned the tricolor because it allowed police to remove any flag that could cause "a breach of the peace" with the exemption of the Union Jack. The act was repealed in 1987.) So the flag flew as a powerful symbol between a British Army base and the Bogside. At the time, though, it wasn't exactly a field of dreams.

"There was a lot of gunfire between both," explained Danny Cassidy, a longtime club member. "So it was not a good place to be."

While imagining the past might have been difficult for me, the people here knew it all too well. History wasn't easily forgotten, especially with the annual summer marching season. Two Protestant organizations—the Orange Order and the Apprentice Boys of Derry—commemorated victories from the seventeenth century by strutting into Catholic neighborhoods. Bands wearing military-style uniforms banged large, double-sided Lambeg drums and caused fifes and flutes to play uplifting, rallying tunes. Men followed decked in dark suits, orange or crimson sashes, white gloves, black bowler hats and they carried closed umbrellas, flags and banners. The themes ranged from Biblical subjects to Royalty figures to war depictions.

In the hot spots, police lined the sidewalks in riot gear as nationalists jeered. The Parades Commission, an independent, quasi-judicial body set up in 1997 to rule on contentious parades, sometimes banned certain routes and restricted music, much to the dismay of the marchers. The violence some years—which also included the Protestant groups against police—was worse than others.

The Derry people were used to turbulence. The majority Catholic population rioted against loyalist groups and British authorities in 1868, 1869, 1870, 1874, 1877, 1883, 1886 and 1905. Things worsened in the twentieth century. Many Protestant-owned businesses wouldn't hire Catholics, and the government shut Catholics out of public housing. In the Bogside, as many as seven or eight families were forced to crowd into a home designed for one family. The Ulster Unionist party ran the show and a common phrase was "a Protestant Parliament for a Protestant people." The division extended to the people's pastimes and traditions. I found a quote by Terrence O'Neill, the country's prime minister from 1963-1969, which summed up that social divide:

> "Anyone who thinks the Protestant community in Northern Ireland is ever going to embrace the GAA, the Irish language, and the Fenian Brotherhood is being as realistic as someone who expects one day to see a banner of Queen Victoria carried in a Hiberiran parade."

The line was drawn, and the groups rarely intermingled socially. The GAA players, though, didn't see their games as a subversive or exclusionary act, rather playing Gaelic football and hurling were their *right*.

"There was basically a lid kept on our culture," Cassidy recalled. "And through the conflict you wanted to express your Irishness. You do that through violence—getting involved in the IRA—or you could do that through culture and the language. It's a resistance to people telling you you're British when we're Irish. So, it's an expression of who we are. Sport and your own culture is a great way of getting back at people. But it's the togetherness that creates a sense of identity."

I met Cassidy at the Irish language school in Creggan where he sometimes taught (he also worked for a language organization in the North). A plaque on the building's front honored Joe Walker, an eighteen-year-old IRA volunteer killed nearby in 1973. Violence wasn't the first choice of many people, who just wanted to live their lives undisturbed. In 1967, the Northern Ireland Civil Rights Association (NICRA) formed with members of both religions to campaign for an end to the discrimination of Catholics. They used the slogan "One man, one vote" and sung "We Shall Overcome" on marches. Unfortunately, words weren't enough. Two events in Derry jumpstarted the Troubles. On October 5, 1968, the Royal Ulster Constabulary (RUC), then Northern Ireland's police force, attacked the NICRA on a march banned by the government. The baton beatings were aired worldwide on TV and galvanized support for the movement, much like police using dogs and water cannons had done a decade earlier in Alabama.

In August 1969, the Battle of the Bogside changed things forever. Nationalists pelted the Apprentice Boys of Derry with stones and bottles during a march then retreated into the Bogisde. The police and loyalist mobs chased the nationalists, but couldn't enter the Estate. Residents had erected barricades from rubble, concrete, old cars—anything that could help—at the entrance of the Bogside.

The RUC unleashed tear gas that choked lungs and watered eyes. Residents fought back throwing petrol bombs from the roofs of high apartment buildings. Gravel turned into volcanoes as flames sprouted into the air. For two days, a steady scene of thick smoke, fires and pitter-patter of violence filled the area. Women and children were moved to safer parts of the city or outside areas (although many stayed). The Derry Citizen Defense Association had prepared for a confrontation in the weeks before the march. It setup three makeshift first aid stations. For communication, the leaders acquired walkie-talkie radios and installed transmitters for Radio Free Derry. People hoarded 43,000 milk bottles for bombs. They were ready.

On the third day of the clashes, the British government called in its soldiers to establish order, but they didn't try to enter the Bogside. Catholics welcomed the troops as saviors from the one-sided police. Claiming victory, nationalists laid out more barricades at the entrance of Creggan and other nearby districts making those areas no-go zones soon patrolled by the Irish Republican Army. (The IRA had been a dying military organization as the graffiti went I Ran Away. It split in December 1969 with the Official IRA and the Provisional IRA. The latter pledged to take up arms to defend Catholics and to unite with Ireland, and it quickly gained new recruits.) Masked men with rifles checked visitors seeking to enter. In essence, they succeeded from British rule. Witness, then, the gable that still stood from the side of a demolished building that I saw on my way into the Bogside with the striking declaration, "You Are Now Entering Free Derry."

British troops also arrived in Belfast to quell rioting there. Initially, the grateful Catholics offered tea, but soon saw the Army as an extension of the police. The troops fought with the IRA, searched citizens and more riots ensued. On August 9, 1971, the British started interning detainees without trial, an activation of the Special Powers Act—that had ensnared Sean Dolan a generation earlier—and swooped up suspected terrorists. The police, though, were using outdated intelligence and arrested innocent people while many IRA members fled. (Internment lasted until December 1975 with 1,874 Catholics detained and 107 Protestants held. In that span, detainees were sometimes beaten and treated poorly.)

Internment increased the alienation that everyday Catholics felt with the government. Many participated in rent and work strikes. It also upped the violence. Take the number of shooting incidents—1,756 in 1971 and 10,628 in 1972 (the deadliest time of the Troubles). And in those two years, Republican groups killed 365 people, Loyalist groups killed 133 and the British forces killed 131.

On July 31, 1972, the British responded to a mass IRA bombing in Belfast by ending Free Derry in Operation Motorman. Over 25,000 troops—including the Ulster Defence Regiment used exclusively in the North—aided by tanks and bulldozers infiltrated the no-go Catholic ghettos (including the handful in Belfast). The IRA couldn't offer resistance in the face of that firepower. The takeover allowed the security forces to monitor the people's lives more closely than ever. Team Sean Dolan could not help but be affected.

"Oh God, you'd get stopped when you were playing Gaelic football," remembered Cassidy. "You were put down as a republican sympathizer. That was part and parcel of the game. They saw you play Gaelic, they knew that you were somehow involved in Irish culture and they didn't like Irish culture."

Following Operation Motorman, the British Army built a base less than fifty yards away from Dolans' field with watchtowers looming in the background. Gaelic football became associated with the republican cause. Kicking the wrong shaped ball apparently meant a threat to the state. Players had their homes searched and several were interned. The club—more like a team because they only had about 15-20 players—operated in a dysfunctional way. Soldiers interrupted practices, forcing the fullbacks, midfielders and forwards to answer questions. As it was, training sessions often had meager numbers because players were in prison or on the run. For games, the desperate footballers recruited friends who never played before to patch holes in the lineup just so they wouldn't have to forfeit. Sean Dolans' record wasn't pretty, but winning wasn't the main goal.

"For us, success meant just staying alive and keeping our dream," said Hugh Brady, a former player and current board member who recalled that there was a quiet support in the community. "People were afraid that if they associated with our club they were immediately put down as a member of the IRA—which wasn't true—but that was the perception of the British forces.... You wonder how we managed."

On one hand, it seemed silly that sports would continue through all this violence and tension. If the players knew they were going to get harassed, I thought, why do it? A person could get interned just on suspicion. But to them, the Gaelic football had to go on. Consider it part stubbornness, part Irish way of never accepting being told what to do.

"We wouldn't let them put us off," said Noel McCrystal, the club's current commissioner and a player in the 1970s. "Unless they fired a lot of CS gas and we were smothered like, we would have to move. But when the gas cleared we were back again, playing, finishing the game."

McCrystal didn't exactly go out of his way to tell me about the past. He'd much rather talk about the youth team he's coaching. I tagged along with them later in the week to see the mayor honor the club's youngest players in a ceremony at the Guildhall, a stately, neo-gothic building with stained glass windows inside. (The interior was rebuilt after a 1972 IRA bombing.) True, things were different now, but how they got there was important. Since I asked, he answered. McCrystal told the facts with no trace of embellishment or bravado, as did everyone else I spoke with. They would have rather not lived it. Through their difficulties, though, a spirit emerged among the team.

"When they were trying to oppress Gaelic players and arrest them for one thing or another it made the people more together instead of dividing them," McCrystal continued. "Because if you were going to matches, they'd usually stop your minibus and keep you late for games and arrest people on the bus. So you were going to a match and maybe had enough to field a team and you might get two or three arrested. So the match had to be abandoned, and you had to play on another night. So that's the way we had to do things. That's just the way it was in them times. We had to accept it and go on."

Sean Dolans faced another problem not found in many rural Catholic areas—soccer. In Derry, it was always the sport of choice in the streets and followed by both religions. In a paradox, many Catholic residents opposed English rule, but who nonetheless were die-hard fans of English soccer. I saw their clubhouse packed for an important Manchester United/Arsenal game, with fans wearing the teams' jerseys and oohing and ahhing at all the right times.

I told that to a republican GAA man elsewhere in the North and he shook his head, saying: "That's backwards."

So Sean Dolans had to worry about player recruitment on two fronts. A few developments turned things around: Derry won the All-Ireland title in 1993 for the first time making Gaelic football sexy in the city. The peace process in the late 1990s eased the outside interference. Then, their clubhouse opened in 1998 after seven years of fundraising. The facility attracted non-players happy to support the local team.

One of them was Damien Donaghy, nicknamed Bubbles because he washed windows. The Manchester United fan didn't play GAA sports growing up, but joined Sean Dolans for its camaraderie. The clubhouse was a good place to watch games, drown a few pints with friends and unwind. In a country area, Bubbles might have picked up a hurling stick as a kid.

"I was always a fan of the GAA, but in this town it was more soccer than anything," he told me as we went into a coatroom off to the side, the only place that wasn't noisy after that English soccer game. "GAA would be, say a third sport than a first sport. Soccer would be first and second.... This club here kind of brought the GAA up. You like to see the Dolans doing well. You know everybody that's playing for them."

One reason that I wanted to talk with Bubbles was because he was tied to a defining event of the Troubles. On January 30, 1972, as a fifteen-year-old, he joined an estimated crowd of 10,000 in a peaceful civil rights march in the Bogside to protest internment. The IRA promised to stay away, and the marchers chanted and smiled as they proceeded from the Creggan to the Bogside. At one point, a section broke away to an Army barricade. A confrontation ensued as the Army lit CS gas canisters, and the crowd threw them back. Eventually British paratroopers fired five shots at protestors, fearing they had nail bombs. Bubbles milled in the crowd, throwing stones, but also looking for a way to make a few pounds—searching for rubber bullets to sell to tourists.

"I went to grab one and the next thing I was shot and I was lying on my back," he recalled.

A bullet pierced his right hip and fractured his femur. He needed to stay in the hospital for six months and in a plaster cast for eight months. It all but ended his serious soccer days, and arthritis had never left his leg.

"It still affects me," he lamented. "I have trouble bending it."

A lawyer for the soldiers later conceded that Donaghy did not have a nail bomb or another explosive.

"I threw stones," he said innocently. "You're young. You'd done what everybody else done. I threw stones. Nobody should be shot for throwing stones."

Donaghy was the first, but not the last person shot that day. About fifteen minutes after he went down, troops from the 1st Battalion Parachute Regiment started an arrest operation and fired 108 shots over a thirty-minute period. In all, twenty-seven unarmed marchers were shot—five in the back—and thirteen died. One man later died of his injuries. The troops said they were fired on. Eyewitnesses, backed by facts, contradicted their statements—no guns were discovered and no soldiers were wounded. The event, known as Bloody Sunday, couldn't be understated. It led to a swell in IRA membership, acts of terrorism on both sides and the suspension of the Northern Ireland Parliament in March 1972 as Britain introduced direct rule from London.

An official report released in April 1972 absolved the Army of all blame, but ignored key evidence and eyewitness interviews. Not surprisingly, Catholics dismissed the findings as propaganda. In 1998, British Prime Minister Tony Blair reopened the issue after new evidence and statements emerged. Lord Saville conducted the inquiry that ended in November 2004 at a cost of about £150 million. Now, the families of those involved were eagerly waiting the report, hoping their loved ones were vindicated.

"You cannot forget the people that died," said Bubbles, remembering his friends. "That's what it's all about. It's a reminder. It never lets you forget what people died for…. [The findings] will get their names cleared. It's not about money. I knew a lot of them. The [families] will be happy to get the results to clear the names and clear everybody. Clear the air. Closure—that's what everybody wants."

Bubbles offered to speak to me another time, but he was eager to get back to his friends. They soon engaged in a mock shouting confrontation over soccer teams. Later, he caused people to rush to the window—he was out on the field having a goal-scoring contest.

I marveled at the role of Sean Dolans in helping the community escape the poverty and sadness of the Troubles. The Bogside and Creggan were two of the most economically deprived areas in Northern Ireland. While I was there, newspapers carried stories of intimidation shootings through windows of homes and at a bar's ceiling, and vandals who broke into a school to thrash computers and ransack classrooms. It wasn't uncommon to see soda cans, newspapers and wrappers strewn over the ground, leaving a trail from the Bogside to the Creggan. Houses were small and packed together. Still, this was home for many.

"I personally feel the pride," Cassidy responded, a little offended that someone would suggest this wasn't prime real estate. "I live in Creggan and I wouldn't leave Creggan. So I don't feel deprived. There is depravation. There is poverty, but there is also a sense of community."

For Cassidy, this is the perfect time to raise children and to be part of a GAA club in Derry. Sean Dolans now had 700 members including a women's team that started in 2006 and youth teams from under-6 on up. When I was there, a vacant, overgrown lot stood next to the locker room. A year later, the club built an all-weather, gravel-based field and floodlights after fundraising. Noel McCrystal continually stressed his club's role in helping kids, while not advocating for sectarianism or politics, just for discipline and respect. Other rainbows included Creggan Enterprises, which formed in 1991 to attract investment. The Ráth Mór business park, for example, had created 165 jobs through twenty-eight businesses.

"We have to look forward," Cassidy continued, refusing to gripe about all the things stolen from his generation. "What happened in the past, happened and we have to look forward as a confident people. The man says that was the bad old days. We look to the future. We're confident as a community now. They can't suppress us. They can't tell us what to play and what not to play."

While the harassment by the authorities had stopped, tensions continued. That "Free Seamus Doherty" I saw on my way to the city was for a Derry man arrested in June 2003 for possessing a car bomb. Doherty and republican groups claimed that he was framed, and Doherty was acquitted in November 2004. On the other side, the last remaining Protestant area downtown was the small Fountain Estates on the Foyle's west bank. In the little enclave holding less than 1,000 people you had the Union Jack flying and six rows of defiant white words glowing off a black wall: "Londonderry/West Bank/Loyalists/Still/Under Siege/No Surrender." The area was subjected to sectarian attacks.

Even the name of the city was touchy, which I found out. I got lost after taking a long walk over the Folye and into a unionist neighborhood with the British colors of red, white and blue painted on curbs. A few high school girls asked if I needed help. I said I was staying in Derry.

"You mean Londonderry?"

"Yes, LONDONderry."

They didn't give me a hard time, just the directions I needed and I was on my way. Officially, nationalist politicians changed the name of the political district from Londonderry City Council to Derry City Council in 1984. It wasn't clear, however, if the city's name also automatically changed. The dispute continued for years and eventually went to the High Court in Belfast. In January 2007, a judge ruled that Londonderry would remain as the official name, and additional legislation was needed for a change. Nonetheless, road signs in the Republic referred to it as Derry, while throughout the North it was Londonderry. English newspapers called it Londonderry, Irish papers Derry. Other organizations went with the neutral Foyle such as BBC Radio Foyle, the Foyle Film Festival and the Foyle & District Road Safety Committee.

So the city hadn't quite reached utopia yet, but I sensed a fresh spirit after the dark years. It was common to have a Catholic mayor and the gerrymandering had ended. So had discrimination in housing and employment. Sean Dolans even faced competition, with five other city GAA clubs popping up. I saw hope in the club members' forwardly thinking and in people's dreams for the city's youth.

"All I saw was the conflict," said Cassidy, his words laced with more optimism than regret. "You lost a lot of people. My wife's sister was blown up. My best friend was shot dead. But I want my children to only think about enjoying themselves. Go on holidays, how to better themselves through education.... Not to think of the conflict. Because the conflict is done and dusted. We want the young people now to be more alive, more open thinking, enjoying life. Life's too short."

Crossmaglen

Take away the British Army base's hovering presence, the helicopter landings and beatings of players during games, the battle for field ownership, the destruction of property and the Crossmaglen Rangers Gaelic football team was still a heck of a story.

I left Derry for this small Catholic village—and by then the B&B family had returned—to learn about this football legend for myself. The country club's four

All-Ireland titles and nearly forty County Armagh championships made it one of Ireland's most successful teams. Football here was an addiction.

"At senior level it's a wee bit more than a hobby," Crossmaglen player Michael McNamee told me. "It's sort of like an obsession. You have to really devote much of your time to it, like regards to social life. Girlfriends don't get too happy with the amount of time you have to spend on the field and the amount of time you're around. It's worth it in the end. It's the best years of your life."

Those golden years took place in a peculiar setting, where unwavering Irish patriotism met the British Army. Crossmaglen was located in south Armagh, a 190-mile stretch of farmland famously called "bandit country" in 1975 by Merlyn Rees, then the Northern Ireland Secretary of State. The IRA thrived with its proximity to the Irish border and general remoteness. People could get lost quickly. The back areas doubled as explosive factories for major terrorist operations. Sniper firings at soldiers occurred daily. Eventually, the Army refused to travel on foot and did everything—including taking out the gabarge—by helicopter. During the Troubles, at least 120 British soldiers died here; there were 1,255 bomb attacks and 1,158 shootings.

On the way to Crossmaglen I saw big, block letters—IRA—stapled to telephone poles blending in with the idyllic scenery of rolling land and hills under great big white clouds. The village center was a nifty square named for area native and club member Cardinal Tomás Ó Fiaich, who headed the Roman Catholic Church in Ireland until his death in 1990. Shops ranging from a Chinese takeout to a bakery, a video rental store to a travel agency bordered the square—which once had a British watchtower—and people smiled and went out of their way to answer questions. Offices for nationalist political parties and additional IRA signs abounded. Make no mistake, Irish culture and identity flourished here. Catholics comprised 98.97 percent of the 1,459 residents. The Rangers' social hall was the center of fun in the village. On bingo nights, for example, the large floor overflowed and chairs needed to be set up in the lobby. Mass was even held there when the church closed for repairs in 1966.

So why would a GAA club have any problems in such a patriotic area? A fortified British Army base and police headquarters with high barracks sat past the square, right before the Rangers field. Through the years, Crossmaglen didn't exactly share sugar and throw block parties for their uninvited guests. They staged a bitter, twenty-eight-year struggle for land ownership that involved both the Irish and British governments.

"A lot of people felt the club might have gone out of existence only for the determination of the people within the town to keep it going," reminisced Gene

Duffy, a club official in the 1980s. "And we're convinced the British Army policy was to get us out of existence because they were getting attacked. They were getting hurt. In south Armagh they couldn't travel the roads—so they were going to take it out on somebody. The only people they could take it out on, they felt, was the GAA club because it was sitting at the center of that community.

"… One thing you have to remember is the GAA club at Crossmaglen was the only—and I mean the only—sport and recreation in that entire area. So during the Troubles it was a policy of the British to see how they would hurt the communities. If you were attacking the GAA club, what you were doing then, was you were hurting the community."

The club had owned the field, St. Oliver Plunkett Park, since 1949; the park itself was named after a seventeenth century Catholic archbishop who had been sentenced to death for treason. He was, in fact, canonized in 1975. So the locals already had a rather special attachment to their field. In 1971, a nearby police station expanded to create a landing pad for the British Army. The problems soon started.

At first, the transgressions didn't seem too harmful such as off-duty soldiers playing soccer on the field and refusing to leave when asked. In November 1971, soldiers destroyed a perimeter wall near the entrance and the parking lot to allow easier access to the barracks. After the club repaired the wall, it was destroyed again, then again, despite protests. On May 17, 1972, an Army helicopter landed on the field during a game. A loaded rifle slammed into an opposing player, knocking him unconscious. Several fans were also hit with rifle butts.

Crossmaglen complained to the GAA president, who contacted Ireland's prime minister. The Northern Ireland government, in turn, responded that hooligans attacked the soldiers and the players got in the way of stones. Witnesses, naturally, contradicted that information. Helicopters, their three propellers buzzing, landed on the field during five games in 1972 causing players and spectators to scramble. Nearby residents had their gardens destroyed. A book published by the Rangers in 1987 detailing their history summed the era up:

> "An incident occurs. Club officials make a protest. The army authorities query, sometimes deny and then almost invariably admit the actual occurrence of the incident. Expressions of regret coupled with facile assurance about non-recurrence are issued. An incident free interval follows, a further encroachment takes place and the cycle begins again."

Duffy was able to chuckle when he recalled how Crossmaglen held an advantage over some of their freaked-out opponents.

"When the helicopters would be coming in over the pitch the visiting teams would be looking, but we kept playing on," he said with pride. "It was a policy we had. You never stopped the game.... We were unbeaten at home for two years in the league. We hadn't a good team but people would just say, 'Jesus, this is unreal.'"

If it was hard to imagine Sean Dolans during the Troubles, it was a little less difficult to picture Crossmaglen's situation. Helicopters still flew into the base. During games, the deafening noise momentarily drowned everything out. Troops and police walked through town, holding guns, although not bothering anyone. But it wasn't hard to let your mind slip back thirty or so years and picture much of the day-to-day life coming to a standstill.

"Way back in the '70s, '80s it used to be checkpoint, checkpoint, checkpoint," Rangers chairman Tommie Coleman told me when we spoke in the clubhouse. "The town was actually sealed off at one stage. All the roads were closed. They had a bunker. Your car was searched going in and out every time you left the town."

Additionally, soldiers entered the social hall in the middle of events on the pretext of clearing the building for bomb scares, suspected by the club to be a false excuse. Older people in wheel chairs, though, felt a real panic. Dances, concerts, plays, bingo nights—they all ended. On the sporting side, committee meetings were routinely disrupted, while players were searched and spectators harassed. Wives of club officials were questioned while bringing their children to school. The intimidation continued with a fence being cut. A suspicious fire burned part of the clubhouse the night before a press conference about the field. Soldiers stopped and queried players going to away games. Visiting teams gave Crossmaglen at least an hour grace period from the starting time, and play sometimes began hours later.

In 1974, the British Army seized part of the Rangers' property using the authority of the Northern Ireland Emergency Provisions Act. They requisitioned more land in 1976 and 1980 including sections of the parking lot and social hall. The base eventually expanded to within ten feet from the field, and the Army posted a lookout tower decorating space behind the goal. More than one wayward kick actually hit the wall or flew into the base never to be seen again. The troops entered their headquarters by unnecessarily driving heavy machinery through the field. They bulldozed rubble and mud over the parking lot and entrance, which cost Crossmaglen £15,000 to clear. The club kept competing to maintain a presence, but the truth was, the field was unplayable at times. The muck made it hard to walk across, let alone run.

Con Murphy, then the GAA president, visited Crossmaglen in 1976 and issued a statement:

> "I must truthfully say that I am appalled at what I saw and learned. The complete entrance to the grounds is taken over; entrance gates and fences are damaged; the GAA social centre is damaged and cut off, therefore unusable in the circumstances; and most important of all, about 30 yards of the playing pitch has been destroyed by heavy vehicles, thus rendering the playing field useless. Players and officials are being constantly harassed by the soldiers. In other words, the people of the area are absolutely deprived of their rights."

Crossmaglen had a strict policy: do not respond directly. Unlike other hot spots, there was no stone throwing, no rioting. No matter what the Army did, the players and coaches ignored them and went about their playing. Protests—such as marches—stayed nonviolent. That discipline, in turn, earned Crossmaglen the respect of the Irish government and the GAA. Murphy, the Association's president, set up a lobbying group to aid the Rangers, which lodged all of their complaints to the GAA central office.

The situation became emblematic of what was happening all across Northern Ireland. As a *Time* magazine article observed in January 1976, "Just as the U.S. army learned in Viet Nam, the military's very presence in the area has helped to alienate local residents."

Or as a Crossmaglen bartender said at the time, "They're an army of occupation and we're an occupied country. We're not pro IRA, we're just anti-British. We hate them, and nothing is going to change until they leave."

Duffy recalled when he once walked past a solider near the club.

"Good evening sir," the solider said.

Duffy kept walking.

"Stop there. I said good evening sir, why wouldn't you talk to me?"

"We were always brought up by our parents to never to speak to strangers. That's why I didn't talk to you."

The Crossmaglen Rangers GAA club wasn't going to concede anything to the British Army. The club had put in compensation claims since 1974, but discussions always stalled. Finally in February 1985, after a long day in court, the Rangers received £150,000 from the government as part of a global settlement covering several wrongs such as physical damage and the actual taking of the land. The ruling also contradicted the Army's claim that it never purposely damaged the grounds.

The quality of Crossmaglen's teams, though, had suffered in the interim. Parents were afraid to let their children practice because of the helicopter landings. So the club recruited people to coach the kids, while doubling as their bodyguards, trying to increase the community's involvement. Eventually, their frustrations were transferred into building up the club to become a power once again.

"The start of the great teams that we've had over the last fifteen years in Crossmaglen was a result of the determination by the people in the town not to let the Army win the battle of the minds," Duffy told me.

The club continued to push for its land, aided by a changing political climate. In August 1994, the IRA announced a ceasefire of military operations (that lasted until February 1996). Violence resumed on both sides, but so did negotiations. Former U.S. senator George Mitchell helped broker the Good Friday Agreement on April 11, 1998. The plan created a Northern Ireland assembly at Stormont Castle based on power-sharing between nationalist and unionist groups, and included peace initiatives such as cross-border organizations. Crossmaglen kept the pressure on—all the way to the top. Irish Prime Minister Bertie Ahern said on April 28, 1998, in Parliament that he had raised the Crossmaglen land issue "with everybody in authority, including the British Prime Minister" and hoped that progress could be made. Nothing dramatic happened, but the chipping away paid off. On April 3, 1999, the British finally said it would return the land, and on July 9 the property was derequisitioned. The Army pushed the base back about fifty yards.

The Irish and British governments released a joint report on July 14, 2001, titled "Achievements In Implementation Of The Good Friday Agreement." It listed the returning of the Crossmaglen Rangers land as one of several "security normalisation steps" taken since the Agreement. Also noted was that the British had closed 35 military installations in Northern Ireland since the pact and reopened 102 cross-border roads.

"It was all part of the bigger picture," Gerard Rushe, a Crossmaglen officer and a former player, told me. "The pressure finally paid off.... Our opinion was they shouldn't have had it in the first place."

For the past few years, relations have been warily better.

"We have very little problems with them now, this last while," said Coleman, who played in the bad times. "They don't bother us at all. We don't bother them. [When] a ball goes into the barracks they usually kick it back out again. Sometimes you have to go around and ring the bell and they give it to you that way, but most of the times they kick it back out again. It's not as bad now.... We didn't used to get the ball back."

The club received £450,000 in compensation from the Northern Ireland government for the occupation. The money went back into Crossmaglen's development. Witness two additional practice fields, a new social hall and a spectator area that holds 1,200 fans. (After I left, a lot changed in a year. In fall 2006, the demolishing of the helicopter landing area started. Then a day before Valentine's Day 2007, the dismantling of the army sangar, the temporary fortification base, began.)

"It was a long battle but I think we fought it with dignity and we were proven right in the end because they're gone and we're still here," Duffy declared when I spoke to him in July 2006. "The British Army and authorities underestimated the will of the people in our area to keep our games going."

And the games do go on. I wondered, though, about the separation of sport and politics. I never heard any "United Ireland" chants in the team huddle or coaches giving anti-British sermons before breaking down the opponent's defensive weaknesses. The players spoke about girls and what they were doing on the weekend. The only time politics or nationalism came up was when I asked about it.

"It never seems to arise in football," Coleman said with a shrug. "We probably have thirty on a committee and there could be maybe ten Sinn Féin [the political party associated with the IRA] and twenty SDLP [a moderate nationalist political party] or the other way around, and we have our meetings. It's football. We're here as a football club. Politics doesn't enter the equation here. You just play away and whatever your political belief is you keep that away from the club.... It's just the unionist people would say that because we play Gaelic football we're republicans or we're enemy of the state or something like that, but it's not true. It's our game. It's tradition for over 100 years now."

One summer evening after practice, two young players remained to work on their kicking while two little kids ran along the side. The Army base loomed in the background. These players were the first generation removed from the field battle.

"I wouldn't remember any of that," nineteen-year-old Tony Kernan told me. "When I was eight, for Christmas, I got a Crossmaglen Rangers kit and I was pulled out to a football field on a Sunday morning. I was told this is what you do on a Sunday morning. And ever since that I loved it. I wasn't told that you're doing this for ..."

Kernan paused, stopping short of saying Irish nationalism or putting it to the Brits or something along those lines.

"It's only now you learn that stuff as you get older."

Michael McNamee chimed in.

"The older generation," he said with a nod. "Where as we didn't really grow up with [it]. We grew up near the end of the Troubles. We're only nineteen and twenty. So it hasn't really affected us. Maybe when we were younger, but we've never been stopped from coming onto the field or playing. You get a helicopter flying over there but it doesn't affect us."

Kernan picked up on cue.

"Where as our fathers would have been stopped and searched and really had to struggle for their right to play the national game. Where when we were ten we could have walked up and jumped that wire and played away."

Kernan pointed to the team's fence on the field, then to the older coaches in the locker room.

"Where they would have struggled to play their game," he said with admiration. "It's probably just a testament to the club, and a lot of people in the club that despite having this they just kept going. I suppose looking back you have a lot of respect for them. We probably take our right to play Gaelic football for granted."

Lisburn

Lisburn wasn't on my radar until I saw a TV report in Crossmaglen about a flag controversy. The city council voted to permanently fly the Union Jack flag on its flagpoles. The country's laws, though, say the flag should only be flown on government buildings during seventeen designated days a year that celebrate various Royal birthdays, anniversaries and holidays. While the Union Jack *was* Northern Ireland's official flag, almost half of the country preferred the Irish tricolor flag. Clearly, it was a sensitive issue. I checked the Web site of the local GAA team, St. Patrick's, and learned their field suffered vandalism in the early 1990s and members had to sell the land in fear.

So I went to the city of 71,000 outside Belfast. I wanted to see how a GAA team operated in an area where Catholics were a large minority. The situation differed from the one I encountered in Derry and Crossmaglen, where the GAA players had problems with the authorities, but not their neighbors.

Here, Catholics accounted for 33 percent of the population, but you wouldn't know any existed with the outpouring of affection for Great Britain. Northern Ireland was a country where flags and colors went beyond patriotism—they were important symbols that marked a territory. If you saw green, orange and white, it was a Catholic area. If you saw the Union Jack and red, white and blue painted on curbs and on the bottom of telephone poles, then it was a Protestant area. Lisburn's city center looked neutral with no outward display of colors, but the surrounding streets exploded like a Fourth of July celebration. Instead, the city was expressing alliance to the Queen. A park was named the Diana Princess of Wales Garden, for example, something that wouldn't be found in a Catholic area.

"We are still engulfed by the unionist people," said Peter Mulholland, a long-time member of St. Patrick's. "And we still have to sort of be—not afraid of them—but we're mindful of them. And we don't do anything silly. We don't make silly, stupid public statements that would bring trouble upon ourselves, you know what I mean? We just keep doing our own thing and keep our heads down. As we say, just get on with it. And to be fair, nobody's really bothering us. But nobody is helping us either. They're not supporting us. They're just ignoring us and we're ignoring them."

We were talking in Mulholland's car after a St. Patrick's football game at a nearby parish. The team played in the lowest division and was struggling. Tonight they suffered another blowout loss. But members hoped that a thriving underage program would in time turn things around. Mulholland clung to that hope. His pride in the club was palpable. As soon as I sat down, he showed me a black and white photo of the fourteen-member management committee taken at the St. Patrick's dinner dance twenty-nine years earlier. The fashion time capsule featured long wavy hair and ties filled with broad vertical stripes. Mulholland clutched the photo with just a little less feeling than he would if cradling an infant. His eyes went down memory lane as he nodded to each person noting who was deceased, who was still involved and who had moved where. First, a chuckle. Then a bite of the lower lip and a head shake. Then a hearty laugh.

There was short Gerry McAreavey, standing first on the back row sporting thick mutton chops and a high forehead. In front of him, seated, was Father Emmet Deegans displaying the thick black glasses of the day, and then young Michael Lynch with a pinstriped suit kneeling last on the front row. These were his people. This was his club. St. Patrick's didn't form in 18-something but in the mid-1960s after previous attempts to sustain a club failed. Mulholland first played as a fifteen-year-old in 1973. Six years later, he added board member duties. His crush on the club, and Gaelic football, had never ended.

"I love Ireland," he declared. "I love my country and I wish to see my country united. But I don't want to see it reunited over the graves of thousands of Protestant people. I don't believe in that, you know what I mean? I want to see it united as all people of all culture and creeds in Ireland being united. And there is a difference. There is a difference. But I'm not in the GAA to enhance or to bring about the unification of Ireland. I'm in the GAA, and I take part in doing what I do, because I love the game as you may love American football or baseball. I love Gaelic football and Gaelic games, the way an Englishman loves soccer or loves cricket."

His heart was nearly broken in the early 1990s, a few years after the club bought land outside of the city. Extremists lugging bats attacked club members—who barely escaped—damaged goalposts and put glass on the grass.

"The police came and told us, 'Look these people won't stop until they kill somebody and we can't give you round the clock protection out there to play your games,'" Mulholland said with regret. "Ah, they can't. And we can't expect them to. Nor should they have to. But such is life in the North of Ireland and the politics…. We were forced to sell the land. People's lives were at risk and we just couldn't stand over the possibility of something terrible happening to somebody."

St. Patrick's found itself at a crossroad and in danger of folding. They were having trouble fielding an adult team, let alone children's teams. And the club wasn't growing without a home base. The members decided to invest in the future. In 1998, with the bank interest from the sale, they paid Kevin Madden to become the club's Gaelic games development officer. Madden, a County Antrim football star, brought energy in teaching the sport to gym classes in the city's Catholic schools. The club now fielded teams in under-8, under-10, under-12, under-14, under-16 and under-18. Two years ago, they won the county under-12 title.

I met Madden for lunch a few days before Antrim played an elimination game in the All-Ireland tournament. I knew he had buzzed hair and a typical lean football body from his picture in the *Irish News* that week. Despite the pressure of the game, Madden went out of his way to meet me on his break at a downtown restaurant.

"I found that once I started going in at the very youngest level, started coaching say the six-and seven year-olds and giving them a taste for it," Madden explained, "it was easy enough to get them to come to the club then. But it didn't happen overnight. It took maybe two or three years to get that Gaelic culture into the schools. And it took support from the principals and the teachers as well. It really took them to buy into the idea before the kids would buy into it."

When our talk turned to religion and politics, Madden looked around and lowered his voice, just in case. He never had any problems, but the atmosphere was certainly different here than in his home parish in the country. (Despite good community relations in a town split 50-50, Madden said his club's locker room was burned down by loyalists about five years ago.)

"Since I've been in Lisburn I haven't had a word spoken to me," said Madden, who occasionally wore his yellow Antrim GAA pullover jacket. "Sometimes you get someone maybe looking at you strange. But I never, ever got any verbal or physical attack."

And did the kids have problems?

"No, very rarely. But in saying that, people in Lisburn are very discreet. They're not going to send their kids down the street in Gaelic tops. They're very discreet about where they go with their Gaelic regalia."

Wearing jerseys downtown were a no-no, as was flying Irish or GAA flags or bunting.

"You couldn't do that," Éamonn Ó Faogáin, a teacher in Lisburn, told me. "You could not do that. You just couldn't. Not in Lisburn."

After lunch, I went back with Madden to the elementary school. A bulletin board near the front door displayed pictures of teachers who passed a GAA coaching certification course and snapshots from a fieldtrip to Cork, where the kids met hurling hero Seán Óg Ó hAilpín.

Madden introduced me to Ó Faogáin, as his students downloaded pictures of hurling stars on the Internet during a break. The class favorite was Kilkenny's Henry Shefflin. We conducted an experiment by asking a handful of the kids would they rather be a professional soccer player for Manchester United and make millions, or play hurling for powerhouse Kilkenny but be an amateur. Every one of them answered Kilkenny. To kids, the concepts of money or the sad drama of Irish history weren't factors. They just know what they love doing.

So does Ó Faogáin. He arrived at the school in 1989 and promptly introduced hurling. Some in the community—and this was during the Troubles' dark days—didn't approve. Ó Faogáin recalled the school's goalposts were cut down on three occasions, shaved glass was placed on the field and mobile classrooms were burned.

"When you're thinking back at it, it sounds mad. It's like almost unbelievable people would do that," he told me, still amazed after all these years. "My biggest fear was that they would do something to the children. That if they ever shot over the fence then it wouldn't be me they would hit. They would hit a child. And I don't say that with any sense of sort of bravado or heroism, that was my real fear."

And he had reason to worry. Ó Faogáin received bullets in the mail along with a note warning that they would be used on him if the promotion of the GAA continued. Then, a red taxi drove up to the school and four men tried to take hurling sticks from the children. The staff heard the commotion and dashed out, forcing the cab to pull away. The school didn't make a big deal of the disturbances and continued quietly. Ó Faogáin didn't even consider hanging up the hurley.

"There comes a time when you either lie down and you become a nothing and just sort have people continually abuse you," he said calmly. "Or you stand up for what you believe and say, 'Here I am, this is what I want to do.' I try to do it in a non-offensive way. I don't want to offend anybody. I don't want to hurt anybody, but I'm not going to apologize for breaking the scene we are living in. This is my country and I am prepared to share it. But that means that it's on an equal basis. I respect their culture—I don't care what they do as long as it doesn't affect me or my family."

Eventually, the incidents stopped and the games grew. At another school downtown, a new principal promoted the sports, and the GAA found a steady home.

Nonetheless, a suspicion remained among hardcore loyalists concerning GAA members. It was also, to a softer extent, more in the mainstream. For example, in August 2003, the PSNI (Police Service of Northern Ireland) announced that officers would have to declare if they were members of certain Irish, British, Catholic and Protestant organizations. An official from the Ulster Unionist political party urged that GAA members should be added to that list, noting the GAA was "a quasi-political organization." The statement drew criticisms from nationalist political parties and it was not included. (After threatened court action by two police officers, the PSNI backed off the requirement.)

"Some would say the GAA is the sporting organization of the IRA," said Mulholland of St. Patrick's in an *are they crazy* tone. "And they believe that. They're brainwashed."

That perception existed partly because of a GAA rule that banned British security and police forces personnel from becoming members. After much debate, the law known as Rule 21 was abolished in 2001. The police service, in fact, now fielded GAA teams. Also, it was obvious that mostly Catholics played the sports—including the occasional paramilitary member—giving the appearance of an exclusive fraternity that pushed Irish nationalism. And the reality was few Protestants would consider playing in Northern GAA clubs. But the Association was nonsectarian and open to all religions. A Protestant even graced the name of the All-Ireland football trophy. Granted, Sam Maguire was a member of the Irish Republican Brotherhood and gathered intelligence in London as Ireland fought for its independence in the early 1900s, but he was a Protestant nonetheless. More recently, Jack Boothman, a Protestant from County Wicklow in the Republic, was the GAA president from 1994-1997. (I heard a rumor that the Kilkenny hurling star Henry Shefflin was Protestant too, although he chuckled when I asked him later in the year—hey, sometimes not every tip materializes.)

St. Patrick's members couldn't help but come into contact with unionists. The club rented playing time on a field owned, ironically, by the Ministry of Defense. It sat across the street from the Thiepval Barracks, the headquarters of the British Army in Northern Ireland. Several disparate teams shared the field in harmony. Before a recent St. Patrick's youth game, for instance, a teenage soccer team was practicing during the GAA club's allotted time. The soccer coach approached the St. Patrick's coaches, offering to leave—no problem. Since St. Patrick's was only using three-quarters of the field, they allowed the soccer team to stay. If either team's ball were accidentally kicked over to the other side, it promptly got booted back.

St. Patrick's profile had been on the rise. When Mickey Mac Cú Uladh took over as the club's public relations officer two years ago, he started sending pictures, write-up of games and practice times to the local paper, the *Ulster Star*. Some club members thought that would be an invitation for mischief-makers. But nothing happened, and in ten years St. Patrick's went from losing a field to having hundreds of kids playing on the weekends.

"I believe that people recognize that we're there to stay," Mickey told me.

St. Patrick's still faced a major problem—no land. Fifteen years ago, extremists forced the club to sell in fear. Now, they couldn't afford a home with real estate so expensive. Members would love a clubhouse with a social hall and fields similar to Crossmaglen or Sean Dolans. Then maybe after a tough loss like the one Mulholland just watched, everyone could go back to gripe and gossip before going home. So Mulholland had a message to other GAA clubs who took things for granted.

"Look at what you have," he said, half annoyed and half jealous. "We don't even have a field that we can kick a football on—so stop complaining, you know. It does wear you down when you listen to other members of the Association in other areas that are totally supported moaning about things.... That does wear you down sometimes. But I'm hardened to it. I'm hardened to it so it doesn't really have that much of an effect on me. What gets me down is watching the lads play the way they did tonight, playing so badly. That's what really gets me down now. I'm more worried about that than I am about the other things."

Belfast

As soon as I stepped foot in Belfast, I was introduced to the city's sectarian divide. A mural across from the main bus station's parking lot featured a masked man clutching a rifle with the warning "You are now entering Loyalist Sandy Row" on a light blue background. High and low, the section had flags and murals celebrating paramilitary groups and important victories. A ten-minute walk on Great Victoria Street past the Europa, the most bombed hotel in Europe, and an opera house, took you into downtown Belfast. Here, the city sparkled with restaurants, a large mall and nightclubs. Keep walking, you'd hit Divis Street, which turned into Falls Road. Parallel to that was Shankill Road. A few random turns took you toward Belfast Castle and North Belfast.

Immediately, you knew what neighborhood you were in. The sidewalks shimmered a little less. Falls Road was the Catholic section with murals featuring the 1981 hunger strikers and the IRA. While Shankill Road was the Protestant section awash with murals of the Queen, the Orange Order and loyalist paramilitary groups. North Belfast was mixed, with different streets displaying whatever was the appropriate color.

The 277,391 people of Belfast were evenly split among 48.58 percent Protestant and 47.20 percent Catholic. The city's downtown was neutral—stores sometimes banned the wearing of inflammatory soccer jerseys—and so was Queen's University past Sandy Row. I visited Belfast twice—in June and October—and stayed at a bed and breakfast near the university managed by a man from India, who never heard of Gaelic football or hurling. Instead, old cricket posters adorned the walls. So much for getting an inside feel from a local. He did warn me not to go past the city center at night.

But it wasn't hard to find GAA contacts in Belfast. Somehow, everything in the Gaelic scene was connected. When I visited Cork in late June, I met members of the St. John's club of Belfast in town for a youth hurling tournament. I got phone numbers, and later arranged to meet them at an under-12 game on a breezy autumn afternoon off Falls Road. While this was considered an inner city area, the wrongly named Black Mountain towered in the background adding a homey feel with green scenery. Hurling, unlike figure skating or gymnastics, was a sport where people improved with age because it was so skillful. But I observed some nifty stick work and quick goalie instincts. In general, everyone was having fun as St. John's cruised to a win.

After the game, the two coaches brought me to their clubhouse to talk about the city's history and sport. Located off Falls on Whiterock Road, this was the right place. West Belfast stood at the heart of the Irish republican movement, a place that still had riots, sectarian attacks, doubts about police neutrality and voluntary housing, social and school segregation by religion.

"We're not living in a postmodern Ireland," coach Michael Johnston told me as people poured in to watch games, shoot snooker and have pints. "We're not living in an Ireland that is multicultural. We're not living in an Ireland that is multinational. We're certainly not living in an Ireland that has forgot its Gaelic roots."

Just in case one did, reminders were everywhere. Falls Road, its splinter streets and nearby nationalist areas like Ardoyne in north Belfast were a shrine/national park to the people's leaders, hopes and struggles. Plaques on buildings noted where residents were killed. Large murals provided memorials to murdered taxi drivers and paramilitary heroes, offered claims of collusion against the British and gave nonpolitical messages such as anti-suicide urgings. One large wall of artwork celebrated Gaelic games. Also honored were those whom the locals feel a connection with including Frederick Douglas, Malcolm X and hunger strikers in Turkey. "Boycott Israeli Goods. Free Palestine" was a staple on walls. (The Star of David was found on loyalist symbols, such as the former official flag of Northern Ireland along with a red Saint George's cross—the patron saint of England. Some said that loyalists felt the Ulster province was their promised land, or they'd been persecuted like the Israelis. Or simply, the six points represented the six counties of Northern Ireland. To me, it was just another example of one side saying black, the other white.)

I learned the murals started in 1981 as a show of support for the ongoing hunger strikers. Ten imprisoned men from paramilitary groups starved themselves at different intervals to protest their not receiving political status while in jail. They demanded the right to wear their own clothes, abstention from forced labor, free association with other prisoners, time off for good behavior and the rights to more visits, mail, educational and recreational facilities. The cellblocks of the Maze prison outside Belfast—also known by its previous name of Long Kesh—looked like H's from the air, and the letter became a symbol of support.

The face of the hunger strikers was Bobby Sands, the prison's IRA commander who had served five years of a fourteen-year sentence for possessing a gun. On March 1, he started the campaign after eating an orange. While he was on strike, Sinn Féin, traditionally the political wing of the IRA, nominated Sands for the UK Parliament in a by-election after the incumbent died of a heart attack. Other nationalist political parties withdrew so the Catholic vote wouldn't be split. Sands, under the Anti-H-Block/Armagh Political Prisoner party, won in the

Fermanagh-South Tyrone district by 1,446 votes. Two other prisoners—one a hunger striker—were later elected to Ireland's parliament. But the British government, led by Margaret Thatcher, refused to give in to the prisoners' demands calling the men terrorists.

The twenty-seven-year-old Sands died on May 5 after fasting for sixty-six days. He was buried in the hallowed Milltown Cemetery on Falls Road, which had been compared to a Cenotaph. An estimated 100,000 people attended his funeral and riots erupted in nationalist areas. The strike ended October 3 after 217 days when families of six prisoners still fasting sought medical intervention. Three days later, some of their demands were met including being allowed to wear their civilian clothes at all times, free association in certain areas and 50% lost remission of sentences based on good behavior. Catholics saw the strikers as martyrs, and their actions had a lasting effect—proof that the political process could be an option to violence. Sinn Féin became a player in future elections.

Probably the most famous mural adorned the side of the party's office on Falls Road. A longhaired Sands was surrounded by two of his often-recited quotes: "Everyone, Republican or otherwise, has their own particular role to play" and "Our revenge will be the laughter of our children." Countless other walls had "God Bless Bobby Sands."

The hunger strikes couldn't help but intersect with the GAA, even recently. The government was considering building a sports complex on the closed Maze property, including a possible GAA field. In 2004, a club formed in Sands' home area of Twinbrook in west Belfast in his honor. The Club of the Skylark's crest included two letter H's, prison wire and a large lark, a symbol in a well-known story that Sands wrote in prison. The caged bird never gave up wanting to be free, and refused to give in to its captor.

In August 2006, a rally commemorating the twenty-fifth anniversary of the Hunger Strikes was held at Casement Park—County Antrim's main GAA stadium—against the wishes of the GAA central office in Dublin, which said the rally violated its rule that the Association remain non-party political. The Antrim GAA board, though, didn't object and 20,000 people paid tribute. (The GAA didn't organize the rally, it just provided the venue.) The speakers included Sinn Féin president Gerry Adams as the wants of the locals won out. It showed that the members controlled the GAA, not the other way around.

Casement Park sat on Anderstown Road, an extension of Falls and the republican theme park. Interestingly, the murals were now tourist attractions. Buses stopped at selected images and at peace lines—long walls or fences that separate Catholic and Protestant neighborhoods. Visitors with worldwide accents snapped photos as locals casually returned from food shopping. But to the residents here, the sites had more meaning than just a postcard to e-mail your family. For them, those honored were *their* family and friends. The St. John coaches brought some of those murals to life for me. Martin Flynn, the other skipper, had grown up with hunger striker Kieran Doherty, who won a county under-18 Gaelic football championship with his club St. Theresa's. Doherty, jailed for possession of firearms and explosives and hijacking a car, was the eighth man to die despite lasting the longest at 73 days. A mural honored Doherty across the street from Casement Park. (I attended a couple games there and noticed no one shooting off foghorns or clapping before the national anthem was over, instead standing respectfully still.)

Roger Casement, by the way, was an Irish revolutionary hung by the British for treason in 1916. In America, there aren't too many Nathan Hale arenas—just whatever company paid the highest for the naming rights. Throughout Ireland, stadiums and clubs were named for their patriots. I received a history lesson just learning who everybody was. But I must admit, seeing people honored for committing acts of terrorism, or plain ordinary violence, was somewhat of a jolt. It didn't matter whose side you were on, there was no denying that innocent people were part of the bigotry and 3,500 killed since the Troubles started. Some people's patriots were other people's terrorists.

I had to put everything in perspective. During the Troubles, IRA members considered themselves soldiers on "active duty" in a war. Detonating bombs or sniper shootings or car hijackings, they felt, were all part of the cause to earn independence. The people valued life—suicide bombings weren't an option—and the violence tapered once the British government began negotiations over power sharing and Catholics received civil rights. To get there, however, many believed an armed struggle was necessary. Going to jail wasn't a stigma, but a badge of honor and part of the price. There was even a social club past Falls Road called the Irish Republican Felons Club, in which full membership was granted to serving or former convicted prisoners or internees for crimes committed for the cause (honorary members include Nelson Mandela).

For balance, on Shankill Road the loyalist murals featured in-your-face hostility as masked men from paramilitary groups held rifles straight at you, marking their territory. They went to the grave feeling like they'd protected the union with Britain and had preserved Protestant culture. On the subject of perspective, I once lived in Virginia where nearby high schools were named for Civil War generals Robert E. Lee, Stonewall Jackson and Turner Ashby, people not exactly beloved by all.

So as an outsider visiting for a short time, I couldn't possibly assess who was right or wrong. But since I spent most of my time in the Catholic sections, I saw their way of thinking: their country was occupied, they faced discrimination, had difficultly getting jobs and were unjustly targeted by police (collusion and cooperation between the police and loyalist paramilitary groups such as the Ulster Volunteer Force had been proven). In addition to the more militant sector, the average Joe was hit hard. The 1971 census revealed that Catholics were two and a half times as likely as Protestants to be unemployed and were two and a half times less likely to hold managerial and supervisory positions. Ten years later, those numbers had barley changed. Another report found that Protestants took more of the skilled jobs, while Catholics were held in manual labor professions.

"We were the blacks," said Michael Johnston, after I brought up a similarity to the U.S. civil rights movement.

So as if it were the late 1800s, Northern Ireland nationalists grabbed onto Irish culture. Prison and the streets became classrooms. Flynn's eyes watered as he spoke about his grandmother, who had told him when he was a boy: "I don't care what you do, but never forget your Irish history and never forget your past."

Flynn, sporting a paunch of experience and a strong mustache, remembered the middle of August 1969 when rioting led to the deployment of British troops on the streets like in Derry. He was eighteen then and walking home near the Falls Road after seeing his girlfriend. Armored police cars fired shots, Catholics hurled petrol bombs and Protestants returned the fire. It was impossible to reach the road. He took refuge in an apartment with other terrified nationalists at the edge of a loyalist area. Their only protection were hurling sticks. He remembered staying up all night, hungry, and lying on the floor.

The next morning, he went to the Falls Road.

"It was like a picture out of the Second World War."

Loyalists had burned Catholics out of their homes on nearby Bombay Street. Smoke curled out from the remnants of charred buildings all over the area. People had little protection. Flynn found a busted shotgun that he clutched like a child's security blanket.

"A shot gun with no safety caps," he said shaking his head. "Unbelievable."

Many such images captured the next thirty years in Belfast, a time of bombs and riots. My focus was sport, and I always felt it had the power to mean more than wins and losses. That was confirmed here.

"The GAA inspired people in the six counties," Flynn proudly told to me. "It was nonpolitical, but it inspired people with their culture, with their identity. And it gave them something that they could hold on to that the Brits tried to take away. They tried to take our lives away from us. They tried to take our sport away from us. But we kept the sport. But we kept it at a price."

Playing for a GAA club automatically identified you as a Catholic and an easy target. St. Enda's in north Belfast had been bombed and burnt several times, and five of its members were murdered. Two killings were directly tied to their GAA involvement. In 1993, a loyalist paramilitary group shot the club's president, seventy-two-year-old Sean Fox, in his home. In 1997, the senior team's manager, Gerry Devlin, took seven bullets as he stood by the club's entrance. Two other well-known GAA murders happened outside Belfast. In 1988 a County Tyrone club player, Aidan McAnespie, was shot in daylight as he crossed the border on the way to a Gaelic football game. The British Army said a soldier's finger slipped while he was cleaning his gun causing three shots to accidentally discharge. Also in 1997, a paramilitary group kidnapped Sean Brown, chairman of the Bellaghy Wolfe Tone club in County Derry, while he was locking the field's gate one night. His body with six bullets turned up ten miles away.

With all that violence, the GAA in the North carried a singular resonance. As I traveled throughout Ireland, Gaelic football and hurling were seen by many as just options to soccer and rugby—one player in Dublin went so far as to say the GAA no longer carried the "nationalistic baggage." Sure, there were people who felt pride in playing an Irish sport and knew about the GAA's storied history—but they also didn't have the Union Jack flag flying on the next street. That fact wasn't lost on most people I spoke with in the North.

"The GAA in the occupied six counties, to a large extent, is at the cutting edge of what the founding fathers of the GAA set it up to be," Michael Johnston explained. "So in other words the promotion of the identity, of the language, of the culture, of the games, of this whole separatist movement ... we're probably closer to that than the GAA people who go out on a Sunday morning in Offaly or Cork or Kilkenny to play a game of hurling or a game of football. The GAA to them is a sporting organization, in general. I think when you scrape them deep enough there is still that nationalist identity there."

Here, you didn't have to look.

"The GAA to us is as much about nationalism as it is about games," said Johnston, proud to spread that gospel to his young players and proud to lead them in patriotic songs during trips to other counties.

Johnston and Flynn, both fathers of preteens, know the importance of keeping the youth busy. The electoral district of Belfast West (which included Falls Road and parts of Shankill Road) had 79 percent of its residents living in the most deprived areas in Northern Ireland, with a part of Whiterock Road topping the list. Belfast claimed fifty-six of the hundred worst areas in a deprivation study called the Noble Index based on such factors as income, employment and living environment. It was hard to escape years of oppression and a sense of hopelessness. Like in parts of Derry, or urban American cities, the streets were peppered with tires and ripped shopping bags and crumpled newspapers that floated up against curbs and fences, with smudged graffiti on walls. West Belfast had a suicide rate that nearly doubled the national average and there were *seven* suicides in a single week in mid-April 2005. Joyriding had also been a problem in which young men stole cars and rammed them into buildings before abandoning the heap of metal.

So during the post-Troubles era, the GAA was still needed for inspiration. I just had to look down the street from St. John's for additional proof. MacRory Park, a strip of land with just enough room for a field, was a GAA ground taken over by the British Army in 1972. When the Army left in 1987, sports didn't return. Enter another eyesore for the community—and an opportunity for GAA club Cardinal O'Donnell, one of the smallest of the fifteen near Falls Road.

"People just turned to anti-social activities," club official Gerald McAreavey told me. "That park was just a dumping ground in the area for people to drink, to do drugs, to do whatever. So our objective was to get them away from it."

O'Donnell's didn't have a playing home, so the vacant lot seemed ideal. Unfortunately, the land was valued at over £300,000. The Lord Mayor of Belfast, a Protestant, discovered a clause attached to the property that restricted its use for sporting purposes only, and the price tag dropped to £50,000. The club raised half the money through government and GAA grants and half through general fundraising.

O'Donnell's reopened the field in 2001 making the GAA once again a fixture at the beginning of Whiterock Road. I met McAreavey in the team's clubhouse on Rockmore Road, a few streets down. The sidewalk leading to the entrance was fenced in for several feet, reminding me of a baseball batting cage. A security camera watched everyone going in. Upstairs, people were playing poker against a background of television news. When a bearded Gerry Adams appeared on the screen, the voices stopped and the TV was turned up until he finished speaking, then it was back to the normal chatter. At one point, having a clubhouse was just as important as a place to play.

McAreavey turned expansive as his eyes took in the activity around him.

"During the Troubles there was little or nowhere else to go for entertainment or a social evening because people wouldn't have went into the town," McAreavey said nestled in his safe haven. "People more or less stayed within their own areas. And consequently the GAA clubs at that stage were flourishing. And there was a lot of camaraderie.

"... You knew you were going to be safe. There wasn't going to be any bother or anything like that there. You sat and had a quiet night and enjoyed yourself and that was it. Now people have more of an extended choice where to go. It does hurt GAA clubs financially."

As it was, O'Donnell's struggled to get players who swayed to powerhouses like St. Gall's, runner-up in the All-Ireland club football championship on St. Patrick's Day 2006. While O'Donnell's last won a major title in 1994, it still had a special niche with local school children and dedicated parents giving back.

"We're one of the smaller clubs," said McAreavey, aware of the club's pecking order. "But we've survived since '27 so we'll keep it going."

Like everywhere else in west Belfast, the history reminders were near. A worn Irish flag flew on one side of MacRory Park. Across the street, a mural featured IRA leaders and a Bobby Sands quote: "Never will they label our liberation struggle as criminal." An open hand was releasing a lark, its wings flapping up high, against a backdrop of the Irish flag along with the words "live free!"

The memories remained in paint and in the heart, but everyone I chatted with put the violence in the past tense. Many positive things had occurred in the four months in-between my visits. In late July, the IRA declared it was ending its armed campaign and promised to disarm. The weekend before I arrived in October, inspectors confirmed that the IRA no longer had weapons. On the field, two Northern teams won national titles—Tyrone captured the All-Ireland football title and County Down took the under-18 title. And the GAA college board voted to allow the PSNI training schools to enter competitions. That was significant, considering the contentious relationship that Catholics historically have had with the police and the ban that once excluded security forces members from playing in the GAA.

"It tells you how far the nationalists have traveled," St. John's Michael Johnston told me with each sentence coming out a little faster. "How confident nationalists are about themselves, our identity and how sure we are about where we're going as a people.

"... Our founding fathers—if they came back today—I think would be amazed at the progression of the nationalist people in this part of Ireland and probably would be very proud of the achievements of the people within this club who kept Gaelic games going; who kept the Irish language going; who kept the Irish culture and identity and nationalistic aspirations going when it wasn't popular, when it wasn't good to be a GAA man—when it was dangerous to be a GAA man. It would have been a lot easier to probably lie down."

Now, just like Bobby Sands wanted, the children were able to laugh.

"There's no going back," said Martin Flynn, stating perhaps the post-Troubles mantra. "I'm not going back and especially my kids. They're not going back to be second-class citizens. But I want a better life for everybody. Not just for my kids but for other kids, even the Protestant kids. For everybody."

Chapter 5
The Hidden Language
July: Gaeltacht, west County Kerry

A few hours after arriving in Ireland, I overheard a conversation in a large town and started to get excited—the people were speaking Irish. My first real "I'm in a foreign country moment!" My enthusiasm soon dimmed, however, when I mentioned my eavesdropping to the owner's son at my bed and breakfast.

He rolled his eyes and said, "They were probably speaking German."

Sadly, I figured out later, they were. Throughout my first five months, no one spoke Irish—sometimes called Gaelic—to each other. The newspapers were in English. The TV stations were in English. The food labels—take a guess ... English. The few brushes I had with the language were nothing a visitor couldn't navigate: some unfamiliar names of people and listings on road signs, a few television shows in Irish and GAA game programs with sections written in Irish. It was a good thing I left my bulky dictionary/teach yourself book at home.

I started to wonder if Irish was actually a functioning language, or was it more like a four-leaf clover—sure they exist, but good luck finding one. So I went off in search of hearing a conversation. During my explorations, I discovered Ireland's native language was a tricky thing. In the United States, with the burgeoning Hispanic population, we debate the issues of bilingual education and if English should be "made" the national language. In Ireland, Irish *was* the official language but not everyone embraced it. Only 9 percent of people used Irish daily and less than half of the population could speak it at all.

The government inadvertently created a backlash when it required Irish in schools following the country's independence in 1922. Instead of thriving, the forced learning led to an ambivalent, even resentful attitude in the decades since. For one, the schools didn't teach Irish as a practical language and students had to memorize books and grammar. Once they passed, it was gladly back to English. Many connected the medium with peasants and poverty, not forward thinking and technology as Ireland sought a global footing. Parents encouraged their kids to learn English in order to compete in business. A saying went "Irish does not sell the cow." Children cringed at the prospect of having to take it as a required subject. Critics claimed it was a waste of money and time to teach an archaic language.

So some considered it a burden. Others, a badge of pride. Parents that *wanted* their kids to learn the language were not satisfied with the system and started Irish-only schools that received state funding. Now, over 33,000 children voluntarily attended those schools throughout every county. Names like Aoibh (pronounced Eve) and Aoife (pronounced Ee-fa) were trendy. Sporting heroes and beauty queens spoke it proudly. The European Union just recognized Irish as an official language, and in 2003 the government passed a language rights law requiring that public services be made available in Irish.

"The language has under gone, and I hate to say it, but a re-branding exercise in the last, say, 15 years," Pádhraic Ó Ciardha, a vice president for the Irish TV station TG-4, told me when I picked his brain on the topic. "The profile of Irish has completely changed from being a badge of the civil service and the middle aged and the backwards, if you wish, to being seen as something that's young and vibrant and sexy and confident and dare I say it—profitable. You can make a living out of Irish now, and it's no bad thing."

Just when was I going to hear it?

I headed out west to the Dingle Peninsula in County Kerry, hanging from the bottom left corner of the country. Three things defined the area, and they all melted together: Gaelic football, Irish language and the countryside's uninterrupted beauty. The land's splendor was the first thing you noticed. Green mountains stretched for miles overlooking the blue Atlantic. Grazing sheep and cows never seemed to be too far away. The setting provided a natural movie set, as Hollywood discovered while filming Robert Mitchum's *Ryan's Daughter* and Tom Cruise's *Far and Away* near the beaches and craggy coastline.

In 1927, the jagged cliffs at the western tip were a glorious sight for Charles Lindbergh, struggling to stay awake in the twenty-eighth hour of his solo flight across the Atlantic en route to Paris. The area retained that healing effect on visitors.

Dingle, Europe's most westerly town, sat toward the end of the forty-mile long, ten-mile wide peninsula. Tourists flocked to see Fungie, a bottleneck dolphin living in the harbor, and for outdoor activities like windsurfing and hiking. Stretching west of Dingle to the ocean were tiny villages and open space. The land was littered with relics from the Stone Age, Bronze Age and Iron Age including inscribed stones, monuments, wedge tombs and remains of castles and forts. There were also dozens of twentieth century landmarks—B&Bs. I arrived in mid-July after taking a two-week "vacation" to spend time with my parents visiting from home. I stayed in Ventry, a speck of a village with 413 residents four miles from Dingle. Another way to describe the distance would be a one hour, fifteen-minute walk in which big, scary bees followed you because the road was so narrow, you had no choice but to rub against the multi-colored flowers on the side to avoid cars and cyclists. I realized that except for strolling on the white beaches, walking here wasn't going to work.

I called Liam O Rócháin, chairman of the local GAA club An Gaeltacht (Gwell-Tech). We met at a pub to chat about the team, and without even asking, he generously offered to take me around the peninsula on the Slea Head drive, a touring route along the coast with treacherous stretches leaving just enough room for one car. That might have saved my life.

On paper, the area looked like it could support a thriving suburb of Dingle. But it was actually sprinkled with 1,200 people and underdeveloped.

"See the many houses?" O Rócháin asked me as he pointed to a lonely cottage near a stream with no other dwellings in sight for miles. "This is it. It looks big on the map."

Before TV and radio, people fished, hunted and played Gaelic football—there weren't many other pastimes. The curved grounds made hurling difficult, but football could thrive on the side of a hill. The environment provided the necessities: a ball consisting of a pig bladder stuffed inside a leather hide and miles of open, curvy fields. In a game that predated football called caid, the goal was to carry the ball from one parish to the next without getting your head chopped off. Defenders wrestled or tripped the poor runner to the ground. Players later used a leather ball stuffed with hay. The rough games led to fights and grudges. In 1884, residents adapted to the GAA's formal rules, which of course changed through the years but the football never stopped.

Nor did a simple life through the decades. Locals mostly earned a living by selling mackerel—iced fresh or salted—and other types of fish, or through the benefits of raising cattle and sheep. The Great Famine of 1845-1848 hit the population hard, and many fled overseas for work. The western part of the peninsula was more or less cut off from the rest of the county. Roads weren't tarred until the 1950s and electricity arrived for the masses in the 1960s. The filming of *Ryan's Daughter* in the late '60s helped modernize the area. Now, tourism provided plenty of jobs.

"Nothing over there but the GAA," O Rócháin said as he nodded to the open space, a fantasyland for a suburban mini-mall developer. "The rural community and the GAA. For people my age it would be very important."

The fifty-three-year-old O Rócháin remembered playing fierce, impromptu pick-up games as a boy, even lacing the brownish ball made of pig's hide himself. Priests coached school teams in the early 1950s, but it was hard to get kids to one spot and An Gaeltacht's adult team struggled with no feeder system. Parents couldn't exactly carpool to practice by cycling fifteen miles. As technology entered the parish, Gaelic football improved because everything became more cohesive. By the early 1970s, cars were affordable for many and O Rócháin finally got phone service in 1989 after years of applying.

Now the small club was flourishing. O Rócháin, an elementary school teacher, proudly recalled the methodical climb to the top, the formula no different than from other clubs throughout Ireland. The youth excelled in the 1980s and their skills translated to the adult level. An Gaeltacht rose from a low-level team to winning its first senior county championship in 2001. Last season, they advanced to the All-Ireland club championship on St. Patrick's Day.

As he was talking, O Rócháin pulled over to a small beach. A gray stone monument on a cliff resembling a chair greeted us with the inscription "Some Lands touch the Heart, Dingle touches the Soul." Another mandatory stop was Dunquin Pier across from the Blasket Islands, a now vacant group of islands that Irish speakers inhabited until 1953. We worked our way down the twisting path with the wind buzzing our ears and messing up our hair. The mountains in the background seemed to touch the clouds. In the dead of summer, evenings were cool, especially near the water. After looking at an old wooden sailboat off to the side, O Rócháin recalled a tip he received from a veteran coach before he took over the youth teams in 1983.

"Don't be doing any physical training. They're fit enough from being after the sheep at the side of the mountains, especially in the spring. Divide whatever you have into a group and play matches. They're always in shape."

You must play to your strengths. Activities like fox hunting with beagles and hen farming also hardened football bodies. Residents all over scenic Kerry, a land of lakes with bright blue water and fat mountains, fell in love with Gaelic football. Hurling, soccer and rugby were practically nonexistent. That sole focus and passion developed Kerry into a dynasty. Nicknamed the Kingdom, Kerry captured thirty-five senior All-Ireland championships. The only other team that could claim double-digit titles was Dublin with twenty-two. An Gaeltacht had contributed over forty players to those championship squads, not a bad achievement for a small club.

O Rócháin took me to the team's complex in Gallarus, near a vacant seventh or eighth century stone oratory once used as a Christian church. It looked like an inverted boat, and stood at an angle so the rainwater ran off. The inside remained dark and dry. The field was down a couple roads. On one side stood mountains, horses and sheep; the sheep sprayed with different colors so they could be easily identified if they strayed. Next to the gate were a couple cows with tags in their ears displaying the numbers 0114 and 0116. On the other side, the Atlantic Ocean splashed about twenty yards away. The beach extended to the field's fence, and the daily high tide nearly soaked the grass. A line of rocks helped cut erosion, but couldn't stop wayward balls from flying into the water. Kids would run to retrieve them, not at all concerned about getting wet. Three sisters watched the action. "Three sisters" was what locals called an island in the distance that had three pointed curves, resembling heads from afar. Glorious sunsets were seen here. O Rócháin recalled a popular saying he heard as a child that captured the imagery: *Golden ball of fire slowly sinking into the hazy western Atlantic Ocean.*

The field boosted the club's turnaround because the players finally had a central location. Bought in 1980, it took four months to flatten the sand banks done with mostly voluntary labor. By 1996, An Gaeltacht had its grand opening, and by then added an improved sand-based surface, viewing stands and a complex that included a kitchen, locker rooms and an upstairs meeting room.

A few days later, I went to a practice and the only English I heard came in the form of universal curse words, uttered at well-placed times. Members conducted all team business in the Irish language—the coaching, the pep talks, administrative meetings, even the club's Web site. Finally, I heard the conversation I had been in search of! Not that I could understand anything, but at least I knew that it definitely wasn't German.

The medium was as much a source of local pride as was its football. This western part of the peninsula was in the Gaeltacht, areas orally frozen in time that featured predominately Irish speakers (thus the GAA club's name). The government designated these sections to ensure the language survives as a first means of communication. The Department of Community, Rural & Gaeltacht Affairs provided funding to homeowners, for education and incentives for businesses. Gaeltachts were found mainly on the Western seaboard with pockets in the Northwest and East totaling 2.3 percent of the population.

Once, most of the country spoke Irish. The medium came to Ireland in around 300 BC as part of the six Celtic languages of Britain. It was sometimes called Gaelic, which is the Anglicized word for Gaeilge, meaning Irish Gaelic. (Scottish Gaelic, however, was more commonly known just as Gaelic.) Tablets from the fourth century BC contained the first evidence of Irish writing. The words flowed until English conquests, settlements and anti-language laws in the sixteenth, seventeenth and eighteenth centuries wobbled its popularity. The government and business worlds switched to English, and Irish came to be viewed as a language for commoners. In places like west Kerry, the Irish words never stopped—even on the field.

Before the practice, I chatted with player Seán Mac an tSíthigh, who just had an eye-candy drive along the seashore. He worked on the other side of the peninsula in a small town named Waterville, population 538. The stop on the famed Ring of Kerry scenic tour had a bronze statue near the beach commemorating one of its frequent visitors, Charlie Chaplin. Mac an tSíthigh was a heritage officer promoting the town's culture and folklore. He returned, of course, to play for his home parish of An Gaeltacht. He took pride in speaking his language, which sometimes confused players on other teams.

"[The language] is kind of a badge of our identity, really, and it's a vital aspect of the club," Mac an tSíthigh explained to me leaning against his car. "I wouldn't be militant about it. It's just that I feel that we have a responsibility because we come from this type of culture, and we have a collective responsibility to maintain it. Simply, as a respectful duty to the generations before us, who always maintained their traditions. Especially in a changing society, I think it's important to hold on to whatever unique traditions you have that give you a unique identity within a broader Irish culture. And I think the language is one of those vital strengths."

The GAA was another. Together, they provided inspiration at a crucial time in Irish history. Between 1850 and 1880, at least three major Irish language societies were formed. In 1884, the GAA started, followed by the influential Gaelic League in 1893. Though nonsectarian and nonpolitical, many of that language organization's members helped launch the Irish revolution and played Gaelic sports.

In September, I met legendary GAA announcer Micheál Ó Muircheartaigh at an All-Ireland hurling championship press conference in Cork. Now in his seventies, the native from outside Dingle was one of the country's most famous Irish speakers and known for his pithy and humorous one-liners during games. (He onced described a player named Joe Rabbitte defending Pat Fox as "a Rabbitte chasing a Fox around Croke Park.")

I couldn't pass up a chance to chat with him about the language; it'd be like writing a piece on the theory of relativity and not talking with Einstein, who happened to be standing a few feet away. Ó Muircheartaigh, looking like he could be twenty years younger with few wrinkles and a full head of light brown hair with only specks of white, was happy to tell me that the connection between the Irish language and the GAA was deeply rooted and shouldn't be ignored. That success of the language movement inspired people to preserve their native games, as well. The late 1800s and early 1900s were a time of cultural separation. Literary figures such as Lady Gregory, John Millington Synge and W.B. Yeats launched the Irish Literary Revival and the Abbey Theatre in Dublin. Others saw sport as a vital route to celebrate their Irishness. All of them loved their country, and the common thread in expressing that pride was through the language.

"And I think that still stands," Ó Muircheartaigh proclaimed.

The GAA didn't just pay lip service to preserving Irish customs. Rule 4 of its guidebook said, "The Association shall actively support the Irish language, traditional Irish dancing, music, song, and other aspects of Irish culture."

Since 1969, the GAA sponsored a competition combining those activities called Scór. Events included storytelling, dancing, ballad singing and questions—which was like a written *Jeopardy*. To compete, you'd better brush up on your knowledge of Irish history, the language and the GAA. Clubs fielded teams and the competition followed the same format as in the sporting arena: winners at the county and provincial levels qualified for the All-Ireland tournament.

Additionally, all official GAA business must be signed in Irish; teams had been penalized for not listing its lineups in the medium. The GAA also supported indigenous industry. Irish paper was required for all documents and correspondence, and trophies and playing equipment needed to be made in Ireland. The Association recently printed a 24-page booklet of Irish phrases and vocabulary commonly used in GAA circles. The introduction said, "It is hoped that, if GAA members learn a few phrases from this booklet each day, that their confidence and desire to use the language will increase." Included were:

>Cén dath atá ar gheansaí fhoireann _____? (pronounced with the bold emphasized *ken **dah** ata air **yan**cie **ur**inn _____)
>What color is the _____ jersey?
>
>Pasáil an liathróid (***pwas**sal eh**lay**ridge*)
>Pass the ball!
>
>Ar ór na cruinne ná (*air **ore** na **krin**gyeh na*)

For the love of God (goodness sake) don't ...!

Bhí sibh millteanach falsa *(vee shiv millchinah falseh)*
You were awfully lazy!

Many clubs and county boards advanced the medium through a cultural officer, who organized trivia nights in Irish and language classes. A GAA club, though, wasn't required to do anything in terms of language education. The frequency of events differed from place to place.

"The vast majority of the people who would be involved in the GAA would be supportive of [the language]," said Ciarán Ó Feinneadha, a Dublin-based language activist who has helped promote the medium in the GAA. "But you get people at different times who wouldn't ... regard it as a priority and they wouldn't put much energy into it. In general, the GAA does support the Irish language."

The Association annually gave to a tournament for Irish-speaking teams (it had been €6,350 the last several years). A 2002 in-house strategic review recommended that the GAA should promote the language "as an integral part of the Association's sporting, social, marketing and public relations activities."

But let's be honest: most teams didn't care if their goalie could read an Irish language newspaper. They just wanted him to stop the ball. It wasn't like grammar tests were required along with a physical.

"It's part of the GAA philosophy to help the Irish language, but it's more talked about than actually acted upon," said Diarmuid Ó Tuama, the principal of an Irish language school in Belfast and a supporter of the GAA. "It's a nice ideal but nobody does anything about it. It's easier to play football or hurling than it is to sort of go and learn a language, obviously."

The GAA was a sporting organization, after all, not a language preservationist society.

"It's not the GAA's role to ensure the Irish language survives," Association president Nickey Brennan told me when I met him later in my travels. "The GAA is an organization that unashamedly supports the Irish language and we conduct some of our business in Irish and we use Irish as often as is practical. But we're not in the business of making sure the language survives. That's for other organizations to do."

The government, though, recognized that the GAA brought a coolness factor into language promotion. In turn, it gave money to GAA clubs under various programs and grants. For example, An Gaeltacht received €192,000 for its expansion projects. The Summer Camps Scheme, meanwhile, gave GAA clubs

€40 for each child that attended a sports camp conducted in Irish with the provision that at least 75 percent had to be from a Gaeltacht area. Some camps had rules that briefly penalized kids if they slipped back to English. In a way, it was a little like hiding a pill in ice cream—not that learning the language should feel like taking medicine.

Perhaps the best promotion for the language was when a team like An Gaeltacht succeeded. Then, everyone associated the medium with winners.

"You're representing a whole community of Irish speakers rather than just a parish or a single club," Mac an tSíthigh continued. "So I think that's important on a national scale, as well, and it's good for the language if they see a successful team."

"They" meaning their fellow countrymen who weren't exposed to the language or thought it was just for senior citizens. There was no grander stage than the All-Ireland final. Last year, club member Dara Ó Cinnéide captained Kerry to another title and then gave the traditional victory speech in Irish—a rare occurrence.

"A lot of people were very proud of that," Mac an tSíthigh pointed out. "That he remained true to his people and his language."

While in the area, I heard about Páidí Ó Sé, another star who hadn't forgotten his roots. Ó Sé was a top defender for the legendary Kerry teams in the 1970s and 1980s. Along with four other teammates, he won a record eight senior All-Ireland titles. He later managed Kerry to titles in 1997 and 2000. Last season, he guided County Westmeath to its first Leinster provincial title. He was known for his bluntness and larger-than-life personality. Take his pub just off the beach in Ventry. He laced it with wall-to-wall pictures of big shots, sporting heroes and local fishermen. A large shot of Páidí and Tom Cruise greeted you from behind the bar as you entered. Down a little to the left, a picture showed Dolly Parton singing with Páidí standing next to her. Near the door, was a framed letter from Martin Sheen dated April 18, 1996, with a picture of the actor near a championship cup. The letter said it was a "special pleasure to have met you and your family the other day" and "when I see Tom Cruise I'll tell him we met."

The lighting was just dark enough to create a cozy feel while looking at the eclectic montage of decorations. One picture had Páidí with Irish Prime Minister Bertie Ahern. I spotted a Larry Bird poster signed to Páidí and a picture of a triumphant Joe Frazier knocking down Muhammad Ali in their first fight signed by the referee Arthur Mercante. And there were dozens of pictures commemorating Páidí's greatest moments in the GAA, along with trophies, paintings and framed articles.

Páidí, a short man with a silver crew cut, was often bustling around, picking up dirty glasses or he was in his general store across the street. You just had to catch him at the right time. Eventually, I arranged to meet him but he kept looking at his watch. The pub's twentieth anniversary celebration was that weekend, so I knew I had little time on glad-to-meet yous and small talk like what he spoke to Dolly about.

Páidí told me of his deep pride he had for the area, but also expressed concern for the language's future in Gaeltachts.

"In the '60s and '70s and before that it was very easy to keep the Irish language and Gaelic football alive," Páidí explained. "But now you have other intrusions, foreign intrusions. You have television and the media exposure of other games. And as a result, there's extra pressure on us with our Irish language and our games because of soccer, of rugby and of the active social scene. Take for example in our schools."

Páidí went on to say how people were moving to the Irish-speaking areas who didn't speak the language. The peaceful beauty of the romantic West was a good draw, especially as other areas became more urbanized because of Ireland's strong economy. Consquently, more and more English was being spoken on the playgrounds and at recess. He added that while those people had a right to move in, it chipped away at the language's future and the native speakers had "come under pressure. It's much more difficult now for them to keep the language going because of outside people living in the area."

The erosion of the spoken language was a real concern. Dr. John Harris, a Trinity College professor in Dublin, found that students mastering a "general comprehension of speech" in Gaeltacht schools dropped from 96.3 percent in 1985 to 73.3 percent in 2002. People didn't have to look far to find troubling stats. The 2002 census revealed that 55 percent spoke Irish on a daily basis in Gaeltacht areas, a drop of five percent from the 1996 census. Another report discovered that just a quarter of children left Gaeltacht elementary schools with a reasonable level of Irish. Certain schools had stopped teaching all subjects in the medium.

Then there was the practical financial concern of using the language. The big controversy when I was there involved the 2004 Placenames Order, an extension of the 2003 Official Languages Act. It declared that maps and signposts in Gaeltacht areas be written only in Irish. Dingle—an easily recognizable name in tour books—became An Daingean. Some business owners worried that the unfamiliar name would hurt tourism. Local politicians called for a repeal and a few months later, someone erected a 25-foot "Dingle" sign on a hill overlooking the town, mimicking the Hollywood sign in protest of the name change. It was taken down overnight.

Despite the concerns, the Irish language was as strong here as anywhere else in the country. Dingle's 62.4 percent of Irish speakers was the largest among towns with populations of 1,500 or more. (Dingle had 1,775 residents.) I heard conversations in cab rides that I shared with Irish speakers, in shops, in homes and, of course, between the playing lines. And that, as much as anything, was a good sign for the language's future.

"There's more of an awareness of it in recent times," Páidí finished. "It did take a bit of a lull but it's on the way back. The present generation is bringing it back again. It's become very fashionable out here to speak it."

When I left Kerry after a few weeks to continue my journey, I boarded a bus in triumph—I reached my goal of hearing a conversation. But I didn't want to stop. I had become fascinated by the country's split in favor of the language and the GAA's connection to its growth. This was new to me. I'd never really paid attention to how words were said, just their meanings. Here, both mattered.

In March, the Irish Language Commissioner called for a review of how the medium was taught in schools—which cost the government €500 million a year—after his office released a report. The findings weren't pretty: the students' poor fluency rate led to an insufficient return on investment. In response, an influential politician urged that Irish should be made optional for the last two years of high school.

Language lovers knew about purge attempts. In the 1960s, two of the three major political parties campaigned to do away with teaching Irish in schools except in certain areas. In 1973, the government ruled that the language would still be taught, but a passing grade wasn't needed to graduate. The speaking requirements for civil service jobs were eliminated a year later. (But everybody loves money and Éire—Ireland—was still printed on currency and stamps.)

The grumblings rumbled on. In 2006, I picked up a copy of the *Irish Times* in New York City and read a high school student's "exam diary" in which she rejoiced about never having to speak Irish again, and how her classmates "were dancing on Gaeilge's grave" after finishing their leaving certificate test. Granted, I would have said the same thing after my last algebra or chemistry test. Then again, memorizing the Ion chart was not a matter of national pride. The debate about the language's importance, it seemed, would continue on for generations.

The Irish activists I encountered were realists. They weren't naïve to expect that the language could ever become Ireland's top tongue. Rather, they viewed the medium as a complement to English and as a vital part of Irish culture that must survive. Simply, they wanted to make it relevant. The rise of the language schools, called Gaelscoileanna, was one life support. Their growth since the 1970s went up like a Kerry mountain, and now numbered 163 elementary schools and 38 high schools.

Another weapon was the electronic media. In 1972, an Irish language radio station began airing in west Kerry. Activists next pushed for a TV station. One parent, Ciarán Ó Feinneadha, saw that his young daughter didn't have any role models who spoke Irish. He thought it was "oppressive" that a citizen whose language was the first language of her country and her home couldn't get support.

"People shouldn't be left in a situation where their children are isolated by the state because they're Irish speakers and that basically was what was happening," he recalled when I met him in his Dublin office. "My kids, when they were young, had no heroes in Irish. When we had the campaign, one of the things we placed great emphasis on was that we wanted Irish-speaking heroes for our children. We needed them."

Ó Feinneadha grew up in an Irish-speaking home in south Dublin and remembered his oldest brother's nickname was "Culchie," a sometimes derogatory term for a country boy.

"There's no doubt about it, we were different and unusual at the time," said Ó Feinneadha, who was an income tax consultant with many Irish-speaking clients. "You wouldn't get that sort of reaction today."

As he got older, his love for the language led him to become a firebrand activist. His radical protests included getting arrested for climbing the mast outside RTÉ, which was state supported, and chaining himself to buildings. A rallying cry—and a popular graffiti symbol—was 00.7%, in reference to the percent of shows using the Irish medium on TV at the time.

The drive captured the attention of the mainstream, and by the early 1990s, political parties threw in their support for an Irish station. TnaG debuted in 1996 with two hours of original Irish programming a day. Now called TG-4, the station upped its Irish shows to six hours per day. Though the station's main offices were in Galway's Connemara Gaeltacht, there was also a small Dublin office; and that was where I met Pádhraic Ó Ciardha, one of TG-4's honchos.

"You fire away," Ó Ciardha said as I took out my notepad and tape recorder. "I talk very fast so you may not get everything I say. So feel free to stop me."

His enthusiasm for the language was machine gun style fast. Granted, this was what he got paid to do. But he grew up in the Connemara and speaking Irish was more a lifestyle than a paycheck. He laid out a map of Ireland across his desk and gave me a history lesson of the language movement. A small portion was marked in pink showing the Gaeltachts.

TG-4 aimed for a national audience and perspective, rather than to just cater to its niche market bathed in pink. As the station looked for programming, sports jumped out. Several important GAA competitions were not being aired. So TG-4 bought the rights for the GAA National League, club championship, under-21 and college competitions. In 2002, TG-4 raised its involvement to another level by sponsoring the women's football championship. The final drew the station's highest ratings for the next two years. Now, it added Tour de France and Wimbledon, and occassionly showed overseas soccer matches that weren't picked up by other stations, as well as the Irish semipro soccer league.

"Sport transcends language which is crucial to all of this," Ó Ciardha continued. "The action drives the story. The commentary is secondary to the action."

He was right. I'd watch games, and while I couldn't understand the announcers, it didn't hurt my appreciation of what was happening. The words sounded lyrical and you did focus on the action. In fact, I'd watch TG-4 often. When it wasn't showing Irish programming, it ran American shows and movies in English, including *The Wire* and *Curb Your Enthusiasm*. A year after I left Ireland, TG-4 acquired the rights to dub the first four seasons of *The Simpsons* in Irish. (For the record, "Eat my shorts" was Ith mo fhobhrist, while "D'oh" and "Ay Caramba" did not translate.)

The popular overseas-created shows were needed to keep viewers once the Irish programming ended. TG-4 operated on a €28 million budget. While that sounded like a lot to me, consider what Ó Ciardha said: the BBC spent just that much last year on taxis. The BBC also spent five times more for eighteen days of Olympic coverage than TG-4 did for all their shows.

TG-4 placed its resources into content, not rides. The station received 90 percent of its funding from the government and the rest from commercial revenue, including advertisements for McDonalds in Irish. The audience numbers were small, but growing. In 2006, it grabbed a 3.5 percent share (800,000 viewers) of the national TV market for its best showing ever. The full menu of original programs included a plot-twisting soap, Ros na Rún. The *Irish Independent* carried a headline calling it "The best soap on TV bar none (Even if you don't speak a work of Irish)" after a controversial assisted suicide episode. Shows hit a wide variety of tastes, ranging from news documentaries, cartoons, a Top-40 music video show and traditional Irish music and dancing. People could enjoy those programs in Irish, then still be entertained when the English language shows come on.

"People forget, you know, that Irish speakers don't just speak Irish," Ó Ciardha pointed out. "Someone who can be speaking to you in Páidí's pub in Ventry may have to rush home not to, you know, milk the cow or write a short story in Irish—they may be going home to watch *Coronation Street* [an English soap]. So they're our audience too. Some people, particularly language counters here in Dublin, think that if you're a speaker of Irish in west Kerry that you're only interested in Irish and Irish culture and Gaelic games. You may want to watch Manchester United. Or you may want to watch the Tour de France. So we try to deal with the reality of that rather than isolate people."

And now, children had their Irish-speaking heroes. Hiudai (Hoo-dee), an animated Scandinavian troll resembling a Leprechaun with tall, antenna-like ears, big eyes, a pointy chin and a tomato-like tan nose, was voted the best television personality at the 2000 Irish Film and Television Awards, a surprise to everyone. Hiudai earned his fame as a co-presenter for a kid's show. Then there were Irish-speaking heartthrobs in flesh and blood, including the Rose of Tralee, Aoibhinn Ni Shúilleabháin, the 2003 Miss Ireland/Miss World, Rosanna Davidson, the Kerry football star Dara Ó Cinnéide and Cork hurling captain Seán Óg Ó hAilpín. What was cooler than pin-ups and sporting idols?

"The positive branding that that makes for the language is incalculable," Ó Ciardha was glad to tell me. "They come up and say one of the first things you need to know about me is I'm an Irish speaker and I'm proud of it. That is so different from the role models that were presented in the Irish media, say, fifteen years ago. If you were an Irish pop star [then] and you mentioned that you were fluent in Irish, your PR man would shoot you. *'Don't mention Irish.'* But now it's completely the other way."

A new inferiority complex was developing for some—not knowing the language. Take Ó hAilpín, the Cork hurler. He learned it from his father, who worked overseas for a stretch in the 1970s and 1980s.

"When Dad went working in Australia they thought he was English because of the fact he spoke English," Ó hAilpín told me when I met him in September. "But Dad would say 'No, no I'm Irish.' And they said 'Look we're Italians and we speak Italian. They're Greeks and they speak Greek. How come you speak English and you're Irish?' They couldn't understand it, and Dad felt embarrassed.... It is important because if you're Irish, you speak Irish. When I was younger and had to learn Irish, I didn't see it. But the older I get, the more I appreciate it."

So did many others. Adults were now taking language classes because they wanted to feel a connection with their heritage. I met Pádraic Mac Donncha, the director of the community center in a small Gaeltacht in Ráth Cairn, County Meath, an hour outside of Dublin. He explained that one reason the big city folk were flocking for language classes was that they now had economic independence, and in looking for things to do, they found their own culture. In the lean times of the past, people were more concerned about simply surviving.

That begged the question, in today's nouveau rich and high-tech Ireland, would people's appreciation of their roots continue to grow. Not everyone was optimistic.

"To be quite honest about it, we've gone from a situation where we were in a revivalist movement to a situation now where people are just trying to get the language to hang on," Ciarán Ó Feinneadha told me. "Although there are a lot of advantages over the last few years, the language is still under fierce pressure, fierce pressure to survive."

He thought the overall goodwill to the language was greater, but didn't regard the medium to be as strong today than it was in the mid-1970s because less people spoke it as a natural day-to-day language.

Then again ...

"These things are relative," TG-4's Ó Ciardha said with his half-full viewpoint. "There are 6,000 languages on the earth and the experts tell us that ninety-nine percent of them are in imminent, imminent, danger of extinction. But Irish isn't one of them. Irish is actually in the one percent that isn't. It will never supplant or replace English. I think the intention is that it will always survive and have a prominent place in the culture of the country and in the sport of the country.... I think Irish is in a much stronger position than it was forty years ago. That's what I believe. And I think the games have been very important in bringing that about."

So, like most things ...

"It depends on whether you're an optimist or a pessimist."

Chapter 6
The Gamble

Early August: Kilnadeema/Leitrim, County Galway

Curiosity drove Kevin Boyle into the bookmaker on that early April day in 2003. He wanted to see what the experts thought of his small hurling club's chances in the upcoming County Galway tournament. He immediately was insulted, then intrigued.

The bookies placed Kilnadeema/Leitrim at 33/1 odds of reaching the quarterfinals. *The quarterfinals!?!* Let alone winning the whole thing. To be fair, Boyle knew that his team hadn't earned more respect while competing the last three seasons in the top division. Going winless would do that. In fact, they barely avoided getting sent down. Now, the local newspaper listed them nineteen out of twenty in its preseason ranking. Nobody had a reason to expect a turnaround. The 33/1 odds might have even been too generous.

Yet, Boyle had a feeling. The uplifting preseason produced a buzz of optimism among the team. Players committed to weight training and a proper diet. Practices were sharp, and the club brought in an outside expert on fitness. This was going to be their breakthrough season. They knew it. And to Boyle—who enjoyed a wager here and there—those odds sparkled.

So at the next practice, the feisty fullback announced he was placing a bet, and he'd collect money if anyone else wanted in. It was just something different, and nobody felt pressure to ante up. But did they. Boyle collected at least €50 apiece—some kicked in €100 or more—from twenty-nine players, team officials and coaches. That was that. Details didn't leak as the driven players continued to train relentlessly. The thirty-year-old Boyle didn't even tell his parents. The driving force wasn't money. The hurlers wanted to make a name for their speck of a team. The club formed eight years earlier after two small villages amalgamated because of a dwindling number of bodies. Neither village had much of a main street and a total of one shop. Nearby parishes owned all the bragging rights. Reaching the quarterfinals was a chance for K/L to earn glory with the big boys.

But just making it out of the preliminary stage would be a struggle. The county tournament featured four groups of five teams, with the top two in each section advancing to the quarterfinals. Galway teams routinely contended for All-Ireland championships and the quality ran deep. It equaled a power conference like an ACC, Big 10 or Pac 10. Kilnadeema/Leitrim (pronounced Kill-na-deema Lee-trim), on the other hand, would be a bad mid-major playing out the schedule. Bombshell upsets were needed to merely survive the group.

Their climb began in late April. K/L won its first game in Group C causing a mild surprise. Word soon seeped into the hurling community about the team's all for one bet, amusing many because it seemed so unrealistic. After an expected loss, K/L rebounded to win its third game by two points against a more established club, and things got interesting. Could the small hurling team beat the odds?

Hold on. Shoeless Joe Jackson anyone? Pete Rose? How could betting on yourself be legal?

I had many questions as I arrived in County Galway to retrace Kilnadeema/Leitrim's bet. I became interested after finding an article on the Internet while doing my research back home. Bells rang in my head—*what?* All my life I heard how athletes needed to be separated from betting on their sport for the game's integrity. In Ireland, though, it was perfectly legal. That surprised me as much as the players not getting paid did. My first thought—scandal. *Oops, I missed a kick. Oops, I let the shot in. Too bad. The other team wins. Damn. And how soon can I collect my money?* An especially tempting payday, I thought, for an amateur who could at least get something for his efforts.

But nobody seemed alarmed. Whenever I had asked someone about the possibility of shenanigans, I always got looks like I was crazy to even suggest something improper could happen.

I met Joe Kenny, the manager of Kilnadeema/Leitrim in 2003 and now a coach for his eight-year-old son's team. He emphatically said, "Ab.So.Lutely never. Ever. Ever. It just doesn't happen. No way. I suppose it's very hard for you to understand why. It just does not happen. Good point, but it's us against them. There is no inch given.... It's a manly thing around here. Hurling is a manly thing. If you're not doing so well it's a little kick in the teeth on your ego."

I spoke with Alan Mulholland, the bookmaker whose firm took the bet. I could hear the amusement in his voice as he answered, "I don't think it's an issue. Like I don't think it's a problem. I think bookmakers are cute enough and wise enough to spot if something underhanded is going on. I think there's enough self-regulation. We're not going to lay bets if we knew something was happening.... You're tying yourself up in knots if you try to legislate against it. You're better off keeping it out in the open."

I got the question in to Dessie Farrell, the head of the Gaelic Players' Association, when I met him in late September. The organization boldly fights for player welfare issues. Gambling, though, wasn't even on its agenda. "It hasn't been a concern," Farrell said, not sure why I would bring it up. "I know players have backed themselves and bet on themselves to score the first goal in the game. Or to kick the first point or whatever the case may be. But the other way, the reverse of it, I can't see it.... It would be extremely difficult to orchestrate."

I also asked Nickey Brennan, a longtime GAA administrator who became the Association's President in 2006. To him, my question was a fat softball: "We would have no great fears on that sort. There is too much pride on winning for your parish. I have no concerns whatsoever. It's a non-issue as we call it."

What was going on?

Maybe it was my American cynicism. Maybe it was knowing about the 1919 Chicago Black Sox, or the 1951 college basketball game-fixing scandal that involved seven schools including then-powerhouse City College of New York. Or the Boston College basketball team shaving points in the 1978-79 season orchestrated by the gangsters featured in *Goodfellas*. Or the suspension of NFL stars Paul Hornung and Alex Karras for the 1963 season for betting on league games and consorting with gamblers. Or Major League Baseball suspending Brooklyn Dodgers manager Leo Durocher for the 1947 season for "conduct detrimental to baseball" including associating with gamblers. Or baseball, again, barring Willie Mays in 1979 and Mickey Mantle in 1983 from league activities such as coaching for working as greeters at an Atlantic City hotel, despite both being long retired. (Another commissioner later reinstated them.) And of course, let's not forget Pete Rose, banned from Major League Baseball for life for betting on *his* team while he was the manager of the Cincinnati Reds. Shoot, Las Vegas can't even get a major professional team.

Just the whiff of a gambling connection in American pro sports gets you bounced. In the GAA, though, players were permitted to bet on themselves and there had never been a major scandal. Internet message boards occasionally lit up with rumors of a thrown game, and a newspaper reported unusual betting patterns during National League and club games shortly after I left Ireland. Then-GAA President Seán Kelly dismissed the report, telling the *Irish Independent,* "I simply don't believe it. You would have to have an awful lot of people involved to fix a match and it defies belief that a whole team would be that corrupt. Our games have always had real integrity and I have no doubt that is still the case. I wouldn't give any credence whatsoever to this claim, especially since it is so short on detail."

I was all for believing in the good of human nature, but legal player gambling just seemed a little remarkable to me. Yet in Ireland, people shrugged when I sounded surprised that it was. And that was one of the reasons I came up with why it wasn't a big deal. Wagering was ingrained in the Irish culture. In the sixteenth and seventeenth centuries, English landowners would bet on hurling games. These days, bookmakers had shops in most parishes, or at least a close drive away. They were bright and clean, there was free tea and coffee, and shiny plasma television screens to watch. Some punters—the gambler—popped in and out as if going to a pub for a quick pint.

Seedy bookies with leg breakers on call need not apply.

"It's socially accepted over here," Mulholland told me in a phone interview from his shop in Galway city. "It's out in the open. There's just no stigma associated with gambling. Even in the last decade it's become more socially acceptable."

I noticed that gambling was indeed a part of the background of everyday life, like going to a movie. (Considering the price of popcorn, Good & Plenty and a soda, laying a couple bets might be cheaper.) Bookmakers openly advertised. Newspapers offered contests to win betting slips. People became famous for their ability to pick winners, like the beloved multimillionaire J.P. McManus from Limerick. The annual Festival at Cheltenham in the southwest of England could just as well have been in Ireland. Every March, the national newspapers covered the steeplechase and hurdle horse racing event like a local spectacle, noting large bets and fancy dresses. This fascination with wagering extended to the Gaelic Athletic Association. A bookmaker sponsored Louth's inter-county GAA teams. Players and coaches worked as bookies. Practically every club's chief fundraiser was the lotto draw. Race nights in pubs, where people bet on horses on the television, were also popular. So why shouldn't a player be allowed to back himself?

Now, the GAA didn't exactly encourage gambling. It wasn't like every player always had twenty-five bucks riding on himself for each game. Mulholland said, that in fact, it was a very small percent of his business, before adding, "I don't want to know."

Regulations were in place. Bookies couldn't set up shop at GAA grounds—there was no chance of grabbing a hot dog and soda and laying down €50 on your team to win by four points while on your way back from the concession stand. The GAA also barred horse racing and greyhound racing on its property. Other than that, it was fair game. The grapevine sometimes had chatter about a club coach placing a bet, and then using his winnings to pay for a team trip.

A team trip—not for a new car for himself. And that was the other main reason why gambling was no big deal: the lifeblood of the GAA was the pride of the parish. I know it sounded corny. It reeked of *Hoosiers* and something out of a 1950s sitcom. But that was all I kept hearing—*the pride of the parish.* Then I thought back to when I covered high school football. Bitter rivals would be fifteen minutes down the road and the best reward for winning was bragging rights at the mall for a year. It hit me: that was the GAA mentality. Even though these athletes were grown men, they were still representing their home and past generations of their family. They weren't being paid, and they'd never be traded, so that honor meant everything. Pride trumped money. Integrity was inherent.

"It's very hard to do something like that in a small rural area where you grow up with everyone," Boyle told me, noting that there could be a hundred practices in a season, which builds a close bond. "For the sake of a few euros and you go ahead and do that and it was found out, you'd be disowned—let's put it that way. I never heard of that happening."

If someone discovered that you did throw a game, Boyle recommended that "you would want to be moving out of your parish very quick after that."

Brennan, the GAA president, hammered it home for me, "Winning for your own people is worth more than anything."

Okay, I came to be convinced that players could both gamble on themselves and maintain integrity. Joe Kenny wouldn't let me think otherwise. I met the thirty-eight-year-old Leitrim parish man at his house, a two-minute walk from the field. Kenny was in his front yard hitting a hurling ball with his two young sons, like a father would toss a baseball to his boy. Green farms and healthy cows surrounded us for miles in all directions. That was basically the snapshot of the two villages. I arrived for a couple weeks in mid-August en route to Cork for the All-Ireland hurling final build-up. I needed to stay in the next town of Loughrea, which also wasn't an urban center, but had a long main street and a handful of B&Bs. Kilnadeema and Leitrim acted as forty-minute commuting homes for Galway city, the Gotham of the West. Go even further, and you'd hit the popular tourist stops of Connemara and the Aran Islands, known for their traditional Irish lifestyle. Sport was one of the few things that gave these otherwise cookie-cutter parishes an identity. (Traditional Irish music was another—famous accordion player Joe Burke was from Kilnadeema.) The GAA has always had a hold in the area. Peter Kelly, the Association's third president from 1889-1895, hailed from Kilnadeema. And the first unofficial GAA meeting took pace in Loughrea on August 15, 1884. The plaque marking the spot sat next to a dry cleaner. (Nationalists officially formed the GAA in the billiard room of the Miss Hayes's Commercial Hotel in Thurles, County Tipperary, on November 1, 1884.)

While other parts of the county favored Gaelic football, this eastern section of Galway was a hurling conclave. Powerhouses like Atherny and Sarsfields had a collection of All-Ireland medals. In fact, Galway teams had reached nine of the last fifteen finals with six wins.

"Here is real hurling country," Kenny told me on his couch over tea. "There's no competition. You have no football, you have no rugby and you basically have no soccer. So you really have one game, which is hurling. Parents—they don't mind their children hurling."

The local rivalries were intense, and Kilnadeema and Leitrim used to battle each other in derby games with plenty of extracurricular violence. Through the years, both achieved success at the junior level. In 1975, players put aside their egos to jell into one club because of sparse numbers (that was in a time of high emigration). In 1981, the club split but rejoined in 1995 because both parishes were again having trouble filling teams.

Each season, adult teams were promoted and relegated divisions depending how well they did. In 1999, K/L finally reached the senior level with an intermediate championship, a great moment for the parishes. But the new expectations weren't high. After all, the last senior success occurred in 1908 when Kilnadeema were county runners-up. Nearly a century later, the hurlers struggled with an overall 0-11-1 record in three years during the county tournament's main draw. K/L's success came in dodging demotion and remaining on senior level. (The bottom two teams in each group were placed in a relegation tournament.)

But they saw a light. For one thing, K/L didn't always embarrass itself with several close defeats. Eventually, the players figured, a couple wins had to come just on karma alone. The roster had talent including the four Tierney brothers, headlined by David, a star for Galway's inter-county team. Kenny, the manager, sensed they were on the cusp and brought in a conditioning coach, who stressed a professional approach. The players never before focused on eating the right foods, thinking like winners and sticking to a weight-training regimen. From January to March, the team rented an all-weather playing field in Galway city once a week under floodlights for €100 a session, practiced another day at their home field and strengthened muscles at a gym an additional three nights a week. This was heady stuff for a team not used to perks and giving an all-out commitment.

So internally, no matter the odds, Kilnadeema/Leitrim had high expectations. Throw in the perceived insult of being placed at 33/1—the next closest team in their group was at 6/1 odds—and the hurlers had a motive for success. Then, there was the bet. Everyone in the county seemed to know about it after K/L's two wins. Underdogs were always likable as it was, but K/L had something else going for it.

"A lot of people were rooting for us because the bookmaker wouldn't be the most popular guy anyway—any bookmaker," said Kenny, echoing the same sentiments about anyone trying to take your money whether it was a tax agent or a parking meter checker or a black jack dealer in Atlantic City, not to mention a bookmaker in rural Ireland.

So with the spotlight on, K/L had its chance to jar the odds. The opponent, Carnmore, was an established senior club that reached three finals in the last twelve years. Every season they were a tough out, and this year was no exception. The bookmakers listed them at even money to win the game, while Kilnadeema/Leitrim was at 4/1 odds. In other words, few thought K/L could pull off the stunner. A win or tie would keep them alive, and might be enough to push them through depending on the other results. A loss, and the season was over. The largest crowd K/L ever played before—6,000 fans—packed a neutral venue on a perfect late May evening. People that previously had no interest were there, cheering. Something that was unthinkable at the beginning of the season had occurred: K/L actually became the driver of a bandwagon.

Back and forth they went, neither team pulling away. K/L trailed by one at the end of regulation, and the referee added a couple minutes of injury time. Late in the session, Carnmore committed a foul, thus giving Kilnadeema/Leitrim's Kevin Molloy a free shot from the left side at forty yards away. The angle made its degree of difficulty close to a 10, and the five-foot-seven Molloy had to provide just the right slice. As the logistics danced in his head, a Carnmore coach sidled up to him on the sideline and told him the bet was hanging on the shot and he couldn't handle the pressure. In other words, "Show me the money!" But Molloy was the wrong man to mentally mess with. The thirty-six-year-old waited his whole career for this shot, all the way back to when Leitrim parish played on the junior level and the only spectators were often wives, girlfriends, kids and dogs. Plus, he had a secret weapon: Molloy made hurleys for a living. Nearly ten years ago, the carpenter decided to mix his skills with his passion. He started with a rough piece of wood from a young ash tree and molded it by sawing, shaving and polishing the block into a smooth stick that didn't give splinters. If anyone knew the sweet spot, it would be Molloy, the wood surgeon. Now, it wasn't quite like

The Natural—in which lightning split a tree to create a super baseball bat for Roy Hobbs—but in this instance, Molloy could just as well have been holding a stick of gold with its own GPS system. You don't frazzle a hurley maker. The veteran ignored the quip, looked through the visor of his helmet, knocked the ball inches in the air and connected. The ball flew through the uprights for one point and a tie. Time expired before Carnmore could get a shot off. Kilnadeema/Leitrim upset the odds and advanced. Or did they? Another game needed to determine if K/L would sneak through. One problem: the Galway county board suspended the club hurling tournament while the All-Ireland inter-county championship was on, much to the chagrin of the players. It'd be another four months before K/L knew if they had a fairytale ending.

The players weren't the only ones on edge. Alan Mulholland, the Galway bookmaker, listened to the game on the radio, not wanting to take any abuse in person. For it would be easy to say "I told you so" to the poor bookie.

But if anybody had the credentials to predict a local tournament, it was Mulholland and his family. The clan contained the GAA in their DNA. John Mulholland Bookmaker was into its fourth generation serving Galway's gamblers with the slogan "The Better Bettor." John Senior founded the shop in 1930 and passed the reins on to his son Ned, who won the 1938 All-Ireland football championship with Galway. Ned's son, John Junior, was now the owner and managing director. *His* son, Alan, also worked in the business, in-between his GAA commitments. First, he played on Galway's Gaelic football team from 1987-1997 and now coached the county's under-18 team. Mulholland dismissed any conflict of interest. After all, all GAA men need a job, and he simply entered the family business—no different than a baker or a trophy maker.

In the early 2000s, Mulholland's had eight stores that offered the regular gambling fare of horse races, overseas soccer and inter-county GAA games. But in order to grow, they needed a niche to compete against larger bookmakers like Paddy Power and Boylesports. They turned to their home turf and offered odds on the qualifying stages of the county tournament. The monopoly was great for business, but it also carried some danger. For one, Mulholland's couldn't compare odds with any other bookmaker, so they had no way of knowing if their numbers were too high or low. They also couldn't lay off the bets, a common practice that bookmakers use as a safety net against large prizes. A bookie hedges his bets by betting the other way with another bookmaker. Then the two would split the winning percentage. (Kilnadeema/Leitrim also bet a small amount with

O'Meara's. The small bookmaker accepted bets on request, and took the 33/1 odds.)

Still, Alan Mulholland felt confident even though Kilnadeema/Leitrim had favorable odds. It seemed safe—K/L were the equivalent to a horse running with a 300-pound jockey on top. The hurling dark horses were seemingly fated to struggle in the senior division once again.

One morning, someone put a chunk of money on Kilnadeema/Leitrim. In bookmakers' parlance, that was a siren going off and they often lower the odds with a lot of activity. Mulholland's accepted €600 at 33/1 odds, €600 at 25/1 and €400 at smaller odds. They made a few inquiries and learned that nothing shady was happening.

"It was such an open bet, there was nothing to be hidden, really," Boyle said. "It was such an outside bet. It wasn't like we were going to try and screw the bookies knowing something they didn't know."

At first, Mulholland's was happy to take the cash considering K/L's past record. But then things got a little testy after Kilnadeema/Leitrim remained alive.

"We happened to be caught with our pants down," Mulholland recalled. "We just had to sit and wait. It was a nervous time for us all. I got the brunt of the abuse from our fellow family members. It was my bright idea to make the book."

As Mulholland waited, so did Kilnadeema/Leitrim. The players felt tension, but what could they do? So they continued to practice and hope for the best.

"I'd come home from work," remembered Boyle, a plasterer, "and go to training, get dinner after training, go home go to bed. That was my night for six, seven months of the year."

Finally, the county championship resumed on the last Saturday of September. Kilnadeema/Leitrim had a clear scenario to reach the quarters: Clarinbridge, a powerful parish close to Galway city, needed to beat or tie Carnmore. If Carnmore won, it'd be tied with K/L and the clubs would need a playoff to determine who advanced. Clarinbridge was the group's favorite, fueled by the same players who won the Galway title two years earlier. A subsequent loss in the All-Ireland final only made them hungrier. This year, they had already qualified for the quarters, including a huge win over Kilnadeema/Leitrim. But this wasn't like a pro American team resting starters late in the season after already clinching a playoff berth. Clarinbridge last played four months ago and needed to get back into game mode. They wanted to win.

That day, some Kilnadeema/Leitrim players attended the annual Galway International Oyster Festival, but nobody missed the game. K/L's supporters were suddenly Clarinbridge fans, perhaps for the first time in the club's existence. Conveniently, they shared maroon and white colors. (K/L also bled blue on its uniform). It was another tense affair, with the outcome in doubt. Clarinbridge led most of the way, but Carnmore tied it late.

"We were mid-sweat," Boyle recalled.

It ended in a draw—the best result in Kilnadeema/Leitrim's history and they didn't even play. Afterwards, the players congratulated their new favorite team.

"We went down to their parish and bought a few drinks," said Boyle, happy to re-pay the favor.

Kilnadeema/Leitrim had turned the Galway sporting world upside down and advanced to the quarterfinals. Each K/L member who ponied up—and a handful were sorry they didn't—collected an average of €1,500 or about €15 per practice session. One daring coach won €5,000. So the money wasn't life-changing, just a nice ski trip to the Alps or car payment. As a symbol, it was priceless.

For Mulholland, it was a cost of doing business.

"Ah what could you do? When you're caught, you're caught," he rationalized. "It was painful at the time, but what could you do? If you're grumpy about it, they're not going to give you back the money. That's what you're there for."

Mulholland presented the players with an oversized check for €42,000. (The club also won €8,000 with the smaller bookmaker.) Mulholland even threw in drinks at a pub.

"I don't remember them buying one back," he deadpanned.

No, few were ever worried about the bookie. The firm made out okay, though. It now expanded to eighteen shops, stretching into nearby County Mayo.

"To tell you the truth, the publicity we got helped," Mulholland recalled with a laugh. "We've become known as the guys to go to for the local championships."

Mulholland had no problems coming up with self-defacing or tongue-in-cheek quips, such as: "It wasn't €40,000 worth of advertising." Or, "I have no doubt that they were the first semiprofessional athletes in the GAA. It had a major influence on their training methods."

So Kilnadeema/Leitrim, not exactly a rag-tag collection of hurlers but the worms trying to beat the birds, the club counted out by the experts, had reached the quarterfinals, set the bookies straight and gained respect. But the story wasn't over. Powerful Sarsfields waited. *Sarsfields.* Just that name alone brought fear onto the field. The K/L players grew up watching the nearby parish dominate for much of the 1990s. Led by star forward Joe Cooney (selected to the county's team of the century), Sarsfields became the first squad to win back-to-back All-

Irelands in 1993 and 1994, and it added another one in 1997. They had tradition, expectations and talent every year. If this was the NCAA basketball tournament, K/L was George Mason and Sarsfields was Connecticut. And remember what happened there?

The tranquil hurling conditions of summer gave way to the wet and windy Ireland of October. At times, it seemed like a hand was in the sky moving balls awry. About midway through the first half, and the score knotted at four, Kevin Molloy fired a well-placed goal and K/L took a four-point lead at halftime. In the second half, the teams traded points as Joe Cooney and his teammates desperately tried to close the gap. The favorites couldn't find any heroics. K/L held on to win by three points. The victory was as surprising—and sweeter—than just advancing to the quarterfinals. They were now legit. They took out the kingpins.

"That was our biggest day," said Kenny, the pride swelling in his voice.

Now, was it possible a club expected to lose all their games could actually win the tournament, one of the toughest in the country? Their semifinal opponent was Loughrea, from right down the road. Kilnadeema sat south of Loughrea. Leitrim was to the east. If the boundaries were drawn differently, the parishes could easily have been part of the town of over 5,000 people. Kilnadeema/Leitrim had a population of approximately 1,500, making it one of the smallest of the senior teams.

But for its size, Loughrea hadn't dominated. Its last senior championship came in 1941. Other sports like rugby, soccer and Gaelic football cut into hurling's hold in the town. This was a winnable game for Kilnadeema/Leitrim. With eleven minutes left, K/L led by three points. A spot in the finals seemed certain. But things have a way of changing quickly in sports. A Kilnadeema/Leitrim forward got smacked in the head. His teammates looked on in concern as he withered in pain. After five minutes, he groggily went off. The delay sapped away K/L's momentum and spirit. Loughrea scored a point, then another and things slowly started to slip away for K/L. Loughrea dominated down the stretch en route to an eight-point victory. Again, think George Mason. The mid-major school had its improbable 2006 NCAA basketball tournament run end with a tough loss in the semis to Florida. K/L, too, couldn't reach the final.

"Inexperience caught us on the day," Kenny chagrined. "And I don't know if we fully believed we could do it. Belief is a huge thing. I don't think we believed fully that we could actually do it."

Looking back, the loss was nothing to be ashamed of. Loughrea started a run of reaching three county finals in four years. In 2006, the town finally won the championship and reached the All-Ireland final. Kilnadeema/Leitrim, on the other hand, went in the opposite direction. It got relegated back to the intermediate division after one win in 2004, despite returning most of the players. The off-season preparation wasn't nearly as intense. As Boyle admitted, "it was just a complete anticlimax."

I found club members optimistic that they could soon return to the senior level and make another run. They were also realistic. The club's player pool remained small compared to larger parishes. Plus, it was difficult sacrificing time from work and your family every season.

"Hard to do it every year in a small club," explained Kenny, who didn't mince words. "Hard to do it. You'll get that kind of effort once every three, four, five years. You won't get it every year because it takes serious training. Serious gym work. Serious organization. Serious commitment from players. No alcohol. Three to four days a week training. Teamwork. You know, huge, huge effort. Can be done, but you won't do it on small numbers in a small area over a period of time. The successful parishes have better numbers, higher quality players and don't have to do as much as we have to do to get there."

Two-thousand-and-three showed Kilnadeema/Leitrim could challenge at the highest hurling level. And while the money was nice, it didn't appear in the record books. The club's thorough Web site didn't even mention it. The oversized check wasn't framed and mounted at the field. Rather, it sat in Boyle's basement against the wall near a snooker table.

"The money was of course brilliant when it happened, but the fact of getting to the quarterfinal—that alone was fantastic," Boyle said. "We would have given up all the money to get that far."

"It wasn't the money," Kenny confirmed. "It wasn't that big a deal. It was lovely to win it, but nobody really did it for the money."

He stopped for a second, wanting to make sure that I understood him.

"You might find that hard to believe, and it's a strange thing for you," he continued. "It was lovely to get a couple quid out of it on the finish, but it was very small on the list. The achievement was the achievement on the game. How well the team did, how well the club did. The feel-good factor. Your area—county semifinal."

The *county semifinal.* To the members of these two small villages, the county semifinal's importance equaled a Super Bowl appearance.

"It's a huge county," said Kenny, proud to the end. "You were there in the last four. It was brilliant."

Before I left, I noticed that a former player had donated a greyhound racing dog to the club for a raffle fundraiser. So why didn't the team just run the dog and raise money by backing it?

"He wasn't good enough," Boyle said with a laugh. "Ah, but he's not too bad. He's a good breed."

Chapter 7
Hurling Under Bright Lights
Mid-August to mid-September: Cork city

Lunch hour at a popular restaurant seemed like a harmless meeting spot to interview Seán Óg Ó hAilpín. But with the All-Ireland final in eight days, it would have turned into anonymity suicide for the Cork hurling captain. Everyone had an opinion, everyone had a game plan, everyone wanted to wish him luck. So Ó hAilpín decided to pass on a sandwich after surveying the people starting to roll in. He motioned for me to get into his car and performed a U-turn to the back parking lot.

He joked that his freshly trimmed curly dark locks was for undercover purposes. Very funny. What newspaper didn't show his picture in the last few weeks? Later in the year, RTÉ named Ó hAilpín (pronounced O-Hal-Peen) Ireland's sports Personality of the Year, and a political party recruited him to run for office. Ó hAilpín appreciated all the attention, but right now he just wanted to focus on the upcoming final against Galway. A crowd of over 80,000 was expected to jam Croke Park. A pair of tickets were listed for €1,200 on eBay. The press box was full.

Ó hAilpín, though, faced distractions everywhere. Last week, he gave interviews during his day job as a commercial lender and took time off to attend a press conference. As the captain, he couldn't blow off a request. He also couldn't ignore his clients and their questions. On the Monday before the final, he planned on staying a few hours late to finish loan applications. To clear his mind, Ó hAilpín would be using three vacation days before the game. Then, he hoped to take the following week off for either celebrating or moping, but first had to check in with his secretary to see how busy they were.

Ó hAilpín was telling me this in the safety of the back parking lot, several rows deep. His cover lasted only a few minutes. A butcher he knew waved. Others noticed him, whispered, but left him alone.

One woman couldn't resist and tentatively walked over.

"Sorry, Seán can you give my twins your autograph?"

"Yeah, do you have a ..."

Ó hAilpín searched around for a pen and a paper. He asked for the spellings of the eight-year-old boys' names, and prepared the treasured keepsakes. The woman moved her closed lips slightly up, sending two signals—she was surprised and impressed. The two boys reverentially kept their distance but came in for a glimpse.

"And hopefully they'll be like you now someday because they're playing for Na Piarsaigh."

Na Piarsaigh was Ó hAilpín's club team, based in the city's northside. He asked who their coaches are.

"Oh, yeah I know those guys, good guys."

Mom, being an adoring mother, needed to get a plug in.

"Timothy will be out playing hurling at ten past eight in the morning."

"Oh yeah, before school? Get on."

"He loves the hurling."

Ó hAilpín reached through the passenger window.

"There we are. That one's for Tristan—the first one—then Timothy."

"Thanks very much."

"OK, good stuff."

Adoration like that wasn't so terrible, and it brought benefits like when Ulster Bank recruited him a few years ago from another bank.

"That's the perks with the job," Ó hAilpín conceded. "When you are noticed and you have a bit of a profile it gets your foot in the door in a lot of things, but then again that only gets you so much. You've got to have the experience and the know-how to do business. Just because you're a good hurler doesn't mean you're going to be a good banker."

A client might be honored to meet you, but after that, he's more concerned that his €250,000 loan funds properly. Because when you're dealing with money, being an all-star banker is more important than someone who's idolized for swinging a stick at a little ball.

Welcome to the big time in the GAA. In 2005, the senior All-Ireland hurling and football tournaments drew 1.8 million fans and brought in €22 million in gate receipts. The finals always attract high TV ratings. Huge expectations are placed on inter-county players. Many live Draconian lifestyles during the season, practicing or working out every night, observing strict diets and abstaining from alcohol. They go to work sore and bruised, and are vilified if something goes wrong on the field.

See where the amateur status might clash with the cash register?

The GAA was among the world's last major sporting organizations to remain amateur. Ten years ago, the international Rugby Union went professional, and American Olympic medal winners were now paid bonuses by the U.S. Olympic Committee. In Ireland, though, the GAA player must dip into his own pocket and suffer at work in order to compete.

"It's like hang on a wee second here," Antrim football captain Kevin Madden told me a few months earlier. "We're bringing in all this money for the GAA and it's actually costing us? We're providing the entertainment. It's going everywhere except into our pockets. There has to be a happy medium somewhere."

Finding that medium was the latest dilemma in the GAA. It went beyond greed. For years, players felt like they'd been taken advantage of by not always receiving proper expenses for travel, uniforms, healthcare and not being allowed to take endorsement money. A players' association formed in late 1999 to look after the athletes' welfare and to establish a set of standards for each inter-county team. Polls found that the majority of players wanted to make the GAA semiprofessional. The GAA administrators, however, argued that it must remain amateur because volunteerism was the strength of the organization. Plus, there wasn't enough money to sustain professionalism on the small island. The Association, in turn, annually pumped millions back to the counties and into the games' development—just not into individual pockets.

The clash over the cash often involved the Cork hurling team, a storied and high-profile squad chock full of stars. So this was the right place to examine the issue of creeping professionalism in the GAA. I went to Cork for the buildup to the All-Ireland hurling championship on, of all days, September 11.

"You're from the Garden State, aren't you?"

I was impressed that Ó hAilpín knew my home state's nickname, let alone where New Jersey was located.

"I know there's an airport there," he said, searching for the name before remembering Newark. "When I was in America I tried to get familiar with the geography of the place."

A few years ago, he spent the summer in New York, learning about American athletes like big NFL lineman Tony Siragusa and surly pitcher Randy Johnson. I told Ó hAilpín he was sort of like an Irish Derek Jeter.

"That's wishful thinking," he said. "Wishful thinking, wishful thinking."

But that was a good comparison in many ways. Ó hAilpín's got a clean-cut, hard working image and he doesn't drink. The morning after Cork won the All-Ireland title last year, Ó hAilpín stunned nearly everyone by showing up for breakfast in workout clothes—he'd just come back from a run.

His allure included an exotic mix and women adored his olive skin. His mother was from the small Fiji island of Rotuma, his father from County Fermanagh in Northern Ireland. They met while his dad worked as a laborer in Australia during the 1970s. Ó hAilpín grew up in Sydney and played Gaelic football with other Irish ex-pat kids. The family moved back to Ireland, choosing Cork when Ó hAilpín was ten, and he added hurling, the city's game of choice. He immediately excelled with his work ethic and naturally athletic body. He made the Cork football and hurling teams, becoming a rare dual player on the inter-county level. After a knee injury in a 2001 car accident, Ó hAilpín focused on hurling. Last season, journalists named the twenty-eight-year-old the Player of the Year after leading Cork to its record twenty-ninth All-Ireland title. He also captured the county title with Na Piarsaigh, thus earning Cork's captaincy this year. (In Cork, the county champions get to select the inter-county team's captain with one of its members. The criteria differed among counties.)

I asked Ó hAilpín about the professionalism issue. He recalled when an uncle visited from Vancouver, Canada, a few years ago. Ó hAilpín was still living at home and unable to afford a car.

"He couldn't believe it," Ó hAilpín remembered. "He fucking couldn't believe it. I was like twenty-one, twenty-two years of age and he said 'You're still living at home with all the money you're making?' I said 'No Peter, I don't make any money from it.'"

The uncle was dumbfounded.

"He said, 'You're not like the ice hockey players back home?,'" Ó hAilpín recalled. "I said 'No Peter, it's different here.'"

I had the same reaction as his uncle did back in the summer of 2002 when I was first introduced to the GAA's setup. At the time, though, I wondered if it was more like the players don't get paid, *wink wink*. I imagined a system similar to SMU football in the 1980s and in other college recruiting scandals where a fat cat booster gave a star €50,000 and a car just for being a nice guy. In essence, the players were fulltime pros, but everything was done under the table.

So, I kept my ears open, sort of conducting my own Woodward/Bernstein investigation. Now, seven months into my trip, I still hadn't discovered any juicy details or sensational nuggets. I decided to tell Ó hAilpín my theory anyway.

"No, that's not like that for me," Ó hAilpín replied, more amused than defensive. "No, no, no, no. I wish it was. It's not like that for me. When I work it's full on.... I'd love for someone to give me thirty grand in the morning but it doesn't happen."

Well, of course he wouldn't admit it, but my investigative efforts went nowhere. There were no brown envelopes, just perks. Most of the top players got a free automobile and that was about it. The parking lot of a Cork practice displayed dozens of cars with sponsor names and phone numbers across their bodies. Ó hAilpín drove a red Ford Focus Zetec with "Courtesy Car Compliments Of CAB Cavanaghs At Blackrock" painted on its side along with the dealership's Web site. Instead of coming off as tacky, the cars and their advertisements were almost like a trophy, seen as a reward and recognition of your worth. Some elite players had deals with clothing and shoe companies—Ó hAilpín got Adidas gear for free—and teams received benefits from their sponsors. For example, O2 phone company gave Cork players free cell phones (but not free service). Stars might appear in commercials. A potato chip ad recently featured Ó hAilpín, for which he said he received a couple thousand euros. A nice bonus, but not enough to pay the mortgage. So Ó hAilpín must work 9 to 5 like any other schlep. But he was in the spotlight just like any other millionaire athlete.

"They want it both ways," he said in a can't win tone.

The conflict was especially difficult in the run-up to the All-Ireland final with the hype everywhere.

"There's so much pressure you can't walk down the street," Ó hAilpín explained. "'You going to win it this year?' 'You going to win it this year?' There's a lot of pressure. The manager, like if we lose Sunday week, he'd be seen as a failure even though we got to the final. I'd be very happy to train once a week if there wasn't so much made out of winning the All-Ireland. But because there's a lot of pressure, you have to train professionally to win it. You're wasting your time [otherwise] because other counties are doing it—because *they're* put under a lot of pressure. It's very competitive. It's a dogfight."

So in a world of oxymorons, the elite players had voluntarily become professional amateurs because they had no other choice.

"There's no gun put to your head to eat properly, but it's back to the professional thing," he continued. "If you want to compete and play well because of the pressure that's put on you, you've got to eat well. I'd love to eat chips every day. I'd eat chips every day and burgers. I have no problem, like. But if I eat chips or whatever, I won't perform properly. You've got to eat pasta, rice, potatoes, vegetables, fruit, chicken, lean red meat, cereals. No fries, no anything. No cakes. No chocolates. No sweets, no nothing."

Ó hAilpín played the GAA sports instead of soccer or rugby for a specific reason. He told me, "Dad wanted me to play hurling and Gaelic just to keep the Irish culture going." Ó hAilpín felt a connection to his heritage. Remember, he spoke Irish fluently and enjoyed reading books in the language. He also took pride in his county.

"Whenever you wear a Cork jersey you're always reminded of the great men that wore it before you," said Ó hAilpín, pausing to take a sip of water. "You're always compared to past players like 'that guy reminds of me Willie Walsh who used to play for Cork in the '50s.' It is a huge honor."

So Ó hAilpín wouldn't be playing if he didn't want to. But when he saw the money that was out there, when 82,000 fans paid €60 a ticket to watch his team play in the final, he wondered why players couldn't get a percentage of the gate. Especially, when he gives up his weekends and misses family events for games and training.

Ó hAilpín knew about the other side. His two younger brothers, Setanta and Aisake, played professional Australian rules football. Setanta signed two years ago, leaving the Cork hurling team. Aisake followed a year later. The moves weren't perceived as a slap to Irish culture. Players and fans showed support, and newspapers monitored their progress.

"I was the first to shake [Setanta's] hand," Ó hAilpín proudly said. "I said 'I hope you make it and I'm 100 percent behind you.' He was kind of unsure about leaving here because Australia's a long way away. I said, 'Look, you only get very rare opportunities in your life and this is an opportunity—go for it.'"

The GAA occasionally lost players to Australia or to professional soccer, both overseas and in the domestic league. If given a financial choice, those athletes might never have left.

"My brother said if the GAA was paying him, he'd get up at three o'clock in the morning. He'd have no problem."

As our chat was coming to an end, still in Ó hAilpín's car tucked in the restaurant's back parking lot, I noticed two CDs between the seats—the best of the Bangles and Simon & Garfunkel. Not exactly the trendiest of music for a young athletic idol. You figure he'd have Eminem or 50 Cent or maybe a Nirvana or Beastie Boys CD, if you want to go back to recent retro cool. Nah, he went with the soft stuff your mother listens to. He pulled out more CDs from the glove compartment and the side door pocket—Billy Joel, Boyz II Men, Nelly, Bananarama, Huey Lewis & The News and famous Irish band The Pogues. We talked about his varied musical tastes and he performed a mini concert, popping in discs and churning out choruses. His voice didn't quite make the windows crack, but I'm afraid Simon Cowell wouldn't be too pleased. Ó hAilpín's not at all embarrassed, and as he belted out the songs, he stopped to mention which among the artists wrote their own songs and played instruments. Still, what if his fans saw him singing these songs?

"They'd tell me to get my balls reattached," he said, shrugging. "I like talent. But guys my age, they'd laugh at me. It's not like pop or rock, but I appreciate true class."

Cork had many high-profile players, but perhaps first-year manager John Allen dangled on the hottest stove. The fans expected a repeat, and it was his leadership that would be analyzed.

Allen agreed to meet me five days before the championship at the elementary school where he taught. He was dressed in a light pink shirt and a blue tie featuring an interesting square pattern. Not wild, just interesting. He wore glasses, and the distance from his nose to ear seemed longer than usual, and the extended frames gave him the look of a deep thinker. Near the school's entrance were photos of students and two pictures showing cutout heads—of Irish presidents and GAA presidents. The red and white colors of Cork were bursting everywhere, from balloons taped to the windows to intertwined looping bunting.

"It's like Santa's kingdom," Allen commented as we passed a bulletin board with streamers and Cork flags on the way to room No. 5 on the second floor.

I didn't see a creaky blackboard with chalk, just a sleek, shiny white board and markers. A couple hurling helmets still in the plastic wrapper sat in one corner next to a sliotar, the hurling ball. Posters hung on the wall showing Munster provincial football and hurling all-stars. Basic conversational phrases and the months of the year were written in Irish on the board. The chairs rested on top of each desk, the students long gone. Allen had an hour to chat before he needed to leave for a school meeting. Later, he'd head to the evening practice and pick the starting team for the final along with his assistants.

Coaching kept him busy, no?

"Oh, jeez, it takes over every moment, really, once you start playing the championship series—all your days and all your nights," Allen told me as he clutched his folded knee, sitting slightly slouched on a chair. "You're either planning or you're at meetings or you're at training or you're watching videos or you're watching games. So it does. It's fulltime in every respect."

The school was near his club, St. Finbarr's on the city's southside. It wasn't far from the airport and a wildlife reserve, where the silver maples and turkey oaks lined a lake that housed various species of geese, swans and ducks all peacefully co-existing. Allen played both football and hurling, compiling a haul of medals, including the 1976 and 1978 hurling All-Ireland championships with Cork. If he wasn't coaching, he'd be a Cork fan. Allen loved that connection you kept with your hometown team.

"There's a fierce sense of loyalty to that," he said before laying out a nightmare scenario for him: the players got paid and another county team enticed one of his guys with cash and a loophole—like his mother was born there—that made it legal for him to switch counties. "You've then broken that great county loyalty or parish loyalty and then it starts. Somebody else buys somebody else. And then you have what happens in the soccer, where this fella plays with this team for two years and then he moves on. Then the fans boo him and they give him the finger and there's trouble amongst the fans in the terraces because they all hate this player who was their hero two years ago."

I knew what he meant. We had the NFL, Major League Baseball, NBA, NHL, and even NASCAR. Just look at baseball star Johnny Damon who jumped from the Boston Red Sox to their nemesis, the New York Yankees, for more money in the winter of 2005. But imagine if baseball was an Irish sport for a second. Damon would never have even made it to Boston, but instead would still be playing for the small-market Kansas City Royals where he started his career. Just think about an international soccer star like David Beckham, who could wind up in of all places shiny Los Angeles.

Allen would hate to see that movement occur in the GAA.

"You would then lose that sense of parochialism and parish. And I could see then how one of our big players, [star defender] Diarmuid O'Sullivan or Seán Óg moves to Clare and we would all hate him then."

Loathing Seán Óg—unimaginable in Cork. So from a fan's perspective, the GAA system was great. A boy could cheer for his hero and then not have to worry about him fleeing the next year for greener pastures. The manager, though, was still scrutinized like in the U.S. Take the All-Ireland semifinal on August 14, when Cork rallied to edge upset-minded Clare by a single point. Allen made two surprise substitutions in the second half, moves which sparked the tight win. If it didn't work, Allen's head would have been on the chopping block.

Despite the pressure, he didn't expect to be rewarded financially.

"I wouldn't be for professionalism, per se," said Allen, not even tempted by the fruits of a bidding war between rich owners. "The players do need to be treated a bit better with their expenses. But realistically, how much money is available for that? How much money is actually available in each club, considering you have got many, many volunteers in every club who train the teams and put out the nets and who cut the fields and who run the lotto. They don't get paid. Nobody gets paid anything. They all do it voluntarily. So there is a lot more to this professionalism than meets the eye."

Ironically, the GAA turned a blind eye to managers getting paid. Some teams brought in top tacticians from other counties and put down several thousand under "expenses." Usually, if someone managed his own county's team he wouldn't get paid, like Allen. So the Cork skipper continued on in what was a dream job for many, chalking up the time commitment as a necessary cost.

"Sport and music are my passions," Allen concluded. "I like mixing with sports people. There are a lot of good things that go with being a manager. You get free tickets to concerts or the odd meal now and then. And lots of people want to talk to you, you know, when you're winning."

Unfortunately, I didn't get a mini-concert of his favorite tunes. But while Allen was now the toast of Cork, what would fans say if they lost on Sunday?

"Get rid of him. Anything less is not good enough for them."

Allen said that with a chuckle. He knew the score and didn't mind.

The player movement that started in the late 1990s actually had its roots a century ago. In 1908, four Cork hurlers went on strike before a Munster championship. Star player Jamesy Kelleher wrote to *The Cork Sportsman* complaining of waking up at six in the morning for a game, walking six miles to a train station, then trekking half a mile to play before reversing the entire routine to finally arrive home at three in the morning.

"Give me the name of the County Board man who will do it?" he wrote. "I have seen, to my disgust, the players draw the crowds, make the money and lose their sweat in many a hard game, while the gentlemen at the head of affairs take charge of the bag and jump into their cars before the match is over to head back to their hotel to count the coin made by the rank and file."

Players are still drawing crowds and losing their sweat, while county officials count the coin. But it was a different era back then. The country was so poor that getting paid just wasn't an option. Players worked long, hard hours, usually in blue collar and farm jobs. Training regiments weren't nearly as sophisticated or time consuming. Donning a county jersey was seen as payment in itself. Their sporting fame helped players secure jobs, even run for political office. Through the 1970s and 1980s, the games' popularity continued to grow, as did player resentment.

"The players were sort of frowned upon," said Dessie Farrell, today the Gaelic Players' Association (GPA) chief executive. "The great catch phrase that has been used on a regular basis every year, I think—'Wouldn't it be a great association except for the players.'"

The GAA had to change with the times and finally allowed team commercial sponsorship in 1991, and individual endorsements in 1997. In stark contrast to U.S. pro teams, business names were displayed across jersey fronts instead of the city or team name. Current ones ranged from a whiskey maker to a mineral water company. Every major competition was also sponsored, similar to American college football bowl games. It was the Guinness All-Ireland Hurling. The Bank of Ireland football. Allianz did the national leagues. A.I.B. Bank took care of the club championship. Vodafone sponsored the all-stars and the player of the month awards. Coca Cola splurged for the international rules series against Australia and for an under-14 competition. Toyota presented a car to the senior All-Ireland finalists and to the club and national league champions (the winners usually raffled the cars as fundraisers). Cadbury did the under-21 football championships. Erin, a food company, the under-21 hurling. Electricity Supply Board, a utility company, handled the under-18 football and hurling championships. Datapac, an IT business, the college championship. McDonalds sponsored a skills competition. M. Donnelly & Co. Ltd, a power tools distributor, sponsored the interprovincial tournament. Vhi Healthcare did the summer camps.

Millions more were pumped into the GAA through clothing companies and from the radio and TV stations airing games.

The players saw all that money swirling about and started to question how they were treated. In 1986, athletes formed a short-lived players' association, but it folded because of player disinterest. In September 1999, the GPA organized. Their goal wasn't a pay-for-play stance, but rather player welfare issues such as out-of-pocket expenses and proper facilities. But the GAA refused to recognize it, and administrators and coaches attacked the union in the press. The GAA even re-formed its own player council, which the athletes largely ignored. This time, their voices were here to stay. The bookmaker Paddy Power offered 50/1 odds on whether the GAA would turn professional before 2005. While that proved to be a losing bet, the players made financial strides.

"We've had our ups and downs," Farrell reflected as the sixth-year anniversary of the GPA approached. "It has been very difficult to take on the might of the GAA and the strength and influence that they can bring to bear on any particular situation. But nonetheless we've succeeded. And I think our greatest success is the fact that we have established ourselves and we're still in existence six years down the line.... I think our players are more militant now and see the commercial merry-go-round for what it is."

From the beginning, the GPA challenged the status quo. In early 2000, the GAA established an endorsement policy in which all deals must go through their hired sponsorship agency. A player kept 50 percent of the money with 30 percent going to a team fund, 10 percent to a hardship fund for current or former players and 10 percent to a general fund that would benefit the players. The GPA said wait a minute, the player should keep more and negotiated its own deal with another agency in which ten stars got to keep 80 percent (20 percent went to the GPA). The GAA threatened suspensions, but nothing happened and it abandoned its policy two years later.

More battles with the GAA ensued. Some were successful, some not. A campaign to get county players a weekly €127 allowance failed, as did securing tax breaks for the athletes. Other things worked, like getting mileage reimbursements raised from a low of ten cents per mile for some counties to the current fifty cents per mile set in 2004. Not every county board treated its teams the same, so the GPA lobbied for—and received—a uniform set of standards covering post-practice meals, proper allocation of equipment, warm-up clothes and the number of tickets each player gets.

The GPA needed to fund itself, and using the GAA mentality of self-reliance, accepted €350,000 in July 2002 to officially be known as "The Carphone Warehouse Sponsored GPA." The bravado of the GPA emboldened its members, which found loopholes like a good accountant. GAA rules stated that players must wear uniforms made by Irish companies, but didn't mention cleats. So, six stars signed with Puma in 2003 in the first individual shoe deals for a reported €6,000 to €7,000 per year. When it came to branding names on playing gear, just the manufacturer and the squad's official sponsor were permitted. Jerseys, shorts, socks, tracksuits and duffle bags were specifically included, but hurleys weren't. So three players—including Ó hAilpín—accepted €750 each to advertise a bookmaker's name on their sticks for a 2003 All-Ireland semifinal. Though they were threatened with suspension, nothing happened. A furious GAA President Seán Kelly ripped the bookmaker, calling it "ambush marketing" and "a cheap shot" and "unprofessional" because it circumvented the intent of the GAA's rules and it wasn't officially approved. Plus, it'd probably draw the ire of the GAA's paying sponsors. The message was sent: additional players pulled out of the deal for the following weekend's other semifinal game. Nobody, though, could claim victory. Commentators thought the players were exploited because of the low payment and used terms like "fall guys" and "pawns." A sports management consultant criticized the GPA for not looking after the players' commercial interests.

The controversies continued while I was in Ireland. Big money wasn't involved, but instead revealed what amateur athletes were willing to do to earn some cash. I couldn't help but contrast their struggles to grab three or four figures to former NBA player Latrell Sprewell's plight in the fall of 2004. Sprewell, who was making $14.6 million a year, turned down a three-year contract extension reportedly worth $21 million a season saying, "I've got my family to feed."

Sometimes, you don't know how good you have it. I observed GAA stars of Sprewell's stature battling RTÉ to hold bottles of the sports drink Club Energise during interviews for €500 per game. RTÉ banned the display saying it doesn't allow product placement. Players involved, including several Cork hurlers, subsequently refused the microphone and a whole mess ensued. RTÉ and GPA eventually brokered a deal whereby the players wouldn't drink Club Energise on the air. RTÉ, in return, would provide benefits to the GPA, including coverage of its events.

Then, in almost a repeat of the 2003 incident of players advertising on their sticks, two Cork hurlers sported Corona Extra on their cleats during the quarter-final for a reported €500 each. GAA officials complained that it clashed with Guinness' sponsorship of the All-Ireland tournament. Commentators again claimed the players were exploited for the low amount. The GAA promised to clear up any ambiguities in the rulebook, but one thing was clear: players still felt they deserved some of the money that was out there.

The GPA, which stayed clear of the beer controversy, strived to make sure the players weren't taken advantage of. Shortly after I left Ireland, the first-ever GAA PlayStation 2 game was released. The GPA blocked Sony from using individual players in the game because they couldn't work out a deal over image rights.

Farrell, a former Dublin football captain, was the face of the players during these rows. GPA members voted the thirty-four-year-old—once a nurse in a psychiatric hospital—their first chairman in 2000. In May 2002, he was named the first GPA chief executive in a fulltime and paid position. In June, the GAA appointed him as the player representative to its Central Council, an unofficial recognition of the GPA's influence and presence. An afternoon text message breaking the news to GPA members was the equivalent of the excited shout of a town crier.

I met Farrell in the GPA office in Dublin on Lower Drumcondra Road, not far from Croke Park. This was a splendidly busy time for Farrell. His club team was competing in the Dublin championships. His autobiography was being serialized the following week in Dublin's *Evening Herald*. It caused a stir with several juicy details, including that Farrell tried to organize a players' revolt against Dublin manager Tommy Lyons—a different Tommy Lyons than the one who managed Ballina—in 2003 because of clashes with the coach's attitude and decisions. He also wrote how his dedication to football was one of the factors in breaking up his marriage.

So Farrell understood what players endured. As Seán Óg Ó hAilpín told me, the time commitment does not go unnoticed in the work world. Having a GAA "name" helped in certain professions, particularly in sales where you were using any advantage to close the deal, but it didn't aid everywhere.

"The word coming back is, you know, it's not necessarily the greatest thing to have on your CV," Farrell warned, "that you're an inter-county player that trains five, six times a week and might be wrecked on a Monday morning or injured for part of the year because of your football or hurling commitments. [But given] the level of commitment required, sacrifices have to be made somewhere. And they generally tend to be at home or in the workplace."

The GPA didn't just lobby for the star players. For example, it gave out college scholarships in conjunction with Club Energise, and a percentage of each bottle sold went to the GPA. The majority of players would never see endorsement money.

"If you were to examine it very closely, I'd imagine the teams operating at the lower levels have more to gain than the teams, for example, who play at Croke Park on Sunday," said Farrell, pausing to take a post-lunch yawn. "Or, some of the better, high-profile teams because they tend to be very well looked after anyway as regards to player welfare.... We're trying to raise the bar for [everyone else]."

A GPA survey found that 70 percent of players thought the GAA should move to semiprofessionalism and two-thirds believed the Association could sustain it. Other findings: 92 percent of the respondents felt they should be reimbursed for loss of earnings; 75 percent attended more than five training sessions a week and played over thirty games a year; 62 percent reported that their personal life suffered from their GAA involvement, but 50 percent found that it benefited their professional life. Almost half had suffered financially as a result of injuries.

Antrim's Kevin Madden found similar views in his dissertation for a graduate degree at the University of Ulster. In 2004, the footballer surveyed three teams in the Ulster province that competed in different divisions of the National League: Tyrone, Derry and Antrim. He discovered that 69 percent wanted the GAA to turn semiprofessional.

Madden's thesis recommended that each county give their players a car and a fuel card for the season with the insurance and taxes pre-paid, a pension scheme to pay into, a cell phone and service, gym membership, a preseason vacation, private health care and special deals with mortgage companies.

Perks like those could keep the GAA amateur and the players happy. Critics of full professionalism fear the club games wouldn't be as important and go by the wayside. Farrell, himself dedicated to Dublin club Na Fianna, conceded, "there has to be a happy medium." But nobody had any solutions, and barring inter-county players from club games hadn't entered the conversation yet.

Even politicians weighed in on the touchy subject. Prime Minister Bertie Ahern said in a RTÉ Radio interview that he supported the players getting expenses, "But ask me would I like to see professionalism or semiprofessionalism with signed contracts and players bringing in their agents and I'd have to say I just can't take it. The day that will happen, when I go down to see my native Dubs and see five Cork guys and a few from Galway, Tyrone and Armagh, well, that's a wrong thing and would be a bad, bad day."

Ahern's views were the same as Cork manager John Allen. In other words, he'd hate to see the pure loyalty to one's county broken. Having a team full of stars from several different counties would be like a Lakers team with Shaq, Karl Malone and Kobe managed by Phil Jackson.

Ó hAilpín could only see the GAA having to eventually make a decision: either go back to where the games were fifty years ago, in which the players didn't put as much into training, or, make it professional in some form.

"One or the other," he proclaimed. "You can't be leaving these double standards."

In the midst of All-Ireland fever in Cork, though, the most important thing for players and fans was the upcoming game. All that other stuff might have a place, but not now. The talk focused on how Cork was going to beat Galway for its thirtieth championship. A few thousand fans attended the open practices, stopping their stars for autographs before they entered the locker room. Little kids even ran onto the field, swatting balls to one another and dreaming of one day wearing the famed red jersey.

Some players arrived early, others hustled in from work still wearing their business suits. Depending on their needs, they saw different people. Two masseurs waited. So did a team doctor. A physiotherapist. Every muscle was loosened and limbered out. This was no time for an injury.

John Allen also received help. His four assistants, called selectors, each had a different responsibility. These included working with the goalkeepers, handling the media, making sure equipment was available and helping with the logistics of organizing transportation and meals. Additionally, two trainers ran all the physical workouts and running drills. Throw in a team manager and a statistician, and the team didn't lack for support.

"There's no doubt that it's an amateur sport, but we do the whole job professionally," Mick Dolan, the county board liaison for hurling, told me at Cork's stadium and practice grounds, Páirc Uí Chaoimh, with the All-Ireland final in a few days. His phone rang nonstop with desperate fans giving it one last try for tickets.

Cork was considered to be one of the most supported and professionally run GAA teams. Especially since a sensational player strike in late November 2002. The hurlers walked out, soon joined by the footballers, in protest over player welfare issues. Specifically, the hurlers were upset at having to travel across the country for a game by coach bus instead of flying, thus having to miss a day of work, and without a team doctor. During the game, a player needed stitches for a facial injury, and the wound reopened during the bus ride home. Other problems persisted: unhealthy post-practice meals, low mileage rates, not getting gym memberships, poor facilities in the canteen area and unhappiness with the four remaining assistant coaches—the manager already quit.

After two weeks, the coaches resigned and the players got most of their demands including promises to upgrade facilities and to have a doctor at all games.

"We decided if we didn't act, we had only ourselves to blame," said Ó hAilpín, one who's never willing to take things lying down.

The strike was a bold move against an organization that usually held the power. The GAA was a fascinating mix between a democracy, socialism and big business. Every spring, the Association held a congress in which each county sent delegates to vote on GAA laws ranging from playing rules to off-the-field issues. But each province, county and club also had its own elected governing board with its unique traditions and rules. In lieu of an owner or general manager, the board took care of everything from running its teams' finances to selecting the manager (who then picked the players along with the other selectors).

The GAA central office, by comparison to American standards, seemed more fan-friendly. It admitted and apologized for the high ticket prices charged during a 2004 hurling quarterfinal replay game—€35 for seats and €20 for terraces (standing room). It also froze the All-Ireland final ticket prices for the past two years at €60 a seat. In February 2006, GAA President Seán Kelly told the *Irish Independent*, "Our financial position is strong so we don't see any need for price hikes." Yeah, that might happen in the NFL.

But where did all of the money from the GAA's fat wallet go? I wondered if someone was driving a fancy new car, while the players got screwed. So I looked at the annual report. In 2005, the GAA made €35.4 million but kept only €333,030. Just over €25 million went to expenditure costs including marketing expenses and stadium rent. (Croke Park was a subsidiary of the GAA, and the Association must pay to play there.) Also included was €2 million in salaries to fulltime employees and €840,569 in their pension costs.

Most of the dough went back into the sports—a chief GAA argument for remaining amateur. The biggest expenditure was €7,090,006 under "Games Development" and much of the €10 million operating surplus was also filed under development. Projects ranged from coaching clinics to putting heart defibrillators at county stadiums to field improvement and floodlights at provincial stadiums to giving out hurling helmets (a recent rule made it mandatory for players twenty-one and under).

The Association pumped an additional €1,195,618 million under "Grants and Donations" to places such as the provincial councils, women's Gaelic football and hurling, agricultural colleges and elementary schools. County boards received €2.4 million to cover expenses (travel, overnight stays, etc.). Included in that figure was the All-Ireland finalists receiving €80,000 for their holiday fund. The Cork hurlers, for example, were going to South Africa this winter, and in the past two years went to New Zealand, Vietnam and Thailand. The GAA also paid €1.3 million for a players injury scheme in which premiums were paid for by the county or club, assisted by a proportion of gate receipts.

So all that added up. Nickey Brennan, the GAA president beginning in April 2006, was quick to point out some of those benefits to me.

"The people who are doing all the support work and the behind the scenes are also working on a voluntary basis," Brennan noted. "It is worth bearing in mind that in 2005 counties spent in the region of 20 million looking after teams. So I think they're pretty well looked after now, despite what people might think."

The problem—costs continued to rise. The *Irish Independent* reported that county boards spent €16.7 million on teams in 2005, up 88 percent from 2001. That figure ranged from Cork's €1.2 million to Leitrim's €235,000. GAA payments did not cover a county's budget for its eight teams in hurling and football—senior, under-21, minors (under-18) and junior (lower-level adult). Financial survival, therefore, was up to each county. Not having salaries to pay helped, of course, but unlike in the U.S., teams didn't receive big bucks for selling its TV and radio rights, or even a huge share of the ticket sales. That money went straight to the GAA. For example, the GAA took in €3.6 million in ticket sales for the 2005 hurling final and €1.2 million for Cork's semifinal. The GAA paid Cork €230,839 in expenses and finalist grants, but for all its teams, not just hurling. By the time the equipment and gym memberships were paid for, Cork made a profit of €38,144, but a dozen counties lost money.

So each county and club must constantly use creative thinking. Cork raffled off the Toyota it received for reaching the championship with €100 tickets. It also sold raffles to win a house and ran golf classics in places ranging from Dublin to America. On a quick browse among teams' Web sites, I found credit unions, fast food joints, fresh fruit and vegetable shops, hotels, oil companies, an FM radio station and construction companies all sponsoring local tournaments or leagues throughout the country.

A recent, yet not widespread, fundraiser was akin to striking oil—real estate. Many GAA clubs have owned their fields for decades. In Ireland's development boom of the early 21st century, the once prime farmland suddenly sat near city centers, shopping malls and golf courses. Clubs and county boards were receiving offers to sell their club, and in some cases a deal to exchange their land for money and another piece of property in a less plum area. As I was finishing writing in early 2007, I read that Portlaoise—the team that Ballina beat in the All-Ireland club final—sold its 18-acre land for €19 million to developers planning a shopping and residential area. In turn, the club was expecting to spend €10 million on a new state-of-the-art facility.

Those sales, though, were rare and clubs needed to fend for themselves. If you wanted to develop and renovate, it was usually a case of sounds good and good luck—let us know how it goes. The GAA central office might dole out a small grant. The government's Department of Arts, Sport & Tourism gave out larger sums funded by lottery earnings, but it was never enough.

As it was, clubs weren't cheap to run. Take Na Piarsaigh (Na-peer-sig), covering Cork's gritty northside sections of Fairhill and Farranere. While it fielded football teams, the nearby North Monastery school was famed for producing young hurling talent. In 1943, a club using some of the North Mon's players split, and fifteen men led by teachers met under a lamppost on No. 3 Redemption Road to form their own club. (They had a patriotic spirit and named themselves after Padraig Pearse, who declared Ireland a sovereign nation in the 1916

Easter Rising. Their crest was a bit unusual—the red hand of Ulster with a severed thumb. The legend went, the hand was Ireland and the thumb represented the six counties of Northern Ireland. When Ireland is united, then the hand will be completed.)

Na Piarsaigh slowly grew and acquired grounds in 1957. Nowadays, it cost between €170,00 to €200,000 to run everything. Buses for kids' teams alone cost €18,000. Some years the club might make a small profit of €1,000, but be down the next year, then go up again—everything evens out. The typical revenue makers were the bread-and-butter of every GAA club: weekly lotto draws, bingo night, profits from the clubhouse bar, sponsorship from local businesses.

In 1999, the club ambitiously opened the country's first indoor hurling field at a cost of a million pounds (euros didn't become Ireland's currency until 2002). Na Piarsaigh needed bank loans of £450,000, which took five years to pay off. Few complained. Hurling morphed from a summer game into a year-round sport. Players walked out of the cold and into an arena with an ice hockey feel—with synthetic turf replacing the ice, of course. A see-through wall and fifty seats allowed parents to comfortably watch the action. The complex included a gym and sauna. Naturally, the playing demand increased, so why stop there? Na Piarsaigh was now in the midst of a three-stage development plan that was expected to cost over €4 million. The final result would be an all-weather outdoor field, two additional adult fields, a children's field and training area, floodlights, extra locker rooms and office and meeting rooms. The club had so far received €680,000 from the government. It needed to take out a €1 million bank loan.

So why do it all?

"If you stand still you go backwards," Paddy Connery, the club chairman told me. "So you have to keep pushing the boundaries and trying to improve your facilities."

Cork, being a city, had more to offer than a rural area. The several GAA clubs competed with soccer, rugby and minor sports like swimming. Na Piarsaigh needed a selling point. Kids just wouldn't come because it was the thing to do. In a way, it was similar to American pro teams building lavish new stadiums to attract fans. An owner might threaten to move his team across country and then hold out until he received full public funding. You couldn't do that in the GAA. Na Piarsaigh was also not interested in moving to another part of Cork for big bucks.

It's like a gardener planting his own tomatoes or peppers, and then checking every few days to see the growth until the produce looks juicy and plump. You take pride in starting something from the beginning, then seeing it fully develop. It means a little more than just buying a bag from a supermarket. Same thing when developing a GAA club—it is yours. In times of need, the people come together and a spirit and camaraderie emerge. Somehow, everything gets taken care of financially. For example, when the club built the indoor arena, it offered a square meter of the field for £100, and made £50,000 from the drive.

"We're where we want to be," Connery said of his home, the club that his father Liam helped start. "We're in our parish and our parish means a lot."

All the money spent, all the work exerted, went into competing for an All-Ireland championship. The hurling final was the first or second Sunday of September, and the football championship took place the third or fourth Sunday. Picture two Super Bowls back-to-back. It never gets old, no matter how many championships you win.

At the beginning of the hurling season, most observers expected a rematch from last year's final in which Cork edged Kilkenny. In the semifinal on August 21, however, upstart Galway stunned Kilkenny by three points in a high-scoring contest that was called one of the greatest games ever. Consequently, the bookies and most commentators installed Cork as the favorites.

I couldn't help but get caught up in the All-Ireland fervor. But to appreciate what a win would really mean to the people, I first had to learn about the history of the city and its past legends. For example, you don't just show up in Chapel Hill, North Carolina, to follow Tar Heels basketball without knowing the names of Dean Smith, Michael Jordan and Tobacco Road, or even the history of the South.

One thing I quickly noticed was how Cork residents took pride in being independent. Red T-shirts proclaimed it the "People's Republic of Cork." Like Chicago, Cork was a second city—119,418 people compared to Dublin's 506,211—and carried a bit of a chip on its shoulder. Pub-goers even sipped locally brewed Murphy's or Beamish over Dublin's Guinness.

The city had an attitude, promoted by the success of its athletic teams but with roots set into its tormented history. During the War of Independence from January 1919-July 1921, Cork defied British rule and acted as a stronghold of the Irish Republican Army (city native Michael Collins was the IRA's director of intelligence). The brutal fighting tested the people's will. A mayor was murdered and another died on a hunger strike. The Black and Tans, a British paramilitary force, burned the city center on December 11, 1920, razing hundreds of buildings. For all the pain, Cork couldn't be broken and earned the nickname of the

Rebel County. (They were also called the Leesiders, because two strands of the River Lee flowed through town.)

When the fighting stopped, the people's spirit continued and Cork flourished as a sporting city, full of GAA clubs, soccer teams and it hosts an international track and field meet every summer. Notable natives include distance runner Sonia O'Sullivan, winner of a silver medal in the 2000 Olympics, and former Manchester United captain Roy Keane. In Gaelic football, the Nemo Rangers, based south of downtown, owned a record seven All-Ireland club titles.

Hurling, though, was king. The city's famed southside teams of Blackrock and St. Finbarr's first played in 1876, even before the formation of the GAA. The fabled northside club of Glen Rovers dominated the 1930s, 1940s and 1950s. Songs and poems celebrating famous victories and teams were written through the years. Even today, your turf mattered.

"You have your own little identity in the middle of a big city," Michael Finn, a member of St. Finbarr's, told me as the club whooped it up in its social hall after an important win in the county hurling tournament.

Then there was the legendary Christy Ring, considered the Babe Ruth of hurling. During a career that spanned from the late 1930s to the early 1960s, he won a record eight All-Ireland inter-county titles and also bagged fourteen county championships with the Glen Rovers. Ring—known for his artistry and accuracy—was teammates and close friends with Jack Lynch, who later served two terms as the country's prime minister. Ring's premature death in 1979 of a heart attack at age fifty-eight stunned the nation; Lynch gave a moving graveside oration at the funeral proclaiming, "as long as hurling is played the story of Christy Ring will be told. And that will be forever."

You could still find him all over the city. A statue of Ring sat at the Cork Airport, while a field and a bridge took his name. Countless pictures decorated the pubs, including one with Bobby Kennedy.

Ring led Cork to an unprecedented four titles in a row from 1941-1944, a feat that had never been matched. Now, the current generation was trying to make their mark. A win would give Cork its first back-to-back championships since 1978, adding extra excitement to the game. No matter what club you claim—or what sporting code you play—everyone came together when it was All-Ireland time. Local adult soccer leagues even postponed its slate for the weekend.

So on the second Sunday of September, fans packed Cork's pubs and GAA clubs in anticipation of the traditional lead-in to an All-Ireland final. For decades, the teams got announced, conducted a warm-up, were introduced to the dignitaries like the Irish president, paraded behind the Artane Boys Band in their blue and scarlet uniforms, stood for the national anthem and then started the game before a howling crowd.

Cork fans flew their red county flags, but really, anything of that color would do including American Confederate flags, Japanese Rising Sun flags, Ferrari flags and the Canadian flag—talk about an interesting mix. Meanwhile, Galway fans waved their maroon flags. No dark colors were to be found.

While waiting for the opening drop, antsy players pushed one another near midfield. Before all mayhem ensured, the referee released the sliotar and sticks were a swinging. In the first minute, a Galway shot went wide to the relieved fans in red. Cork came right back with a point sailing fifty yards for an early lead. In the sixteenth minute, the Leesiders' Ben O'Connor struck a bullet into the lower right corner of the net for the game's first goal and a six-point lead for Cork. Galway, undeterred, charged downfield with a close shot at goal. Cork keeper Donal Óg Cusack dropped to his left and knocked the ball away as the crowd erupted. Cork set the tempo early, never trailed and cruised to a five-point victory. As players mobbed one another, Ó hAilpín accepted the Liam McCathy Cup on the Hogan Stand. He smiled, pumped his left fist into the air and delivered the victory speech in Irish, proclaiming, "This is the stuff dreams are made of." Late afternoon shadows partly covered the thousands of fans on the field, who jumped and went nuts during each of Ó hAilpín's pauses. He ended with the traditional three hip-hip hoorays for the losing team.

The two local daily newspapers, the *Irish Examiner* and *Evening Echo* carried comprehensive coverage that would normally be reserved if man walked on Mars. Before the game, they broke down every conceivable angle, ran features on the five previous Cork/Galway championship games, ran countdown boxes with X days to go and had a contest to win a helicopter trip to the game. Afterwards, their sections had photo galleries, player rankings and posters.

The day after the win, 50,000 of Cork's closest fans greeted the hurlers back in the city, capped with a parade through downtown. Five rows of bagpipers wearing kilts preceded a double-decker bus of players, who peered out from the open top. They wore tan suits and waved and pumped fists to the masses. The thousands lining the streets swung flags, snapped photos and a couple starry-eyed teenagers held "will you marry me" signs directed to their favorite player. And now, Ó hAilpín did not mind being seen.

Chapter 8
A Sporting Battlefield
Late September to early October: Dublin city

During my eight-month stay, one team brought residents in the Republic together. No matter what county, what parish, what age, they all stopped to collectively watch and curse or high-five. The team: Ireland. The sports: soccer and rugby. Because for all the passion that hurling and Gaelic football elicited, it mostly didn't leave the island. Sure, beating your neighbor was great, but global pride added another dimension. Fans in faraway continents might not know that Cork won the All-Ireland hurling title, but they could recite Éire football's World Cup record. Soccer, over the past twenty-five years, was as much an Irish export as U2, fancy crystal or dark beer.

The glamorous English Premiership added to soccer's luster. The league rivaled the GAA in media coverage. Fans developed deep loyalties to Arsenal, Chelsea, Manchester United and other teams with high-paid stars that the English tabloids covered like young Hollywood heiresses. A kid could dream of being both an international hero and a millionaire. Rugby, too. The men in green carrying the oval ball also crossed the sporting divide, especially when they had grudge matches against England and Scotland.

The GAA faced the biggest crunch in Dublin. Ireland's happening cosmopolitan capital offered activities for all tastes. The deep athletic menu included soccer and rugby, but also basketball, baseball, cricket, American football, sailing, water polo, boxing, lawn tennis, karate, judo—you name it.

"Every sport under the sun is played in Dublin at this stage," said Philip Darcy, an athlete I met who spurned the GAA for ice hockey and kickboxing.

Now, don't fret over the GAA in Dublin just yet. A fierce club scene and a prominent inter-county squad supported by passionate, vocal fans gave Dublin a front-page presence. Amateur glory lived—you were still rooting for your own. But the gloves were off, especially in the last ten to twenty years as the GAA's challengers grew stronger.

I came to Dublin on the East Coast in my final month to see just how big a threat the GAA faced. The subculture of the four major American sports, with its national teams and local leagues, also intrigued me. Just how the heck did ice hockey, baseball, American football and basketball find their way to Ireland?

Dublin was a city of choices. James Joyce or W.B. Yeats? St. Patrick's Cathedral or the Christ Church Cathedral? Guinness' St. James's Gate Brewery or Old Jameson Distillery? The Abbey Theatre or the National Gallery? These days you could add Burger King or McDonald's?

Something was always going on in a lively place that exploded at the city center. O'Connell Street zipped through downtown and jiggled on both sides. The tall space needle-like Spire, built as part of the 2000 Millennium celebration, stood in the middle of the action. Designer clothing boutiques and art galleries abounded. In 2005, Dublin tied with New York as the thirteenth most expensive city to live in—just behind Paris and Milan. Chic company, indeed. I was a long way from the rural soil of Annaduff, Kilnadeema and Quilty. Even so, Dublin was a manageable, walkable city with the River Liffey running through, and unlike urban American cities, there were no skyscrapers.

The playing fields, too, boogied with activity because of athletes like Robert Fitzgerald. On an unseasonably warm Saturday in early October, the college freshman spent the morning coaching his former high school's under-16 rugby team's practice (they needed a hand for the season and Fitzgerald wanted to give back). After an hour power nap, he rushed to play for his Gaelic football club. On Sunday, he had another football game. If you wanted to play something, the options were nearly as plentiful as mailboxes. Fitzgerald squeezed me in as he walked from the locker room to the parking lot to wait for his ride after Saturday's game in south Dublin.

"I'm used to it," he said shrugging. "I've been doing it my whole life—juggling from one game to another game. Get a lift. All that kind of stuff."

He glanced down to check his cell phone for missed calls, then stretched his neck to see if his girlfriend pulled into the lot yet.

"Soccer, Gaelic, rugby, hurling—there's everything within ten minutes of my house," Fitzgerald continued. "So it's whatever you're into. It's whatever your parents bring you to, that's what you'll play."

On the surface, Fitzgerald's juggling of sports was admirable, but not noteworthy. Athletes all over America made similar sacrifices. What caught my interest was that Fitzgerald, who also played soccer when he was younger, didn't think twice about competing in Gaelic football *and* rugby. He simply found the sports exciting and a challenge to be fit. Factors such as his political views or what his friends thought had no bearing on his decisions.

Once, they might have. The GAA traditionally held an iron-like grip over its players and facilities. The Association's rules, strict from American standards, helped stunt the growth of other sports for generations while establishing hurling and Gaelic football as a vital part of Irish life. Rule 27—known as the Ban—barred GAA members from playing or attending any foreign game. Or, more specifically: rugby, soccer, cricket and field hockey. You were either with us or against us. Introduced in 1902, it made sense as Ireland sought to strike its own identity from England. On the other side of the cultural war, the British banned GAA games in 1918, an act ignored.

After Ireland won its independence in the early 1920s, some saw that thinking as narrow-minded. Members debated the rule every three years, but little changed. In 1938, for example, the GAA removed Ireland's president Dr. Douglas Hyde as its patron for attending an international soccer game. Even a top political official performing a ceremonial role wasn't spared. Suspensions of double-dipping athletes continued through the decades, including star Waterford hurler Tom Cheasty being forced to miss the 1963 National League final for going to a dance held by a soccer club. You couldn't even two-step on the wrong floor. Some teams looked the other way, but just to be safe you'd better wear a fake mustache. A Vigilance Committee, sort of the Ban police, staked out soccer and rugby games to bust GAA members. In the late 1960s, a committee re-examined the issue, and in 1971 the Ban was unanimously lifted. Soccer and rugby had long stopped being viewed as sports of the enemy—just other fast-paced activities. It wasn't as if Irish babies were born with genes disliking rugby.

The floodgates opened for dual players who gravitated—at least legally—to those sports in the off-season to stay in shape. Conveniently, the GAA ran from late winter to the fall, the opposite of soccer and rugby, which were played on the soft ground in the cold. Some used Gaelic football as a résumé builder, including Kevin Moran, who won two All-Ireland championships with Dublin in 1976 and 1977. Moran, now an agent for international soccer stars, later played for Manchester United. In rugby, Mick Galwey captured an All-Ireland championship with Kerry in 1986, then went on to captain the Irish national rugby team. Still, the Irish psyche was stubborn enough that it took a while for soccer and rugby to fully grab the people's imagination.

By the time I got to Dublin in mid-September, everyone had soccer on their minds—but it wasn't a good thought. France had just edged Ireland 1-0 for the first time in Dublin since 1953 in a key World Cup qualifier. The crushing defeat all but ended Ireland's chances of advancing to the mega tournament in 2006. The 82,300-seat Croke Park went dead quiet. But that was only because the anticipated game took place at the much smaller 36,000-seat Lansdowne Road stadium in south Dublin. It wasn't for a lack of interest, rather GAA Rule 42 states that its grounds should be used for GAA games "and for such other purposes not in conflict with the aims and objects of the Association." Read: no soccer and rugby. Other stuff, no problem. Croke Park had hosted concerts, boxing (Muhammad Ali beat Al "Blue" Lewis in 1972), American football games (the Chicago Bears played the Pittsburgh Steelers in 1997 and Notre Dame played Navy in 1996) and the opening ceremonies of the 2003 Special Olympics World Summer Games. But soccer and rugby fell into a different category.

The decision, rooted in nationalism, was later supported with practical arguments. Chiefly, why should the GAA help its competition? It was, after all, a small island and survival of the fittest ruled. The GAA central office wouldn't even budge to allow benefit soccer games after an August 1998 terrorist bombing in Omagh, County Tyrone, by the Real IRA—an extremist splinter group—that killed twenty-nine people and injured 250. For that, the Association was heavily criticized, including by its own members. But the organization's constitution wasn't a fickle thing, and good or bad, procedures were followed to give every county a voice.

That democracy was on display in 2005 as the GAA tried to maneuver out of another pickle. Lansdowne Road was scheduled for renovations in 2007, and that meant the Irish soccer and rugby teams would be homeless. Enter Croke Park, a logical temporary venue as Ireland's showcase stadium. Outsiders couldn't understand why the GAA wouldn't help their fellow countrymen and avoid the embarrassment of "home" soccer and rugby games in the United Kingdom. But they underestimated the special bond GAA people had with their stadium, like a fan did with his team or a child with a pet. Sometimes called Croker or Headquarters, the place bled with Irish history and represented all the good of Gaelic games. In 1913, the GAA bought the land in Dublin's northside for £3,500. Members built the original stands behind one goal from the rubble of the 1916 Easter Rising and called it Hill 16. (Republicans took over the city's General Post Office and declared Ireland a sovereign republic as several buildings burned during the week's street fighting.) Fans watched their sacred game on sacred ground. During the War of Independence on November 21, 1920, England's Black and Tans opened fire during a Dublin/Tipperary Gaelic football game in retaliation for the Irish forces killing fourteen spies earlier that morning. A reciprocal fourteen people were killed including Tipperary player Michael Hogan in an event known as Bloody Sunday (the first one). The Hogan Stand, where the winning captain accepts the All-Ireland trophy, was named in his memory. Another part of the stadium was titled for GAA founder Michael Cusack. The stadium itself honored Dr. Thomas Croke, the Archbishop of Cashel and the GAA's first patron. His rousing letter of acceptance became the GAA's unofficial charter.

But it wasn't just a park of faded history (although the past lived in an adjacent museum). Croker evolved into a modern facility with corporate boxes, video scoreboards and the third-highest capacity in Europe. The GAA, and the GAA alone, decided to redevelop Croke Park in the early 1990s over a twelve-year period that cost €260 million (the government provided over €100 million in aid). Members, from the smallest remote clubs up to the sophisticated city boys, took pride that their amateur organization developed such a wonderful stadium. All glowed over it. I remembered having lunch with a GAA man, and watching him debate with the waiter—a non-GAA man—about how no one could tell the GAA what to do with its property. And why didn't soccer and rugby do likewise and build up their grounds?

Members in favor of opening Croke Park pointed to the financial windfall the Association would get for renting the stadium—it wouldn't be a pro bono act. Throw in the positive PR and a chance for an international audience to see their home, and momentum grew to opening Croker up. Plus, many in the GAA were also earnest Irish soccer and rugby fans.

After months of debate and uncertainty, the issue was decided in June at the GAA's annual congress. Delegates from each county voted 227-97 to allow those Irish teams to play in Croke Park during Lansdowne Road's renovation (a two-thirds majority was required). In 2007, the GAA extended the invitation for another year. This was groundbreaking stuff. Traditionalists couldn't bear to hear *God Save The Queen* roaring from the Croke Park speakers when England came to town. Nonetheless, ten games were scheduled ranging from Six Nation rugby contests to World Cup soccer qualifiers.

The Irish soccer and rugby governing bodies said they would pay the GAA either 25 percent of the gross gate or €1.25 million per game, likely bringing in between €8 and €10 million each year for the GAA. However, it was a temporary move and local GAA fields remained just that—for the GAA.

America's awakening to the World's Most Popular game took place in the 1970s when Pele and the New York Cosmos stormed into popular culture. Ireland's soccer explosion arrived a decade later. Aging, imported stars weren't needed. Rather, vibrant talent with Irish blood earned international success. Soccer didn't suddenly appear overnight. The first Dublin club formed in 1883, and the sport always had a niche pocket in working class areas. But the bulk of the country had nothing to get excited about. The best players went to England, Ireland's semipro league drew only scant interest and the national team struggled. Struggled as in never qualifying for the final stages of a major competition.

In 1988, former English star Jack Charlton took a team of the post-Ban generation players to the European Championships—Ireland's first big tournament. That was an achievement in itself, but they reached icon status after defeating England in the opening game. It didn't matter that Ireland failed to advance out of the group stages. Nearly 200,000 fans lined Dublin streets to welcome home their heroes. This was before the Celtic Tiger in a time of high emigration, when Ireland was not yet on the verge of cracking anyone's top-ten lists as the best place to live in the universe. Soccer provided a reason to cheer and to wave the green, orange and white.

The stage got even bigger. Two years later, Ireland rolled into its first World Cup and surprisingly advanced to the quarterfinals with a 5-4 victory in penalty kicks over Romania. A 1-0 loss to Italy didn't diminish the euphoria the country felt. Soon, adult and youth leagues began to swell with new teams. Unlike in the United States, soccer fever didn't disappear. In the 1994 World Cup, Ireland paid back Italy with a 1-0 victory in the opening game at Giants Stadium, and advanced to the round of 16 before losing 2-0 to the Netherlands. That Italy win, though, cemented Ireland as a serious contender—even though it failed to qualify in 1998.

I got an idea of the national team's hold when I glanced at the arts section in February and learned that *I, Keano* was opening in Dublin's Olympia Theatre. The comedic musical based its plot on an incident at the 2002 World Cup. On the eve of Ireland's first game, captain Roy Keane quit the team upset over the squad's poor training facilities and other slights. His confidants persuaded him to stay. Keane subsequently criticized the management in a newspaper interview with popular *Irish Times* columnist Tom Humphries, and then verbally berated manager Mick McCarthy in front of the team. McCarthy kicked Keane off, and fans split over who was at fault. *I, Keano* traded in a soccer setting for a Roman battle and a star warrior bickering with his general.

Without Keane, Ireland dramatically tied Germany in the final minute, and advanced to the round of 16. There, Ireland lost a heartbreaker on penalty kicks to Spain. Over 100,000 people greeted the team at Dublin's Phoenix Park. If you didn't know better, you'd have thought Ireland were world champs while watching the hundreds of balloons and flags in the air. The pride of a small nation earning success against mega powers never gets old.

Rugby, minus the large parades, also united the country. Shortly after I arrived in the winter, the annual Six Nations tournament involving England, France, Italy, Scotland and Wales started. The national anthems before games featured moving scenes. Rugged players with no neck and cauliflower ears locked arms and swayed while mouthing the words of their country. Like the GAA, there was one Irish national rugby team for all thirty-two counties. The team used a song called *Ireland's Call* as its anthem. (In international soccer, a separate Northern Ireland team competed.)

Historically, the GAA and rugby setups didn't have much in common (although GAA founder Michael Cusack first played rugby). Outsiders viewed rugby as a snooty sport for the professional classes. Elite, fee-paying high schools such as Dublin's Blackrock College attracted the rugby class. Today, the popular school finals every St. Patrick's Day drew up to 20,000 fans.

Like soccer, Irish rugby struggled on the world stage, lacking a buzz. But in the last five years, the Irish Rugby Football Union had been in attack mode to counter its not-for-the-masses image. It targeted areas where rugby was an afterthought, pumping in money for coaches and developmental programs. Take Tallaght, a south Dublin area with a strong GAA and soccer community. In ten years, Tallaght went from nearly zero to 3,000 kids playing rugby during school. That was the aim of Irish rugby—as well as soccer—get the youth playing and then hopefully keep them as adults.

No matter why he first played, a child continued on because he had fun. Sport extended to having heroes and cheering with friends and having your imagination captured. Gaelic football had that hold in Dublin. (Hurling was less popular and the inter-county team hadn't challenged nationally for some time.) Football fever engulfed the city during the All-Ireland tournament. For outsiders, Dublin was the team you loved to hate, the big bad city boys inflated by hype because they resided in the media capital.

In the 1970s, after a down period, the Dubs restored football as a trendy glam sport with six straight All-Ireland final appearances from 1974-1979 and three championships. That included four duels against Kerry. Fans called themselves Heffo's Army—after revered manager Kevin Heffernan—and jammed Hill 16, while singing the Liverpool soccer anthem, *You'll Never Walk Alone*. They became the Cameron Crazies of the GAA. Some say Heffernan and Dublin's success saved Gaelic football in the city and held off soccer's popularity for a while longer. The stars became media darlings, molded by Heffo and his physically demanding practices and technical acumen. After a 1983 title, the medals stopped with just one other championship in 1995. But what a summer. An eighteen-year-old dynamo named Jason Sherlock turned icon with exciting goals as Dublin once again captured the city.

Jayo, as he was called, inspired kids, who dreamed of one day donning the blue jersey of Dublin. One of those boys was Robert Fitzgerald, who heard Sherlock speak at his elementary school in south Dublin. Smitten, he trained with images of All-Ireland glory in his head. Fitzgerald especially followed the inter-county players from his club, St. Brigid's in the Castleknock section of Dublin. In high school, he added rugby and as a senior led Belvedere to a Leinster schools championship. When he went to University College Dublin this fall, Fitzgerald knew he had to focus on a single sport to reach the highest level. And he knew what was in his heart.

"I knew from day one," he told me of his decision to drop rugby. "There was no kind of indecision or anything."

The fact that Gaelic football was amateur didn't affect his thinking. Nor did a big contract to play overseas for one of Ireland's provincial teams. What did was one day winning an All-Ireland for his home team and being the next Jayo.

"You love playing the Gaelic," declared Fitzgerald, a member of Dublin's under-21 squad. "There's a passion for it. It doesn't make a difference if you don't get paid for it."

I wondered if some of his rugby friends ever gave him a hard time for choosing football. In other words, was there still a stigma like in the old days?

"Not really, but they might slag you or something like that," said Fitzgerald, knowing it was just boys will be boys instead of nationalism. "But there's nothing vindictive or bad about it. Then some of them would go to your game."

During my travels, I never heard politics mentioned as the reason for playing—or not playing. Just the typical macho talk like "Gaelic football's a real man's game" or "a lot of those GAA guys wouldn't be skillful enough to play soccer. They're just big lumps." It was like when I wrestled in high school. We'd tweak the basketball players, but it would be more in good fun than pure meanness.

So the codes did seem to get along. For example, I got Fitzgerald's name from his high school rugby coach, Andrew Kenny, who now guided the under-20 squad for the Clontarf rugby club. Kenny realized that he'd occasionally lose a Robert Fitzgerald, but it was no different than someone choosing track over baseball in the States.

"There isn't *that* much of a conflict," said Kenny, dismissing any hostilities between the players. "Like, OK, we lose a few players to Gaelic football and vice versa in Dublin. But you just accept that. You win some, you lose some. Glad they're still playing sports, you're happy for them. I don't think there's any animosity or problem."

Clontarf was typical of the dozens of sporting clusters throughout Dublin. I stopped by after noticing several fields on a random stroll in the northside, not far from Croke Park and a twenty-minute walk from the city center. Brawls and bloodsucking had a long history there. On Good Friday 1014, Vikings invaded the turf in a final attempt to conquer King Brian Boru and his troops. Boru lost his own life, but his men killed 6,000 Vikings, their dream ultimately defeated. The Battle of Clontarf went down as one of Ireland's most legendary tussles. The district was also the birthplace of Bram Stoker, the author of *Dracula*.

Now, a millenia later, I tiptoed in, making sure no Viking ghosts remained. I needn't have worried. Violence must be the furthest thing from people's minds here: Clontarf was next to breezy Dublin Bay and its Seafield Drive made for a nice stroll. The Clontarf Yacht & Boat Club dated back to 1875. You'd find two GAA clubs, a rugby and cricket club, a basketball club and about half a dozen adult soccer teams, some with youth divisions. Other nearby districts offered just as many options. This was GAA life in a city, where a club must joust with everyone for players—even other Gaelic clubs.

Unlike in the country, GAA parish lines were blurred and an athlete could go anywhere in the city. Since Dublin was the island's commerce capital, people from all over worked there. A player fell into three categories: the junior-level players would often transfer out of their parish to a city club just to stay active. The more serious players traveled back to their home team no matter the distance, like Leitrim's Dara McKiernan. Some high-level players switched to top Dublin clubs. Opponents whispered about secret payments or compensation like cars given to the stars. The GAA brass, though, has had trouble coming up with hard proof. That hadn't stopped them from considering ways to police outside transfers such as limiting the number of country players per team. Clubs often refused permission for transfers to cross-town teams, meaning the player had to sit out a year before competing again.

I asked Dave Walley, an official at the Scoil Uí Chonaill GAA club off Clontarf's main strip, about the competition they faced. Traditionally, an Irish-speaking school behind Croke Park supplied most of their players. About 20 percent came from an elementary school in Clontarf (the rest play for the Clontarf GAA club whose field and clubhouse were next to the classrooms). We spoke off to the side as an under-13 girls practice was underway.

"There's thirty-five girls here. I guarantee you we can pick five of them out of there, and they'd be from three miles that way," Walley said as he pointed to the right, before moving his hand in a clockwise motion to mark east, west, south and north. "And three miles that way. Three miles that way. Three miles that way. And three miles that way."

The range covered five or six GAA clubs. In a rural area, one GAA club would claim a monopoly on all those athletes. Here, it was the Wild West. Some were powerhouses that got players easily. Others were small clubs like Scoil Uí Chonaill, which couldn't wait for people to come. So they had to market themselves as more than just sports. Don't expect any P.T. Barnum-like stunts, but a mixture of fun events with the serious training was needed. Every summer, for example, Scoil Uí Chonaill had an in-house blitz tournament, in which boys and girls played on the same team. They hosted barbeques and held a social night for older children, disco included. A recent skills competition attracted over 400 players with games like golfing using a hurley. Walley noted they took youth teams on day trips to the country for matches, and it became a memorable experience with talent shows and sing-alongs.

"We put a lot of effort into making it interesting," said Walley, remembering to tell me about a calendar the club was producing that had pictures of every youth player.

The GAA recognized the need to hook kids and provide the means to keep them playing. In 2002, a Strategic Review Committee proposed splitting Dublin into two separate counties for the All-Ireland football tournament. The reasoning: Dublin's GAA resources weren't meeting the city's growth or matching the sporting competition. The motion failed, but the GAA central council made a commitment to nurture the games in Dublin. Beginning in 2005, it pledged to pump €1.6 million into development projects over a three-year period.

So all three of the major sporting codes were making an effort to attract players. With over a million people living in the Dublin region, there seemed to be enough bodies for all activities.

"It's just you don't have time to do everything," Kenny, the rugby skipper, told me. "As a kid they'll play sports seven days a week if they can. But when it gets bigger and it's more physical, you know, you've got to commit to one or the other."

And that was the challenge.

I stumbled upon the four major American professional sports—which had national teams and local leagues—and rounders, an original GAA sport similar to baseball. Maybe it shouldn't have been that surprising to me. NBA, MLB, and even the NFL had long gone global. Diverse languages filled locker rooms, ranging from Chinese to Wolof, an African dialect. American teams now routinely struggled in international competitions. But Ireland? There weren't too many Seamus's in the NBA. And I never heard of baseball academies here that develop talent for the Majors. The Irish Ice Hockey Association's Web site even proclaimed, "Yes, that's right, there is hockey in Ireland." Throw in the constant wetness and a lack of facilities, and it got me curious: Who played the sports? Were they a fad and a carefree novelty, or did players take it serious? Could it ever get to the point of challenging the GAA for players? Would Seamus one day *be* a common name in the NBA?

One athlete who didn't fall under the GAA's spell was Philip Darcy, a compact block of power, built like a Gaelic football defender you didn't want to run into. Growing up in Dublin, he was more interested in kicking people than kicking a ball over a bar. As a six-year-old, Darcy followed people in white suits and black belts entering a senior center and marveled at the high kicks. He, too, began taking karate lessons. He even traced his mother's signature onto the permission form, and hid his uniform at a friend's house. Eventually, Mom came around. The crafty Darcy later switched to kickboxing and competed in international competitions. He added ice hockey after skating at a small rink near his house (that later closed), and made the Irish national team.

"It's all really around where you live and what school you go to," Darcy said of the initial reason for choosing a sport. "It really has a big impact on what you do and what your interests are.... You're going to go somewhere that's local where you're comfortable, you can do it and go home."

Darcy, now in his early twenties, paused for a second, digesting what he just said.

"Now I travel 300 miles to Belfast to play ice hockey for two hours," he told me laughing.

The sporting bug did that to you. In some cases, all it took was getting an introduction. These minor sports still faced disadvantages compared to the GAA—little media coverage, government funding, attendance and tradition. Yet, increased participation and better coaching had strengthened them in the past ten years. The hub for all five was Dublin (including rounders), so it wasn't hard to track down gurus in each code.

One thing I had already discovered was that the Irish liked their sports fast and continuous. Baseball, on one hand, was, uh, slow. I mean I love it and could appreciate the intricacies, but I'd admit it could drag at times. Dragging at times wasn't a sexy selling point for athletes accustomed to nonstop hurling and Gaelic football games. So what hooked them? It happened innocently enough. The American Pastime got rolling in the late 1980s after coed slow-pitch softball games became a tad too serious. Hardball was the natural progression. In 1995, Major League Baseball International sent coaches to instruct the fledging players, and the national team started play a year later. Now, a ten-team league—seven teams in Dublin, two in Belfast and one in Wicklow (a county outside Dublin)—played a twenty-game season. The players were a mix between committed baseball fanatics who trained in the winter to guys who came in hung over. Of the four fields used by the league, only one was an actual baseball diamond, financed by former Los Angles Dodgers owner Peter O'Malley. (In 2006, the Wicklow baseball league was developing a field.)

Internationally, the Irish team—displaying the country's symbol of a harp on its green caps—took a bronze medal in the 2004 European B-Pool championship won by Germany. Ireland defeated Austria, Finland and Serbia-Montenegro along the way. Those countries weren't exactly baseball powerhouses like Cuba or the Dominican Republic, but a win was a win and Ireland's baseball sophistication continued to increase. For example, national team coach Sean Mitchell nearly got ejected from a game on purpose.

"We were getting killed by a couple umpires so I cut loose on them," said Mitchell, spoken like a grizzled baseball lifer. "I was surprised they didn't throw me out, actually. I think it was what we needed to energize our team, you know, get emotion going. We ended up coming back and winning the game, so it was a good motivational trick."

The art of arguing aside, Irish baseball had a way to go from the Major Leagues. The national team's best players were from the United States, usually college or ex-college players with Irish passports and a good curveball (two-thirds of the team must be Irish residents, a rule the country's baseball governing body decided on to encourage homegrown players). While the ringers were nice, the goal was to establish youth programs that would then be turned over to the locals to run. That vision faced a problem because the first generation of Irish players were themselves still competing and weren't available to coach or umpire. As Mitchell, also a catcher, explained, "There's only so much a handful of volunteers with fulltime day jobs can do."

But he cited examples of baseball success stories. Wicklow had a thriving youth program, as did rural Cork, led by of all people, members of the Moldovan national team now living there. In County Antrim, an American ex-pat coached kids. A Webmaster from a Stafford, Virginia, AAU team discovered their Web site, became intrigued and the Virginia Mustangs made the Portstewart Eagles their sister squad. Among other gestures of support, they sent needed equipment as Irish sporting goods stores didn't exactly stock bats or glove conditioner.

The optimistic Mitchell could see baseball and the minor sports finding a niche in Ireland. (Baseball received some pub in the United States when filmmaker John Fitzgerald released a documentary, *The Emerald Diamond,* about the players' struggles and passion shortly after I returned home.)

"In a lot of places, the top twenty kids in a particular community get on the football team and there's nothing for the rest of them, especially a lot of these rural areas in the country where it's just GAA," said Mitchell, offering a convincing sales pitch. "And if they're not good enough to make it onto those teams, there's nothing for them. They might as well play with their PlayStation."

Or, just maybe, they would find baseball. Mitchell was also a realist. He knew that the GAA had a 100-year head start. He also knew it was difficult to attract serious hurlers and footballers because the seasons conflict. In other words, don't expect Ireland to challenge Cuba anytime soon.

"It's very hard to get the word out in terms of press coverage or anything else," he said. "Being a minority sport is a serious challenge. We've been going for ten years and doing our best to publicize things, and we occasionally get spots in the national newspapers. Generally, you meet somebody on the street and they have no idea there's baseball being played in Ireland."

The concept of Irish baseball wasn't entirely foreign. The league's annual awards were named after Irish immigrants who played in the early days of American professional baseball. They included Andy Leonard, a member of the Cincinnati Red Stockings—the first all-professional baseball team in 1869, and "Dirty" Jack Doyle, believed to be baseball's first pinch-hitter.

While that was ancient history to many, I learned that kids grow up playing rounders, a sport that historians say baseball developed from. Witness the same three bases and a home plate, the same nine positions and a hitter and pitcher. The many differences include a different walk and strikeout system, no stolen bases, a hurling ball—smaller and softer than a baseball—and the pitcher threw underhand. (An English version of rounders used five bases with other rules.)

With thoughts of the MLB playoffs about to begin, I had the urge to watch a rounders game. I squeezed in the mixed (coed) final in Kildare, a county outside Dublin known for its horses, on the third Sunday in September. Chairman Margaret Delaney greeted me at a GAA club across from Mondello Park, a racetrack featuring fast cars and motorcycles. A constant vroooooooom serenaded the players for most of the game, which started late because three players were tardy.

Just when I thought I understood what was going on, something happened like a runner—or base holder—advanced on a fly out without tagging up or took first base on the third ball. It could definitely be a cousin of baseball, but a lighter version. Fielders didn't use mitts (just non-mandatory thin gloves that were worn in Gaelic football and handball), didn't wear hats, didn't use spikes and traded in pinstripes for a collared GAA jersey along with shorts or warm-up pants. If the seven-inning game was tied, then two extra innings would be played followed by the next tie-breaking criteria—whoever won the most innings. Failing that, the game must be replayed from the beginning.

I saw rounders played at GAA youth camps during down times—I was stunned that a baseball game broke out during hurling drills. But once puberty hits, the coolness factor was on par with listening to your parents or hanging out with a younger sister.

"People don't take it seriously enough as an actual adult game and that's where the problem lies," said Delaney, who became active when her children played. "'The school yard game' is what they call it. The seniors who play it take our game seriously."

This All-Ireland final *was* serious, with close calls and managers strategizing ala Tony LaRussa. The rosters featured a mix of teenagers to men in their early fifties. A pitcher delivered a baby three weeks ago, but was out there firing away. Some players looked like athletes, others appeared to be professional fast food tasters. That was one appeal of the game, kind of like golf, in that you could play at a high level for a long time without necessarily being super fit.

But for a while, rounders was like the forgotten GAA sport, only popular in pockets of eight counties at the senior level. This summer, after years of trying, GAA president Seán Kelly allowed the rounders all-stars to play in Croke Park at halftime of a Gaelic football game. Delaney said that attention drew many hits to the Rounders Council of Ireland's Web site and inquiries about teams. They welcomed any help. The eleven officers did everything from grounds crew work to making sandwiches and soup for the players to umpiring to deciding on rules interpretations.

"It's the only organization I know of where the chairman comes around and marks the pitches," said Delaney, who doubled as the public relations officer. "All the other chairmen breeze in in their suit on the day and they're mingling. We don't. We have to work and it's because we haven't enough help. A lot of the time you're putting your hand in your own pocket to keep things going."

After the Erne Eagles Rounders Club from County Cavan defeated the Limekiln Rounders Club out of Dublin, the medals were presented. For these players, it wasn't just a kids game. The winning manager Sean Hughes admitted the sport had an image problem because "a lot of guys won't play rounders because they think rounders is a girls game." But he had no problem reveling in winning an All-Ireland title, and confidently declared "when people see rounders played the way we play it, the proper way, it's a completely different game."

In April, an Annaduff Gaelic football player told me he played the American variety for a brief period while he lived in Dublin. *American football?* But the connection made sense. For while the Irish prefer their sports in hyperspeed, they also value toughness and a take-no-prisoners physicality. American football might be stop and go, but it fits the manliness criteria. Hardnosed fans noticed the big bodies smashing in the early 1980s when Irish and English TV stations started airing NFL games. They couldn't resist trying it, and in 1984 formed a team in Dublin. In 1986, the Craigavon Cowboys of County Armagh beat the Dublin Celts 6-0 to win the first Shamrock Bowl. Soon after, the Irish American Football League inaugurated its first full season with eleven teams. The playbooks weren't very sophisticated.

"You just had eleven really big lugs trying to kill each other," said Terry Lynch, an accountant who has played for a team near Belfast since 1989. "That was all it was."

Hey, even pencil pushers need to release aggression. Over time, coaches and players acquired football savvy as teams threw the ball more. But the sport had trouble maintaining players and folded after the 1999 season with only three teams remaining. Dedicated zealots refused to see football die. They revived the league in 2001 with four teams. It grew to six teams in 2005, and upped to nine teams in 2007 for an eight-game season stretching from March to July. All-stars comprised the national squad, which planned to enter European Championships against other developing football countries like Austria, Norway and Serbia. To get an idea of Ireland's level, the all-stars lost to an NCAA Division III team in the last two years: 52-2 to John Carroll (Ohio) and 53-0 to Adrian College

(Michigan). Still, the sport had come a long way since the beginning. (And let's see how well those Adrian boys do in a game of hurling.)

"It's thriving in the sense that it's better organized," said Lynch, a big offensive lineman. "A lot of the guys that are involved have been in it a long time. They know all the pitfalls of the sport. They know the costs of running the sport. They know the facilities.... It's becoming more of an organized sport where as before it was friends in the park playing about."

On the day of the All-Ireland Gaelic football final pitting Kerry against Tyrone before 82,112 people, I went to an all-star American football practice on a simple field in another part of town and chatted with two rookies, Barry Flinn and Sam Hodgins. The high school seniors were just starting their school rugby season.

In both sports, the object was to score touchdowns as muscular, oversized men enjoyed driving you into the ground. Rugby, though, was played nonstop without stoppages for downs or equipment. Thus, bulking up in American football with a helmet and heavy pads became a fun novelty.

"The first time you put [the equipment] on you get the biggest kick out of it ever," said Hodgins, sporting a bandage on his chin from a rugby hit. "I feel safer and can go in harder playing American. I feel safer when I'm smashing around with the pads on then in rugby when I have to smash it up without them."

Hodgins played running back, so he was often the smashee instead of the smasher. Some of his friends saw the armor and concluded that American football was easier. Hodgins, though, would like to point out one thing: "They don't think about the fact that, like the guy hitting you has all the big pads and the helmet to hit you with as well."

The average Irish person acquired his American football IQ through movies like *Any Given Sunday* or other popular culture. Both Flinn and Hodgins fell in love with football after playing Madden on PlayStation and watching NFL games on Sky Sports, an English channel available in Ireland. All it took was an e-mail to the coach of the Dublin Rebels, and soon they were living out their video fantasy.

"The people that we know just think it's cool," Flinn, a wide receiver, told me. "It's a bit different."

He did note that hecklers sometimes drove by their practices shouting "blue 24" and other strange football jargon they picked up from TV. After a while, trying to be clever turned into the same jokes—just another obstacle the Irish American footballers had to deal with.

"They always think they're so original," Flinn grimaced.

By far, the most established American sport was basketball. An Irish army sergeant introduced round ball to his country in the early 1920s. A national governing body formed in 1945. But know this about the Irish basketball squad—it held some of its tryouts in New Jersey. That kind of summed up basketball in Ireland. It was there. There was some interest, but ... the talent still had a way to go. A league creatively called the SuperLeague paid two foreigners (the Irish players got nothing) and attracted crowds ranging from a few hundred to a few thousand per game for the eleven teams. A fledging national team mostly contained players that were raised in the United States and were eligible because they could get Irish passports. The current highest-profile player was the Phoenix Suns' Pat Burke, the first Irish-born player to make the NBA, although he attended high school in Florida. During the fall, Ireland just missed qualifying for the top-level European championship for the first time after a loss to Denmark.

With the SuperLeague starting, I went to see University College Dublin-Marian play (the squad was based at the college, but wasn't a student team). The court reminded me of a small high school gym. Only one side had bleachers. On a second level, fans stood on a mezzanine looking down. The light blue floor resembled a rainbow with orange, yellow, red and green markings on it. Advertisements littered the sides.

After the game, as kids shot around, I waited for the players and stopped one with an American accent. Damion Morbley played NCAA Division I ball for Cal State Northridge, and grew up in Compton, California. I asked him about the court's floor surface, which felt like a mix of a wrestling mat and the hardwood.

"I don't know if it's clay, cement," said Morbley, throwing up his arms. "I have no idea."

The basketball culture differed from the street ball and blacktop courts that Morbley was used to back home. Then again, there weren't too many pick-up Gaelic football games at Long Beach.

"I don't see enough parks here and if I do see a park, the rim is all messed up and there's no net," he said. "If they want to improve they have to get better facilities and they have to put more of an emphasis on it. They might have a few players that make it to the NBA, but as a whole it's not going to become a powerhouse like Serbia."

Indeed, foreign-born players now littered NBA rosters, but they were from the likes of Lithuania, Serbia, and Slovenia. The SuperLeague had trouble attracting higher quality ballers because clubs only paid a couple hundred euros a week. Some also provided jobs coaching in schools over the twenty-eight week time frame. (Mario Elie, though, played for Killester in Clontarf in 1987 before finding fame for the Houston Rockets.)

Basketball—much more than baseball, American football and ice hockey—attracted GAA stars to the SuperLeague. That included the 2006 Gaelic football Player of the Year, Kerry's Kieran Donaghy. (His exploits and the Tralee Tigers were chronicled in the book *Paddy on the Hardwood* by former coach Rus Bradburd, once a New Mexico State and UTEP assistant, which was released about a year after I got back.) The GAA and basketball seasons only overlapped briefly, and hoops was a great way to stay in shape. In the fall and winter, some Bo Jackson-like athletes played basketball one night, then a club football game the next. But there was no mistaking where basketball stood on the pecking order.

"Basketball is sitting comfortably in fifth place in popularity after the two Gaelic sports, soccer and rugby," said Pat Price, the coach of the Cork team in the SuperLeague. "The degrees of separation in Irish basketball is probably about two—'I don't know the guy, but he does.'"

Price, at the Dublin game scouting, also sported a familiar accent. The native of Erie, Pennsylvania, played two years at Penn State-Scranton before coaching high school ball. Coaching camp connections led him to Ireland six seasons ago. He explained that basketball was popular to an extent. The small round ball public devoured the stats, but the overall interest was more laidback. Gaelic football and hurling were serious.

"They do it as a fun, recreational activity," Price had observed. "My own findings are that the people who influence what sports kids play are traditional GAA people like school principals."

Price continued that some schools were receptive to teaching basketball when he approached administrators. But if the principal was a GAA diehard, the reaction might be, *"Sorry lads. No need to come in here. The lads are playing hurling. The lads are playing football."*

"That's what you're up against," Price concluded. "If basketball got even one tenth of the attention that like GAA sports or some other sports get for funding, we'd be fine. Just it's an afterthought with a lot of the people."

Declan King, an official from the Killester team in Clontarf, pointed out that while basketball lags in money, it did have one advantage—little competition. The Irish semipro soccer league and the heart of the GAA took place in the summer. In the winter, spectators were there for the taking. An evening in a warm gym in the cold of December did have a certain appeal.

"A lot of people that I brought along to games from other sports like soccer, rugby, Gaelic football—they love the sport now," he said. "But we've got to get out and spread a gospel of what the sport is all about. The thing that has to get out is there's great entertainment there."

Then you had ice hockey. At first, I wondered if Irish ice hockey was akin to Jamaican bobsledding. There was no snow in Jamaica. And there were no ice rinks in the Republic. But the Irish situation wasn't as dire as the Jamaican sledders.

Dublin once had two small rinks that had been converted from movie theaters. In the early 1980s, locals discovered that ice hockey filled the Irish requirements of speed and violence. They staged rough hockey games, with no equipment and plenty of fighting. If a stick broke, it somehow got fixed and re-shaped, however poorly, and the guys played on.

"Unfortunately I think we had the vision of hockey at the time was supposed to be all fighting," said Cliff Saunders, now the Irish Ice Hockey Association president. "We weren't afraid. We play very physical. As you know, the GAA is a physical game. Playing Gaelic football, you [could get] an elbow in the head. It's natural. You become resilient to it. [Playing ice hockey], we became resilient to the bruises and the busted lips."

Players from both rinks formed one squad and traveled to England and Scotland for games. Saunders became the coach, equipped with knowledge from reading training manuals on the job. The team practiced during the only time slot available: midnight on Sunday for three hours.

"Instead of going to the pub, we played hockey," said Saunders, who I met for an afternoon chat over tea. All I had to do was introduce myself, and he proceeded to tell me the history, current plight and just about everything I wanted to know about Irish ice hockey but was afraid to ask. He often got an audience at International Hockey Federation conferences.

"When we tell the guys the stories," Saunders said with a glow, "even Canada hockey goes, 'Jeez, that's the way it was in our old days.'"

Eventually, hockey-crazed Canadians attending medical school at Dublin's Royal College of Surgeons taught the locals the sport's finer points. In 1997, Ireland joined hockey's international governing body, and received funding and coaching tips. But in 1999 and 2000, after disputes with insurance companies, the Dublin rinks closed. That started the Jamaican bobsled-like chapter of Irish ice hockey. The 200 kids suddenly had no place to practice and the youth programs ended.

The national team's only option for practice was two hours away at Belfast during a less than ideal time—Sunday at five o'clock in the morning. Darcy remembered standing on a cold Dublin street corner at two, waiting to get picked up as drunkards staggered by and stared. The cops, too, wanted to know what someone was doing out at that time covered in a hood and holding a bag. His answer of ice hockey sounded perplexing.

"They used to laugh every time," Darcy told me as we met for a chat in a pub on his way home from an evening kickboxing practice. "They just thought we were mad. They found the humor in it. After a while, they'd drive by and beep at us and wave."

The Irish national team now received better ice time—ten on Tuesday nights and occasionally on Saturday morning at eleven when the Belfast Giants were playing later home games. (The professional Giants played against other teams from the United Kingdom.)

Interestingly, the Irish team included both Catholics and Protestants from the six counties of Northern Ireland. Some members have had Union Jack and Glasgow Rangers tattoos (a soccer team with a Protestant fan base)—not exactly Irish-related symbols. No bother, everyone just wanted to play hockey and teammates from the different backgrounds hang out socially.

"It's sport," said Saunders, only concerned who has the best wrist shot.

Because of the lack of practice time, Ireland struggled internationally and was ranked forty-fourth in the world out of forty-five countries in 2005, only ahead of Armenia. A few months before I spoke with Saunders, Ireland played in the lowest-level world championship and managed to beat Armenia 23-1, but lost to South Africa 5-4, Luxembourg 8-4 and eventual champion Mexico, 6-1. (In 2007, however, Ireland finished second in the tournament and received promotion to the next division.)

The national team operated on a grassroots level. Players needed to pay for trips. Darcy had to show his employer a letter from the ice hockey association so he wouldn't get penalized for missing work.

"The company wasn't happy," recalled Darcy, an electrician. "But at the same time, they were like 'OK, if you're representing your country it's not just a normal everyday thing.' It wasn't a rubbish excuse."

The players didn't mind those inconveniences, but they had concerns over the sport's survival with few kids playing. The hockey association was desperately lobbying to get a new rink built in Dublin. A couple years ago, it ran two outdoor rinks in Dublin for nine weeks near Christmas. They made €1.2 million and bought a Zamboni, the ice resurfacer machine. The Zamboni sadly sat in Mark

Bowes' garden next to produce and flowers. Bowes, the association's general secretary, even had a picture in his cell phone that he showed me like a proud parent.

The hockey nuts weren't giving up. For example, Bowes mortgaged one of his houses and switched telecommunications jobs to free up time, and Saunders was voluntarily working part-time for an insurance company. The two men in their thirties saw it as short-term annoyances on the road to long-term success.

"Ten years and a couple hundred thousand [euros] and we're still here," Bowes proclaimed. "So we're not going to go away."

Epilogue
GAA in America & What I Learned

I flew home from Ireland on a Monday morning, touching down at JFK at noon. That night, I went to a U2 concert at Madison Square Garden and noticed several GAA jerseys. A few weeks later, I attended a New York Giants game and spotted a green County Kerry shirt down the aisle.

Now that my eyes were open to this sort of thing, I saw the Irish everywhere. I even checked my local paper for a hurling column. While there wasn't one, I thought a good way to end my journey would be to explore the Gaelic scene in the United States. It wasn't just a bunch of Irish ex-pats whacking a ball around on a Sunday morning. All activity was connected to the old country. The New York GAA Board and the North American GAA Board (everywhere else) were considered "counties" and received the same voting rights at the Association's annual Congress as did Irish counties. Headquarters in Dublin provided financial support. Surprisingly, New York entered a team—consisting mostly of Irish natives—in the senior All-Ireland provincial tournaments. That was like a Serbian school holding a spot in the NCAA tournament every year.

The Irish, of course, have long been linked with America, and through Ellis Island they brought their sports. The benefits went beyond actually competing. GAA clubs acted as e-mail or a chat room before the Internet.

"It was a huge networking organization when people came here," said North American Board member Eamonn Kelly, a Chicago resident who emigrated from Dublin in the 1950s. "You typically got jobs through connections. As soon as you joined up with a GAA club you became friendly with a lot of people."

But with a better Irish economy in the late 1990s and tougher U.S. immigration laws following 9/11, fewer Irish people were coming, or they were going home. Instead of dying out, though, two trends in the last decade have kept the GAA alive—the rise of American-born players and teams stretching across the country, not just in the original urban enclaves of Irish America. From Portland, Oregon, to Albuquerque, New Mexico, to Charlotte, North Carolina, the ancient Irish games were breathing in modern America.

"Most of the GAA clubs in the U.S. now realize if they are to survive in the future it has to be working at underage levels with American kids," GAA president Nickey Brennan told me.

I met him at the Continental Youth Championships outside Boston at the New England Cultural Centre in Canton, Massachusetts. The third annual tournament drew over 1,000 boys and girls from seven states, Ottawa and London. Ninety-two teams played over 200 games in the three long days. Brennan considered the event so important that he flew in and handed out medals.

Except for the sticky July humidity, he could have been in Dublin, Kilkenny or Clare. Parents rolled in, tugging infants past an Irish tricolor on a high flagpole. Lines formed at the concession stands, where they offered Lucozade energy drink and Tayto chips. On Saturday and Sunday, All-Ireland tournament games aired in the clubhouse. When I arrived, Detroit was playing Denver in an under-16 boys' game and Philadelphia took on San Francisco in an under-12 girls' match. Organizers bounced around, making sure things ran smoothly on the seven playing fields.

Will Gaelic football moms and hurling dads one day be an important demographic? Teams were slowly becoming more diverse. Take the Pittsburgh under-16 football team (which joined forces with Detroit for the weekend because a few players couldn't attend). Johnny Connolly, the thirty-five-year-old coach, recruited about twenty-five kids from his platform as an eighth grade social studies teacher. He'd talk it up and sometimes popped in a DVD of GAA games during study hall or a down time to intrigued students who never heard of it. They were impressed. He's gotten black, bi-racial, Italian and Jewish kids to come out.

"The u-14 kids I'm picking up are a United Nations commercial," said Connolly, one of the many GAA pied pipers in America. "Kids usually love it. I think they just like the sport because it's fast-paced, it's hard-hitting, there's a lot of scoring. It has all the little things that Americans like. It has speed, excitement, hitting, scoring—it's not boring. All these kids prefer it to soccer, that's for sure."

The GAA naturally struggles against the established high school sports, but they have a place. For example, many kids specialize in one sport and play year-round on travel teams. Enter Gaelic football or hurling as an athletic—yet laid-back—way to stay in shape.

"[The other sports] almost become too serious," said Connolly, whose family was from Galway. "I think part of the appeal for Gaelic football is it's fun, but it's low-key. It's not like if you don't show up for one practice and you're done. And that's a good thing. If they end up liking it, they stick with it."

Like Mark Molloy, a rising high school senior in the Boston area, who quit American football in seventh grade when practices interfered with Gaelic football. The glamour of one day playing under those Friday lights didn't mean a thing.

"I kept saying, 'You know Gaelic football's over in a couple weeks I'll get to football then,'" recalled Molloy, whose genes also go back to Ireland. "But then I was so behind on the football team, I was like forget about it."

So he took up soccer, which started later. Now, Gaelic football provided great off-season conditioning, and Molloy would "be hurting for soccer if I didn't do this. I'd probably just sit on the couch." In the spring, he hustles straight from his high school lacrosse practice to Gaelic football training.

"I love it and I wouldn't give it up for anything," he proclaimed.

Many American clubs don't have youth teams, so players join together for tournaments like this. But Molloy intended to play for the New England Celtic, a team comprised of American-born players based in the Canton area. It formed a few years ago, after players had trouble breaking into clubs with Irish-born players.

"It's all ex-athletes," said Mike O'Connor Jr., a veteran on the team. "It's not like the softball league where you go out and the whole idea is to play a few innings and get drunk. It is serious. You can't help but take it serious."

They've had success on the junior level. So much so, O'Connor has noticed opposing teams filled with Irish accents making sure to compete hard against the Yanks.

"When they played us they kind of stepped it up," said O'Connor, proud of that achievement. "They didn't want to lose to these American guys. In the last two years we've been playing, we made it to the final of our division. They put a little extra into it."

But the Americans aren't quite ready to beat the Irish at their own game. The Boston senior league, for example, was 99 percent Irish-born.

"It's going to take probably a good five to ten years before we can get young American kids up to that senior level," Eamonn Kelly, of the North American GAA board, told me.

One way was to try to get it into school gym classes. San Francisco did. In early 2007, the thriving GAA city convinced the YMCA, which ran the city's elementary schools' physical education classes, to teach Gaelic football. Now over 3,000 kids would be getting a taste. One could even read the San Francisco GAA Web site in Spanish—perhaps normal for a soccer team, but unusual for the GAA.

Milwaukee also made news. In 2006, the league's Dave Olsen received a prestigious President's Award from the GAA's Seán Kelly for his work in helping attract nearly 200 American-born players for its hurling league. In other cities, all it took were a handful of GAA diehards to get a club going, and word spread.

The traditional American home of the GAA has been New York, specifically Gaelic Park in the Kingsbridge section of the Bronx at the tip of Manhattan College. Through the decades, it acted as part-social hall and part-Croke Park of North America. Crowds of a few thousand flocked on the weekends to enjoy the games, but also to mingle and attend dances afterward.

Ironically, the GAA flourished in New York when economic times were bad back home. A wave of new immigrants always filled lineups and the stands. The 1947 All-Ireland football final was even played in the Polo Grounds after years of lobbying by ex-pats. Cavan beat Kerry in an exciting game before 34,941 fans. At one point, NY clubs were allowed to fly in top Irish players for important games, giving star power to Gaelic Park.

The key to New York's future success—which includes teams in the metropolitan area of Connecticut, New Jersey and suburban NY—is developing its own players. Since the Celtic Tiger of the late 1990s, less and less immigrants were leaving. (About 150 Irish college students, though, still come for the summer.)

In 2007, New York needed to withdraw from the Ulster provincial hurling tournament because many players went back to Ireland. In the past three years, eight clubs whittled to four. But the games have a heartbeat. For one, Gaelic football was remaining steady in participation numbers with one merger in the last two years. Another plus was a new artificial turf playing surface at Gaelic Park and floodlights. Then, New York GAA held children's camps for the first time in the summer of 2007. So while they may no longer be able to draw 30,000 fans to a baseball stadium, the games do live for a new generation.

"We're reasonably healthy," said GAA board member Larry McCarthy. "The interest is there. The kids are there."

It was fitting that I met Eamonn Kelly, the North American GAA officer, in Massachusetts. He was the first person I contacted in spring 2004—if Kelly blew me off, I might have never followed through. Fortunately, he offered tips and directed me to Fergal McGill of the GAA office in Dublin (another helpful resource).

So I considered my journey having come full circle, from a vague idea in a Virginia apartment to eight months in Ireland to watching the GAA back home. Now, it was time to assess my trip and what I learned.

I more or less stuck to my blueprint, sampling a cross section of the country. But I didn't exactly travel in luxury. My entourage consisted of a suitcase, a computer carrying case stuffed with papers and knickknacks and a shopping bag full of newspapers in my best bag lady imitation (it didn't occur to me that I could get most of the articles on the Net), as I traveled by Bus Éireann from cheap B&B to cheap B&B across the flat of the land.

I was in Ireland for a purpose and spent my time wisely. Research won out over pub hopping and gulping black jugs of beer. However, if I was with sources that were drinking, I felt I had to down a couple in the name of reporting, of course. That also meant tasting poitín—moonshine. Woooooowzer!!! A sip of the homemade whiskey acted as my flu shot for the year. If the strong and bitter Guinness put hair on my chest, poitín took it right off.

And talking about alcohol, Ireland had a strict smoking ban in workplaces, which extended to pubs. It was the first country to enact such a law in March 2004. Everywhere I went, no matter how small a place, people automatically sauntered outside to smoke without trying to cheat. One night, though, I found a loophole after last call. Around 1, the doors bolted with two-dozen regulars still remaining. Nearly everyone whipped out cigarettes and puffed away. Pints were flowing. Around two thirty, the crooners belted out traditional Irish songs, which only made the night cooler. I don't smoke, but to be a bad ass, I held a cigarette in my hand and waited for it to melt down to my fingers before grabbing another one. I coughed harshly, though, at each puff attempt—I could honestly say I didn't inhale.

So nothing came to faze me. For example, I nearly lost my way in March when returning by bus from Dublin to Ballina, Mayo, after the club championship. We stopped in County Longford for a changeover, and I went into the restroom. I emerged a couple minutes later to see the bus pulling out.

"That's the bus for Ballina?"

"Yeah, go, you might catch it!"

I sprinted, the prospects not good. I could barely outrun a slug on a stroll, let alone a bus with a four-car head start. I waddled with eight newspapers flapping in the wind. Notepads and loose papers were bouncing out of my jacket. Fortunately, the bus stopped at a red light and I hopped on, winded. It was the last bus to Ballina for the evening so it would have been a looooooong night in Longford.

And because sport is unpredictable, I had to scrap an entire chapter. In August, I went to Cork to write about the city's hurling hysteria. Then, it was on to Kilkenny for the All-Ireland hurling buildup and a look at professionalism in the GAA. It seemed a safe bet with powerhouse Kilkenny having reached the last three All-Ireland hurling finals. I never made it. Kilkenny, naturally, was upset by Galway in the semifinals in a classic, gasping, high-scoring affair. I wasn't celebrating. I had even arranged for my brother and his girlfriend to visit me in Kilkenny, known as the Medieval capital of Ireland for its preserved castles.

After a mild panic, I remained in Cork, which advanced to the All-Ireland final with a narrow win in the semis. I switched the focus of the chapter from Cork club hurling to the inter-county championship buildup and how money was entering the game. My understanding brother quickly changed hotels, and while he missed the twelfth-century Kilkenny Castle, he got to kiss the Blarney Stone—not a bad turn of events.

But I still wanted to meet Kilkenny's Henry Shefflin. He was the star who inspired me by playing a week after nearly losing his eye. Fortunately, the Kilkenny club semifinals were scheduled for my last full day in Ireland. That morning I had an interview with Dublin's hurling coach Tommy Naughton, but if I hustled I would make the bus for the two-hour ride to Kilkenny. Naughton answered what I wanted to know, and as I was leaving, I picked up a hurley on the ground to take a final swing. He caught that from the corner of his eye and told me to follow him to his car. Naughton shuffled a few hurleys in his trunk before handing me one to keep—a gift to a guest. I was floored, and after saying, Are you sure? several times, I gratefully clutched the stick and ran to the bus station.

I made it just in time (and didn't venture to the bathroom as those buses don't wait for anything). Carrying the stick led to a fantasy. I noticed people staring at me—women peered, boys fawned, older men nodded. Perhaps they mistook me for a top free taker? In my mind, I had just won an All-Ireland medal. One man even said, "You've got quite a weapon there."

I felt like a member of an exclusive fraternity and received more nods in Kilkenny, so infatuated with hurling it was the only county to not enter a team in the All-Ireland football tournament. Consider this: the semifinals drew 10,000 fans in a county of 87,000 residents. (That would be like 700,000 people going to a New York Knicks game.) In the first semifinal, Shefflin and the Ballyhale Shamrocks emerged victorious. He then ventured to the stands to scout the second contest. I had my chance. At halftime, I introduced myself and asked him about getting injured in the 2004 All-Ireland quarterfinal. Shefflin told me he underwent surgery that evening at eleven to repair a severed tear duct. He didn't embellish and brag like a high school football star telling a tale twenty years later at a reunion. He simply recalled what happened.

"I wanted to play, obviously, and the surgeon was very good. And I had to bandage up and I had a couple stitches. You do those things, you know?"

Well, no. I once got a paper cut on my right hand—my writing hand—and after drowning the quarter-inch wound with Neosporin, I tried doing all non-writing things with my left hand for the day, like eating. I decided to hold that info back as he continued.

"I had a big black eye on me and obviously it was the talk of the place," said Shefflin, who now logically works as a salesman for a medical company. "I'm used to that and that's the way it goes. We won the match the following week so that made it all the better."

He added: "We love the game and that's why we play the game. It's a great thing for us as amateur players to play in Croke Park. I think that's worth more than gold."

That was the passion and pride that drove me to Ireland in the first place. I had been stuck in my job as a sportswriter and hoped that the GAA player's zeal would shatter my inertia. I was looking for something big, but what I found were the small things.

Like a tired Shefflin, named the 2006 Hurler of the Year, handing out medals at a youth banquet hours after his semifinal win.

Or Annaduff coach Eugene Cox arriving at the empty field two hours before games to line the chalk because somebody had to do it. He could have easily sent some kid, but Cox felt responsible because *his* team was playing.

Or Mickey Mac Cú Uladh, the public relations officer for St. Patrick's in Lisburn, taking me to a game, then waiting in his car for an hour as I interviewed an older member of the club. Mickey didn't want any credit, just that I got the best information about what he loved.

For eight months, I watched coaches and players devote that kind of attention to their calling. I gained a better appreciation for sport and what it takes to be great. For one thing, it's about approaching minutia in the same way you would approach an All-Ireland final. That can be applied to any craft, including writing. I felt revitalized as I boarded the plane, and thought recapturing that love was what my adventure was all about.

Acknowledgments

Whew! I never thought I would get to this point. I have so many people to thank, it's overwhelming. They fall into two categories: people from Ireland and people who helped with the writing.

The Irish Thanks: Everybody's name that I mentioned in the book deserves a tremendous thank you and bow down. They all gave me their time and hospitality and went out of their way to help me. So thank you.

Unfortunately, because of space and focus, I needed to cut things. So I'm also indebted to everyone whose name did not get in. Those are the people I'll mention here. Two intended chapters got the ax: Women's GAA and College GAA. Both were important and interesting, but I couldn't delve as deeply into the topics as I wanted to. I'd like to thank Dublin's camogie (women's hurling) captain Eimear Brannigan and the camogie PRO Máire Uí Scolaí for their time. As well as Limerick IT GAA board members Seoirse Bulfin, Jimmy Browne and Liam Kelly. Sorry I couldn't tell your stories, but a writer has to make some tough cuts, like a manager filling out his lineup. Also deserving thanks are Pádraic Mac Donncha from Ráth Cairn and Diarmuid Ó Tuama from Belfast for information on the language movement in their areas. The following people earned my gratitude: Danny Flynn took me on a tour of the Nemo Rangers, Christy Hughes gave me rounders info over tea at his home, Michael Hogan and Noel Hogan—no relation—gave me boxing info, Alan Matthews, an economics professor at Trinity College, helped with the Celtic Tiger background via e-mail, coaching great John O'Mahony, the lotto committee at Kilmurry-Ibrickane, Irish national team point guard Lorcan Precious, Michael McCormack from Killester and David Crowe from Clontarf soccer.

The additional people took a crazy call out of the blue from an American and didn't hang up: Gillian Talty, John Healy, Padraig Prendergast, Michael O Meara, Phil DeMonte and Paddy Connery (who gets additional props for letting me crash in an extra bedroom after the Munster hurling final, thus saving me from being eaten by a cow). Kilkenny secretary Pat Dunphy was my first overseas call to Ireland, and he offered access and insight. New Yorker Dick Lyons helped me in America, and even sent me a hurling book and tape unsolicited. Larry McCarthy of New York GAA also helped with info on the U.S. Gaelic scene. Helping me from Boston were Sean Flynn, Ann Marie McDonagh and Michael O'Connor.

I must thank the Daly kin of Maire, John, Donal and Micheál for making my stay in Kilmurry more enjoyable; and Peggy Melvin in Ballina for her conversation, sweets and Easter dinner. And in Leitrim, the whole clan of Coxes—I'd run out of paper if I mentioned them all. I will thank Catherine and Kenneth, because I promised I would.

Finally, Fergal McGill of the GAA office quickly answered all of my questions and checked facts for me when I'm sure he had a million other things to do, so: Tréaslaím libh an obair a dhéanann sibh!

Writing Help: I don't have enough space to mention every single friend and inspiration—maybe for my next book—so I'll begin with a blanket thank you to everyone who supported me. I know, a cop-out, but I'm genuinely appreciative to the people in my life. George Stapleton gets a mention for introducing me to Ireland and attending my first hurling game with me, and being a good friend in general. Avi Salzman stepped up with his stellar—and pro bono—editing/suggestions for the early chapters and long phone calls (after the free minutes kicked in) and being my go-to guy to bounce ideas off of. Also offering valuable input were Mike Barber, Kevin Callahan, John Davis and Luke Vilelle (and I can't mention Luke without the other old DNR staffers Will Bottinick and Tom Stevens). I have to thank Chris Simmons for making me a better writer while in Harrisonburg, and Susan Leon for her editing and getting me to think of it as a book instead of a long article.

Then, of course, there's my brother Rick and parents, Ed and Ronnie. Sometimes I don't always show my appreciation for their unwavering support, but it means a lot knowing they're always there for me.

If there's anyone I missed, I'll get you next time.

Note on Sources

I got most of my information from personal interviews and observations. However, I consulted books for historical and background info. I found the Terrence O'Neill quote used in Chapter Four from: *A History of Northern Ireland 1920-1996*, by Thomas Hennessey, St. Martin's Press, 1997. I plucked the Cuimín tale from Chapter Two out of two books: *History and Legends of the Civil Parish of Kilcummin* by Sean Lavin, N.T. 1986 and *Tales of the West of Ireland* by Sean Henry, Mercier Press, 1999.

The following books were helpful for getting a feel of a particular scene, statistics or just plain enjoyment:

A History of Gaelic Football, by Jack Mahon, Gill & Macmillan, 2000

A History of Hurling, by Seamus J. King, Gill & Macmillan, 1996

For the Cause of Liberty: A Thousand Years of Ireland's Heroes, by Terry Golway, Touchstone, 2000

Bandit Country, the IRA & South Armagh, by Toby Harnden, Coronet Books LIR Hodder & Stoughton, 1999

Bear in mind these dead ... An Index of Deaths from the Conflict in Ireland 1969-1993, by Malcolm Sutton, Beyond the Pale Publications, 1994

Everything Irish, The History, Literature, Art, Music, People and Places of Ireland, from A to Z, Edited by Lelia Ruckenstein and James A. O'Malley, Ballantine Books, 2003

Gaelic Games and the Gaelic Athletic Association, by Paul Healy, Mercier Press 1998

Green Fields: Gaelic Sport in Ireland, by Tom Humphries, Orion Publishing Co, 1996

How the GAA survived the Troubles, by Desmond Fahy, Wolfhound Press, 2001

Ireland and the Irish, Portrait of a Changing Society, by John Ardagh, Penguin Putnam, 1997

Northern Ireland: A Report on the Conflict, by The London Sunday Times Insight Team, Random House, 1972

O'Brien Pocket History of Gaelic Sport, by Eamonn Sweeney, The O'Brien Press, 2004

O'Brien Pocket History of The Troubles, by Brian Feeney, The O'Brien Press, 2004

O'Brien Pocket History of The IRA, by Brendan O'Brien, The O'Brien Press, 2005

Scéal Club Eanach Dubh: A History of GAA Activity in Annaduff Parish 1889-1983, edited by Des Guckian, printed by the Westmeath Examiner Ltd., 1983

The Crossmaglen G.A.A. Story 1887-1987, by Con Short, Raonaithe na Croise, 1987

The Goal of Victory: History of Ballina Stephenites 1886-1986, by Terry Reilly, printing by Western People, 1986

The IRA: A History, by Tim Pat Coogan, Roberts Rinehart Publishers, 1993

The Irish Troubles, by J. Bowyer Bell, St. Martin's Press, 1993

The Lifelong Season: At the Heart of Gaelic Games, by Keith Duggan, TownHouse, 2004

The Republic of Ireland; its Government and Politics, by Morley Ayearst, New York University Press, 1970

The Road to Croker: A GAA Fanatic on the Championship Trail, by Eamonn Sweeney, Hodder LIR, 2004

The Ultimate Encyclopedia of Gaelic Football & Hurling, by Martin Breheny & Donal Keenan, Carlton Books, 2001

Those Are Real Bullets: Bloody Sunday, Derry, 1972, by Peter Pringle and Philip Jacobson, Grove Press, 2000

1001 Things Everyone Should Know About Irish American History, by Edward T. O'Donnell, Broadway Books, 2002

Newspapers were also helpful including: *The Belfast Telegraph, The Clare Champion, Derry Journal, Irish Daily Star, The Irish Examiner, The Irish News, The Irish Times, Leitrim Observer, The Mayo News, The Sunday Business Post, Sunday Tribune* and *The Western People*. Since they had a free archive and it was easily accessible by date, the *Irish Independent* received the most clicks. A great Web site I used for background on the Troubles was http://cain.ulst.ac.uk, produced at the University of Ulster. I also found www.museumoffreederry.org/, www.udr.talktalk.net/ and www.northantrim.com/giantscauseway.htm useful. Finally, the Ireland and Northern Ireland census came in handy.

Final Note

If anyone has any comments, feel free to tell me at proamateurs@Hotmail.com. Please check out www.AndyMendlowitz.com for additional information on my Irish journey.

Ireland has its unique vocabulary and speech patterns. For familiarity, I mostly followed the American way of talking, except putting County and River before the name.

I found it interesting how much the English language could differ from country to country. Consider this my unofficial, incomplete musings on the differences between American English and Irish English, and other cultural variations:

The name Padraig is sometimes pronounced Pad-rake, sometimes it's Poor-rig. Quay is pronounced key. Eamonn is pronounced A-man. People say bye, bye, bye when hanging up. Cookies are called biscuits. Biro is a pen. A row is a dispute. A jerk is a bollox. A car trunk is a boot. Tires are spelled tyres. Weight is measured in stones (14 pounds=1 stone). Grand and lovely are constantly used to describe things from food to people. Napys are diapers. Something dear is expensive. A vacation is a holiday. Garbage is rubbish. A sweater is a jumper. A five-dollar bill is a fiver. A ten, a tenner. High school is secondary school or community college. Mr or Mrs has no period. French Fries are chips. A lawyer is a solicitor. A field is a pitch. Potato chips are crisps. Crack—spelled craic—is a good time. Me is often substituted for my. Spring officially begins February 1. A team roster is a panel. A team's schedule is a fixture. Restrooms are simply toilets. Petrol is gas. Cell phones are mobile phones. Sixth century castles replace Cracker Barrel or gas station signs at the side of the road. Fans replace "up" for "go" while rooting, as in Up Dublin. Roundabouts replace U-turns. An upset win is a shock win. A historic win is a famous win. A parking lot is a car park. If you're drunk, you're pissed. To let a building is to rent it. Togging out is changing into your uniform. Or, playing in the game such as Henry Shefflin togged out for Kilkenny on Sunday. The police are called the Garda, and they don't carry guns or wear badges. A truck is a lorry. Firstly and whilst are common words. A microcassette tape recorder is a dictaphone. A college freshman is a fresher. Television shows don't always begin on the hour and half-hour, instead possibly starting at :05, :10, :15, :20, :25, :35, :45 or :55 past the hour. The dates and days are switched, so it would be 5 January 2007 or 5/1/07. There are 9 digits in a phone number instead of 10 (except for cell phones). It's amazing how little things stand out when you're not used to them.

978-0-595-45684-0
0-595-45684-7

Printed in the United States
201837BV00004B/142-261/A